How to Get a JOB

How to Get a Job

James Bramlett

ZondervanPublishingHouse
Grand Rapids, Michigan

A Division of HarperCollins*Publishers*

How to Get a Job
Copyright © 1986, 1991 by James D. Bramlett

Requests for information should be addressed to:
Zondervan Publishing House
1415 Lake Drive S.E.
Grand Rapids, Michigan 49506

Library of Congress Cataloging-in-Publication Data

Bramlett, James D.
  How to get a job : an updated edition of Finding work / James D.
Bramlett.
    p. cm.
  Rev. ed. of: Finding work. ©1986.
  ISBN 0-310-39051-6 (pbk.)
    1. Job hunting—United States. 2. Vocational guidance—United
States. 3. Work (Theology) 4. Christian life—1960– I. Bramlett,
James D. Finding work. II. Title.
  HF5382.75.U6B73 1991
  650.14—dc20   91–18854
                                                          CIP

Unless otherwise indicated, the Scripture text used is the New American Standard Bible, copyright © 1960, 1962, 1963, 1968, 1971, 1972, 1973, 1975 by the Lockman Foundation, La Habra, California.

Scripture quotations marked KJV are taken from the King James Version of the Bible. Quotations marked RSV are from the Revised Standard Version.

Edited by David Hazard and Mary McCormick
Cover Design by Terry Dugan

Printed in the United States of America

91 92 93 94 95 96 / AM / 10 9 8 7 6 5 4 3 2 1

*Dedicated to
my three sons:
Jim, Steve, and Scott.*

Contents

APPENDIXES

Foreword

Next to the decision to commit your life to Christ, you will perhaps make no greater decison than that of your life's vocation. For some, the decision is easy; you have always known what you wanted to do. For others, choosing a life's work is a great struggle.

As Christians we are privileged to have the guidance of the Holy Spirit in making these important life decisions. We also have Christ's command to "Go and make disciples of all nations." When we are gripped with the urgency of reaching the world for Christ, this becomes the basis upon which we determine our priorities in life and work.

As a young businessman I dreamed of becoming successful in business and living a life of wealth and prestige, but when I met Christ, my goals and my life's direction were transformed. God led me to serve him full-time in evangelism and discipleship. Along with the joy of seeing lives transformed by Christ, God has brought me fulfillment in my work beyond my wildest dreams.

Whatever God leads you to do, rest assured that if you are walking in His will, He has plans for you, "to give you a future and a hope" (Jer. 29:11). This book will help you discover your gifts and determine your direction, based on clear principles from God's Word.

May you discover the joy of being in the center of God's will and the thrill of seeing your life count for Christ wherever He leads you!

Bill Bright
Founder and President
Campus Crusade for Christ International

Introduction _____

You need this book if you are a Christian and are going to be looking for any kind of job.

You especially need this book if you are a Christian and are considering a Christian vocation or if you are planning on going to college.

This book is unique for Christians, covering the subject of vocational guidance and job hunting from A to Z—from discerning God's calling and will for your life, to preparing resumés and interviewing, to knowing how to act on the job once you get it.

I saw the need for such a volume several years ago. As a personnel director and vice-president of human resources in one of the nation's largest Christian organizations, I screened tens of thousands of applicants for thousands of jobs over a period of years. I saw applicants do it the wrong way; I saw them do it the right way. Many times I thought, *How nice it would be if everyone looking for a job, especially those hoping to enter a Christian vocation could have a handbook to guide them.*

Well, this is it. You will find hundreds of suggestions. Any one of them may be the difference in getting the position you desire. But more important, I have included some valuable spiritual guidance that I have learned over the years, some from other people and some the hard way via my own experience. You will discover how the Lord fits into your vocational planning and job-hunting process.

There are many stages in the vocational decision-making process, and you may be at any one of them. Maybe you are just recently out of school and have never held a job before. Perhaps you are an old hand but are starting to feel a restless nudge to do something else with your life. No matter where you are, there is something here for you.

I have included many real-life situations, using the experiences of real people to illustrate some of the principles. Appendix C is a collection of some especially interesting real-life employment situations. In most cases throughout the book, fictitious names have been used.

While the book was being written, I had the opportunity to share my vision for it with some longtime friends, a pastor and his wife. Wilma immediately saw the potential and exclaimed, "This is really needed. I've known so many people, especially in the Christian college I attended, who needed something like this. Because of family pressures or a lack of guidance, many of them were planning to enter ministry work for which they weren't called or talented. This could really be a help to so many people."

That is my prayer.

James Bramlett

PART I

Finding God's Will

Chapter 1 _____
HOW TO DETERMINE
A CALLING

Most of us have heard the term "calling." Perhaps you've heard it used in referring to your pastor's being called to your church. Or perhaps you may have heard about dear old brother so-and-so who felt a "call" to preach and headed off to Bible college or seminary on his way to the pulpit.

Perhaps you have asked yourself, "Will I ever hear 'the call'?" And maybe, "What will it sound like if I hear it? Will I hear a voice or see handwriting on the wall?" You may even be a little scared: You may see yourself some day at a good, fulfilling job when suddenly you hear a call to go to Africa and live a life of total deprivation.

Usually when you think of receiving a call, you conjure up a mental image of preaching from the pulpit of a nice, neat church or of going to the bush country of Africa. After all, is there really anything in between?

That's what happened to me. I felt a call when I was a teenager. I envisioned myself either in a pulpit or in Africa. Somehow by God's grace, I pursued neither as God's will for me. Sometimes I had pangs of guilt when I thought about not being a preacher or a missionary. These feelings were caused by misunderstanding the incredibly wide scope and variety of God's many kinds of callings. For years the call was clear but not the *calling,* a concept to be pursued in a moment.

My guilt feelings were caused also by the Holy Spirit's

promptings that He wanted a deeper commitment and a closer walk with me at that time, although I didn't interpret it that way. Surely I had many areas of needed improvement, but either because of my hardheadedness or improper teaching, I did not perceive how to have a closer walk. I have since learned to trust God's sovereignty in these matters; He has a timing and a progression for us.

God was molding me, just as He is molding you. With His power, He has absolutely no problem communicating with us whenever He wants. Paul's dramatic encounter on the road to Damascus is a prime example. For Paul God had a *priority* message that came with such speed and force that Paul had to pick himself up from the ground and say, "Who are you, Lord?" Of course, God doesn't speak to us exactly the same way He spoke to Paul. The point is, God can penetrate our thick skulls any time He chooses, and more often than not, His messages are softer and gentler. Later, I will discuss some of the ways He gets His messages to us.

The vital thing to know is this: *Every believer has a calling of some kind.* God has a unique plan for each of us. Your own calling, whatever it is, is every bit as important as any other. It may include employment in a Christian or secular organization, a Christian or secular vocation, or both; spare-time activities, or your role as full-time homemaker—really, any area worthy of endeavor.

On the one hand, there are many who are called to full-time Christian work. On the other hand, I know people who, in God's perfect will and calling for their lives, are in secular employment and whose church responsibilities are an avocation. You probably know many of them, too. Nevertheless, God has called everyone to be salt and light in the world, and if all believers were encapsulated in Christian organizations, what would happen? It's scary to think what government or business would be like if there were no Christians there.

So, if you are asking yourself, "Do I have a calling?" the answer is yes! Instead of comparing yourself with others or trying to follow their paths, you have to discover where God wants *you* to be.

Though God's callings are varied, I would never minimize a call to full-time Christian work. It is true that a Christian vocation is a place of special service, where no one should be just for the income but for God's plan and also for the ministry in which he serves. On occasion I have known people who have worked for Christian organizations for the wrong reasons, such as prestige or power, with awful results. John was one of those men.

John supposedly had superior skills in his vocation and was hired in spite of problems with his references and one manager's perception that he was not right for the organization. John was later promoted and given wide-ranging responsibilities and authority.

It soon became apparent that John's motives were not to serve God but were self-serving, and he exhibited signs of neurotic behavior. Now the organization had a problem. Havoc broke out in the departments: Those oppressed under John's management were resigning en masse; those who remained were crying for help. Marriages were strained, and two cases of immorality emerged. The entire organization was being hurt operationally by the strife.

Not long thereafter, John and the manager who hired him were discharged. Although their departure brought a rapid return to tranquility, employee stability, and increased operational effectiveness, it was too late to stop the damage to many lives or prevent wounds that left lasting scars.

This is an extreme example, a vivid example, of how things do not go right when you miss God's calling and enter into a Christian vocation without spiritual commitment.

More typically, there is the case of Robert.

Robert was called by the Lord to fill a professional position in a Christian organization. His inner sense of calling prompted him to apply. During the screening, it became obvious to everyone that Robert was God's man for the job. Robert, too, felt he was led to leave his business and enter full-time Christian service in this particular organization, even though his previous annual income was nearly $100,000 and this organization could not come close to that salary.

Nonetheless, Robert and his family calculated their needs to determine the very least he could make and still survive. He had a postgraduate degree and several years of top professional experience, but to Robert that was not important. He prayerfully concluded that he and his family could sacrifice and get by on $15,000 a year at the very least. Even so, he felt a little selfish by establishing even that low figure, so he did not mention it during follow-up interviews. He was determined that money would not stand in the way of God's calling for him.

During the final meeting, in which a job offer was made, Robert was still praying that his figure of $15,000 was not too much. Of course, the company officials did not know about that figure and the depth of his commitment. They offered him an annual salary of $30,000—high for that company, but low compared with what Robert's skill and experience would demand elsewhere.

Surprised, Robert wept tears of joy at God's goodness. He perceived it as a great blessing, even though it was only about 30 percent of what he was making before. He was sure God had seen his heart and honored his commitment.

Furthermore, both Robert and the ministry have been rewarded. His efforts have resulted in much unity, efficiency, and peace. He was later promoted and his salary raised. Robert was called, and he responded in meekness and humility.

Someone has said that the Lord really desires a radical

commitment. The world is full of radicals, mar
are radically committed to destroying God's ki
His people. In response, God's people need to I
faith and love, as well as a radical commitme
Him. And that raises a very important question: How can
you really tell whether you have a calling into a full-time
Christian vocation? Through my own past struggles with
this question, the following simple truths emerged:

God will begin to reveal it deep in your spirit.

*It will become a longing and a desire put there by God
Himself.*

*It will be somewhat like the pull of a magnet: You can
resist it but you really do not want to.*

It will be like an itch, needing relief through fulfillment.

*It will not be coercive: The Holy Spirit is gentle; your will
must still come into play.*

*The end result of the direction of these feelings will be to
glorify the Father and the Son rather than yourself.*

During one of my early struggles to determine God's will
for my life, I decided to seek the counsel of my pastor, a
learned and impressive servant of God, several years my
senior. A few days later, seated in his office, I was sure I
was going to hear God speak through this wise man. After
a minimum of small talk I asked, "Dr. Martin, how can a
person know if he has a calling from God?"

I fully expected a long and scholarly dissertation from
this educated gentleman. He might even pull down one or
two of the thick books that lined his shelves and go over
some theological points with me. However, he replied,

imply, "You know you have a calling when it is something you just have to do or else you will be miserable."

That's it! That's really all the advice I received, but I learned something else that has been confirmed many times since: *Spiritual truth is typically succinct and to the point.*

God does not need to waste words and apparently is not interested in impressing us with His vocabulary. He gave us only one Book; he could have given us a library (libraries have been filled with man's attempts to improve on what He said). Jesus, too, you remember, was very much to the point.

Truth is simple; people complicate things. I knew I had my answer. Maybe you do, too.

NOTICE

For special, additional insight on knowing God's calling and will for your life, see the soul-stirring letter from Dr. Bill Bright, President of Campus Crusade for Christ International, included as Appendix B.

Chapter 2 _____
HOW
GOL

Some people seek and labor for years to find God's will, but they don't have to. It's really easy. The secret is in acknowledging that God *is* God, recognizing His lordship in your life while, at the same time, not trusting in your own understanding. Does that sound familiar? It's the wisdom of Solomon.

> Trust in the Lord with all your heart, and do not lean on your own understanding. In all your ways acknowledge Him, and He will make your paths straight (Prov. 3:5–6).

Some people argue that God gave us reason and understanding, so shouldn't we "lean" on it just a little bit? Admittedly, there is an argument for that. According to your faith, be it unto you. But frankly, I recommend that you read on.

THAT FIRST CRUCIAL STEP

The very first crucial step in finding God's will is to *make a decision in your heart that His will is what you really want*. That may sound simple, but it's critical. You have to decide if you really want His will and are willing to trust Him for your future. What better deal could you have than to be in the will of One who is total love, total caring, and

21

cern for your good? There really is no reasonable
...tive.

...you agree, He already sees your heart. Still, it would
...good to say a simple prayer, because He likes to hear
from you—something like this one:

> "Lord, as of this moment, I want Your will to be done in my
> life. Amen."

As soon as you sincerely do this, something astounding
happens. Suddenly you have released the reins of your life
to Him, and He has taken them. You can relax, knowing
that He has it all under control: You are exactly where He
wants you *today* and you will be where He wants you
tomorrow. You no longer have to worry or be anxious if,
suppose, two years ago you "blew it," made a bad
decision, and feel you are not in the right place today. Your
prayer has just made where you are the right place to be.
He will redeem the past to optimize the future for you
because your God is sovereign in all things.

Do you really want God's will? Did you pray that
prayer? Well, you asked for it, and for all practical
purposes, you've got it!

WAYS IN WHICH HE SPEAKS TO US

Isn't it nice to have the One who created and rules the
whole universe interested in your individual life so much
that He guides your every step and direction? His purposes
are always good; thus, all His direction is for your ultimate
benefit, the benefit of others, and for His glory. What a
deal!

Nevertheless, many Christians have trouble finding
God's guidance on specific matters and day-to-day decisions, such as what to study in school, where to apply for a
job, or which job to pursue. It is easy to discern God's will

in general terms but sometimes more difficult to translate it into specific applications. Let's discuss several ways in which God speaks to us, generally as well as specifically.

HE SPEAKS THROUGH HIS WORD

When facing a decision, pray and then do some Bible reading. Expect a possible answer. Sometimes the answer to a specific need comes from a particular passage; other times it proceeds from the context in a place where you never thought possible. It happens, and when it does, it is an awesome feeling to realize the sheer power of the Word and how God uses it.

One day at work I was facing a tough decision. I really was struggling, still carrying the burden at quitting time, as I walked to my car to drive home.

The incredible happened the moment I turned on the ignition. I had left the radio switch on, and the tuner was set at a secular station. At that precise second, words from the Bible came blaring through my speakers—the Word of God from a secular station and through a secular song. And it directly addressed my situation, giving me a very precise answer to a difficult matter. I have rarely been so awed at God's concern for me and at His power. He is truly the God of the incredible. Instances such as this have clearly shown me that God can be with each of us in everyday situations. He doesn't reveal Himself only when we are in our prayer closets and when we are reading the Bible. But I do not recommend that you wait to hear God's voice come spontaneously from your radio. I suspect that normally He prefers you to open and use the Bible. It is important to know that God uses His Word to give us specific guidance.

No matter how God communicates a message of guidance to us, He *will not* violate His Word, even though He may stir our spirits in other ways.

HE SPEAKS IN YOUR SPIRIT

It is impossible to describe methodically how a transcendent God communicates to our inner person, but He does. Sometimes, you just have a "knowing." It may be a "still, small voice" or a booming voice within you. Some call it an "inner witness."

This inner steering mechanism that you have is one of the least understood and appreciated of God's methods but probably the most important. It is important because it is basic to the New Covenant, in which God has chosen to make His own dwelling place within us, the mystery that Paul talks about as "Christ in you" (Col. 1:27). It may be easily accepted with the mind but too profound and mysterious for the heart. Nonetheless, it is true.

The human tendency is to look to outside sources—but Jesus came to replace external religion and form with internal reality. Under the New Covenant, He communicates with us, ". . . not with ink, but with the Spirit of the living God, not on tablets of stone, but on tablets of human hearts" (2 Cor. 3:3).

He lives within you! The Captain of your soul is at the steering wheel. Is He capable of steering this unwieldy and awkward vessel? You bet He is, more than you could ever imagine.

In my experience, God's message in my spirit is the key to His guidance, but it is usually combined with one or more of some other methods.

HE SPEAKS THROUGH OTHERS

Interaction with the corporate body of Christ is very important to God. That's just the way He likes it, undoubtedly because it involves relationships, which are at the top of His priority list. He often chooses to speak through others to get a message to us.

His guidance may come through the counsel of a pastor, elder, or a Christian friend. In fact, it would be wise to seek counsel and prayer support from these people on important decisions, such as vocational direction. "In the multitude of counselors there is safety" (Prov. 11:14 KJV). This is certainly a biblical approach.

God may also speak through others in a most unexpected way, and often in the unexpectedness, the timing and relevance of a message will manifest its own authentication, causing your spirit to leap. This may come in a meeting of believers as someone delivers a general message, and suddenly you know it is intended for you. Or it may come directly from a person who knows he has a "word" for you, and when he speaks, you sense that you have just heard from the throne of God. Remember, too, that the Lord once spoke through the jaws of an ass, another reminder that He is not limited. Tune into the divine wavelength and always be expectant.

If you are married, discussion and unity with your spouse are desirable. God will often use a spouse to guide us. Similarly, He may choose to speak through parents, who often have keen insight. Respect for their God-given wisdom and role is important.

I must add a word of caution: Always be careful in seeking advice from others. For some, it's a cop-out for seeking God Himself. Many are always looking for advice about what to do and will leap at the first suggestion. There are times when one may have to act courageously and contrary to the advice of others to do God's will. To do this is difficult but sometimes necessary.

Never use this means solely for guidance. Check it carefully against the others.

HE SPEAKS THROUGH CIRCUMSTANCES

God is the God of circumstances; circumstances are not there by accident. They may include opportunity or removed opportunity, perhaps a new geographical location, increased or limited finances.

Weigh everything carefully. Ask yourself, *Which of these circumstances may God have established to direct my steps? Some? All?* God has determined those circumstances for a purpose.

For some of you, God may want you to burst out of your circumstances by faith in His power, defying the natural and seemingly impossible to create a new set of circumstances. This may be true in your vocation if you believe you are locked into a situation from which there appears to be no escape. There *is* an escape. If you feel oppressed by your circumstances, ask for and expect a miracle. Then, by faith, do something bold. The results will glorify Him.

HE SPEAKS THROUGH YOUR DESIRES

Some believe that surely God's will must be undesirable and that unless you are careful, He will probably figure out some way to make you miserable. One day a pastor's wife said to me, "God sure knows how to hurt us!" I was amazed at her lack of understanding of His ways. Such a thought dishonors our Father, who delights in blessing us. We hurt ourselves. Others may hurt us, Satan may try to hurt us—but our Father? Never! His loving-kindness is better than life (Ps. 63:3).

Your heart's desire, once you are oriented toward pleasing God, may be your best indicator of what God's will for your life may be, whether it is in Christian employment per se or in secular employment.

The Lord Himself plants desires within everyone to sense and act upon. Any strong vocational desires which you have may be from Him. With only one condition He will satisfy them.

> Delight yourself in the Lord; And he will give you the desires of your heart (Ps. 37:4).

FINAL KEY

There is one more important key to finding God's will for your vocational life. Use it and you will be launched into an exciting and adventurous future; ignore it and you may be shipwrecked on the shoals of fear, disappointment, and missed opportunity.

I was struggling years ago with questions about direction when I discovered the key that sets all else in motion: Regardless of how much guidance you get, no matter how much or how little, *you have to step out in faith with it.* That's just the way it is. You walk by faith, not by sight, and the Bible says that faith pleases God. When you think you've got it and you know the direction, "Go for it!"

Divine guidance is like the rudder of a boat. When the boat is in motion, the rudder can affect the boat's movements right or left. If the boat is stationary, the rudder has no effect at all.

It is important to be still as you pray, to seek God's voice within, to read His Word, and wait upon Him. But there is a point when you have to get up and start moving. Jesus told His disciples to wait but He also told them to "go." Waiting is scriptural, but if you are waiting for lightning to strike, an audible voice, or the appearance of an angel, you may be waiting forever. Pray through all the aforementioned steps, and you will probably have enough to go on.

The apostle Paul was a man-on-the-move, who did not always know God's entire plan in advance. Once when he started out in one direction to proclaim the gospel, the Holy Spirit let him go a distance before saying, in effect, "Hey, Paul. Stop. Turn. I want you to go that way instead." Paul's rudder was working because Paul was in motion. So, take what you believe to be God's leading and step out with it.

Here is another important point: Once you have sought the Lord's wisdom in the matter, you've received what you believe is the answer and stepped out with it—*do not doubt.*

> But let him ask in faith without any doubting, for the one who doubts is like the surf of the sea driven and tossed by the wind (James 1:6).

Full speed ahead! Doubting thoughts *will* enter your mind, but reject them and press on. Remember, however, that as you are moving forward, like the apostle Paul, the Holy Spirit may divert you and alter your course. That does not mean you started in the wrong direction but that you needed to get moving. You see through a glass darkly and cannot always see very far ahead. The Word is like a lamp unto our feet, not a spotlight shining two hundred yards ahead. God undoubtedly has a purpose in these seemingly circuitous routes.

Someday you will look back and say, "He guided me every step along the way."

NOTICE

For special, additional insight on knowing God's calling and will for your life, see the soul-stirring letter from Dr. Bill Bright, President of Campus Crusade for Christ International, included as Appendix B.

PART II
Finding Yourself

Chapter 3 _____
HOW TO FIND YOUR
GIFTS AND TALENTS

You are a unique creature. There are things about your specific make-up and life experiences that give you an insight and an ability in certain ways that cannot be duplicated by anyone. Your gifts and talents have come from your heavenly Father, and what's more, He has a special plan for your life. He is going to use you in a way that He cannot use anyone else.

I am using the terms "gifts" and "talents" interchangeably and primarily in a vocational sense, though many gifts and talents may go beyond vocation and are manifested in different areas. Both mean abilities that have been given to you. You *are able* to do certain things better than you can do other things; you *enjoy* doing certain things better than you do other things—a distinction that is important.

There is obviously a correlation between what you are *able* to do and what you *enjoy* doing. But there may be some things that you are able to do well but you do not enjoy. Even though you have multiple talents and gifts, you probably should pursue vocationally only that one (or those very few) where both ability and enjoyment coincide.

The things that you are able to do best usually become apparent early in life. Rarely do these gifts result in excellence of performance without the cultivation of training, practice, and experience. You may be highly gifted as a musician, but many hours of study and practice will be necessary to develop this gift. Until the gift is cultivated, it is only a potential.

When you think of gifts, you usually think first of the artistic gifts, such as music and painting, but gifts really include every form of human endeavor. Giftedness includes *what* you can do, *how* you do it, and *how* you relate it to other people. Even your personality can be one of your gifts.

Have you ever noticed a really good salesperson? The amazing thing about a *good* salesperson is that he can sell you something you hadn't planned on buying and make you glad you did. He might even make you think it was your idea and that he's selling it to you as a favor! A gifted salesperson comfortably flows in his interactions with people. Many tend to think of the super-sales type as loud, extroverted, and gregarious, and that's often the case. Still, there are highly successful people who are not outgoing. In both is a common personality ingredient that enables them to *inspire trust* and to *persuade*. Both make it happen. That is, they make the sale.

Let's take a look at an unusual and multi-talented person in the Bible, the wife described in Proverbs 31. Note that among other things she is a salesperson, even making what she sells. She selects wool and flax and works "with hands in delight." She purchases real estate, plants, and trades. In addition to her obvious talents, she also has some admirable personal characteristics that help make her successful. She gets up while it is still dark; she opens her mouth in wisdom; she does not eat the bread of idleness.

This person is a superwoman, someone diligently exercising her God-given gifts and talents. She is in the place of God's will, doing what she is supposed to do.

What is the result? Well, she is obviously well adjusted and happy. She is described as having strength and dignity and "she laughs" when contemplating the future.

Strength and dignity do come from being in the right

place that God has for you. You sense His favor, which brings inner confidence and strength. You know that demands on you may be difficult but you have this indescribable assurance that He will see you through and that He has equipped you for the job. Plus, you can even "laugh at the future" because life and even the unknown have a dimension of merriment brought about by trusting God and knowing that you are in His will. This is joy, a fruit of the Holy Spirit.

Conversely, if you are not exercising your gifts and not in the right place, there can be a dread about work, an uneasiness and apprehension brought about by the requirement for you to do things for which you are ill equipped. You can lose your joy, and your life can become unhappy even though you may not know why.

SPIRITUAL VERSUS VOCATIONAL GIFTS

Can you really differentiate between spiritual and vocational gifts? Not really, since all gifts come from the Father and are, in that sense, spiritual. But there are certain gifts that are primarily for ministry and may or may not be vocationally related, such as those described in Romans 12:6–8, which include prophesying, serving, teaching, encouraging, contributing, leading, and showing mercy. Other gifts, mentioned in 1 Corinthians 12:8–10, are called manifestations of the Spirit, usually thought to be supernatural endowments used when believers are assembled. First Corinthians 12:28 adds some more gifts, or "appointments," and Ephesians 4 adds others that are usually considered ministry offices in the church.

Some of these gifts and appointments can obviously involve a full-time vocational pursuit in a church or church-related occupation. Typically, but not exclusively, this might include serving, teaching, administrating, and evangelizing or pastoring.

Is there anything wrong with earning a livelihood from a spiritual gift in a church-related job? Definitely not. The New Testament is clear on this point. (See 1 Cor. 9:3–12.)

Vocational gifts can include much more. God has placed us in a complex society where there are thousands of types of jobs and needs for varying skills. Someone has estimated that there are about twenty thousand different types of jobs in this country, and I suspect that's conservative. The point is, you can probably *do* a lot of them. But which are best suited for you? Which can you do best? Which will make you the happiest?

FINDING YOUR GIFTS

There are two principal ways of finding your own gifts: Do it yourself through self-analysis, sometimes called self-assessment. Or get outside help with vocational testing and counseling.

You can, of course, combine the two, checking one against the other. Since both methods are imperfect, this would be the surest way to achieve accurate results. (A later chapter is devoted fully to professional testing.)

Right now, let's take a look at some self-assessment techniques. Systematic methods are available commercially to help you do this, and I recommend you give them a try. Here are some of the most popular books: *Self-Assessment and Career Development* by James G. Clawson et al. (Prentice-Hall, Inc., 1985); *What Color Is Your Parachute?* rev. ed. by Richard Nelson Bolles (Ten Speed Press, 1990); *The Truth About You,* written from a Christian perspective, by Arthur F. Miller and Ralph T.

Mattson (Ten Speed Press, 1989) and, by the same authors, *Finding a Job You Can Love* (Thomas Nelson Publishers, 1982); *Discover What You're Best At* by Barry and Linda Gale (Simon and Schuster, Inc., 1990); and *Discover Your God-Given Gifts* by Don and Katie Fortune (Fleming H. Revell Co., 1987). A fun method of self-assessment can be found in the *Quick Job-Hunting Map,* a booklet by Richard N. Bolles and Victoria B. Zenoff (Ten Speed Press). (See back cover of book to learn how to get a free bonus copy of *The Quick Job-Hunting Map.*)

Self-assessment basically means taking inventory of yourself to measure what gifts and talents you really have. You are encouraged to survey your entire life as far back as you can remember to recall activities in which you excelled and/or enjoyed. It sounds simple, and in a way it is. Yet, it can be very time-consuming if you are to achieve truly accurate results.

I am going to give you a taste of the self-assessment method. If you do it correctly and conscientiously, it may give you what you want to know or at least perk your interest enough to pursue this further. I believe it will help you not only to demonstrate the principle of self-assessment but actually to perceive a talent that you may have otherwise taken for granted and thus overlooked.

Start with a prayer, since you will really need the Lord's wisdom. You are going to be looking backward at your entire life and you need the Holy Spirit to assist you.

Then get paper and pen. You can do this alone, although it may help to get input from people who have known you a long time.

STEPS

1. At the top of your paper, write *List 1—Activities At Which I Have Excelled.*

2. Systematically go back in your memory as far back as you can, to preschool if possible. Try to recall every activity or everything you ever did. It will be easier if you try to do it year-by-year, using school years to help you recall. For example, slowly walk through grammar school, then high school. It will help you to recall different residences, schools, friends, neighbors, relatives, or anything that can form an association. During these years, try to recall these areas:

> hobbies
> school subjects of special interest
> extracurricular activities
> favorite books
> favorite games
> heroes or heroines
> special travels
> pastime activities
> favorite movies
> special awards or recognition
> church activities and friends
> jobs held, including summer

3. On your paper, write, no matter how seemingly small or insignificant, *anything you ever did well, ever did better than most other things,* or *ever did better than most of your other friends.* For each item, include the year or your age as a later reminder.

   Don't rush. This may take days. Ponder it; sleep on it. It's worth the time. Let your thoughts flow freely. If in doubt, write it down and judge it later. Prejudging can inhibit thought.

4. On a second sheet of paper, write *List 2—Activities I Have Enjoyed the Most.*

5. Repeat Step 2.

6. On your second piece of paper, write down anything you ever did, no matter how seemingly small or insignificant, *that you seemed to enjoy more than other things, that gave you the most satisfaction,* and *that you were inclined to want to do again because of the enjoyment.* Then review Step 3. The same rules apply to this step. Take your time.

7. On a third sheet of paper, write *List 3—Personal Characteristics.* Write the following categories and rate yourself on a scale of 1 to 5 according to the definitions below:

Analytical. Discovering what, how, why.
Numerical. Good at numbers.
Mechanical. Good with hands, tools, equipment.
Technical. Scientifically oriented.
Organizational. Teamwork, decision-making, leadership.
Interpersonal. Good with people.
Artistic. Good at one or more of the fine arts.
Competitive. Likes to win, excel.
Working independently. Prefers to work alone.
Outdoors. Prefers to work outdoors.

Rating Scale

5. Applies to a very large degree— highly applicable.

4. Applies to an above-average degree.

3. Applies to an average degree.

2. Applies to a below-average degree.

1. Applies to little or no degree.

8. Now take all three lists and lay them out before you. Study them individually and collectively, looking for themes, for commonality, for patterns that are like threads weaving through your life.

   If you have done this exercise carefully, you have painted a picture of yourself. It may be a little rough, but even the most sophisticated methods often produce only a rough picture. Your efforts can be amazingly accurate.

   See what items on List 1 also appear on List 2. Circle them.

   Check the items you have circled against List 3 and the categories in which you have rated yourself a 3 or higher. A 4 or a 5 rating is especially significant.

   What you now have are activities in which you have demonstrated ability *and* enjoyment that also conform to a general category or categories you consider to be descriptive of yourself.

9. All you have to do now is to convert these activities into an occupational category. After you have completed the last steps, such an occupational category (or categories) will probably become obvious.

   If you are still having trouble making occupational associations, go to your library and peruse the two-hundred-fifty occupations listed in the *Occupational Outlook Handbook,* published by the Department of Labor.

10. The final step is eliminating any occupational category not feasible because of your circumstances. For example, the above exercise may have shown that you have a special talent in athletics, but you are now sixty years old. It is unlikely that athletic competition would be a viable vocational alternative for you at this time, but you might consider a sports-related job.

Now, determine which final categories cause your spirit to leap and say, "Yes, this is it!"

Do not be discouraged if you lack refinement in any of these areas, such as training or experience. Take one step at a time. All you have been looking for is latent talent or ability, so all of these need development.

Nevertheless, refined or not, the talent is yours. God gave it, and with His help, it will be brought to fruition.

NOW WHAT?

You have made progress toward deciding upon your specific gifts and talents. You may have even completed the task. If you are still not satisfied, rethink the previous ten steps. Maybe, you did it too hastily. I've given you an outline—a blueprint. You have to fill in the blanks.

You should also consider having some testing done as discussed in the next chapter. You can compare the results of this with what you already have accomplished.

In any case, assessment is foundational to all other steps in the vocational planning process and can affect your whole life. Give it the time and attention it deserves.

Chapter 4

HOW TO USE VOCATIONAL TESTING

Does the term "vocational testing" scare you? It scares some people and can especially rattle you when you are being interviewed for a job and the interviewer says, "Oh, by the way, we have a few questionnaires we would like for you to fill out." Then, he puts you in a private room, gives you some instructions, winds up a timer, and starts to close the door. You object, and he says, "Oh, we just want to know a little more about you, and this is a good way to do it. Besides, everybody takes these, so don't feel bad."

You then stare at the strange-looking form, which seems to have a million short questions on it. You have only twenty minutes to finish.

After it's all over, you decide it wasn't that bad. In fact, it was all pretty interesting. You wonder how you scored. The company may or may not tell you; they may tell you part of the results but not all, depending on their policy. Some consulting psychologists prefer that their test results not be divulged, except possibly in general terms; others are not restrictive.

The company, by using psychological tests, is really trying to look inside your head. They want to find out some things about you that may not otherwise be apparent. When you stop to think about it, it's a little scary. How often does somebody look inside your head?

Well, relax. It's really not all that bad. There is more of a positive than negative side to this. My intent is to remove the mystery for you by explaining what these tests try to do, how they may succeed or fail, and how you can use them to your advantage.

You can initiate the testing process for your own purposes and use it in vocational planning. Do consider this for yourself. Later, you will find suggestions on how to pursue it.

There are many psychological tests available that relate to vocational planning. Many are so-called standard tests that are marketed by their owners or copyright holders and used by counselors and psychologists for their private use. Many others are developed by psychologists for use in their practices. Most tests go through a statistical validation process using large numbers of testees to establish a data base, referred to as the statistical "population." From this data, the test designer calculates important information, such as the test's *reliability* and *validity*—meaning how accurate the test is in describing or predicting whatever it is intended for. Some tests have not been subjected to such statistical rigor. If you ever decide to use psychological testing in your vocational planning, always inquire about this, especially if you are going to pay for it. A reputable counselor will respect your inquiry and be glad to share such data. Frankly, you will probably not be able to understand it, but at least you will have the comfort of knowing it is a professional test.

There are four particular categories of tests that may be of interest to you in vocational planning. They may also be the most likely used by a potential employer.

Tests that help you determine your vocational interests.

Tests that determine your ability to reason.

Tests that determine your personality characteristics.

Tests that determine your aptitude for certain kinds of work.

VOCATIONAL INTEREST TESTS

These tests offer a systematic way of getting you to describe the kinds of work you like and the kinds you do not like. A typical test will give you a large number of questions, each with several choices of jobs. Then, you select the one you "like most" and the one you "like least." The test evaluation correlates all the questions and answers, giving a collective picture of what you have said about your likes and dislikes.

The test results can be amazingly accurate. You are systematically forced to make choices, and interests may emerge that you were never fully aware of.

For example, I took one of these tests several years ago, and the test revealed, among other things, that outdoor activities were high on my preference list. At first I thought the test was inaccurate, because I had never desired or had an outdoor job. I really am not an outdoor person and don't camp, hunt, or fish. I read the interpretive material that went with the test and discovered that an item with a high score represents a "need" that tends to find fulfillment, if not vocationally then in some other way. I read further that those scoring high on "outdoor activities" often had their need met by reading "outdoor magazines," or "building a cottage on a lake."

I was amazed. At that time, I *was* building a cottage on a nearby lake! But that's not all. Months earlier, I responded to a strange impulse and subscribed to both *Organic Gardening* and another outdoor magazine, though I did not even have a garden, nor was I planning one. When the magazines arrived, I perused them, carefully read the good articles, then laid them aside. Yet, somewhere inside my cranium a need for the outdoors was expressing itself. I believe this is related to a later decision to leave the eight-to-five office scene for a different routine that keeps me from being indoors so consistently.

I would never have thought that that particular test result would have had vocational significance in my life, but it did.

Who knows what similar need lies inside your cranium? Would you like to know? I strongly recommend the vocational interest test to help you determine your interests and preferences and to help you find your way into the marketplace. Since there is a correlation between what you are *able* to do and what you *prefer* to do, as previously discussed, these tests can help you uncover your gifts and talents too.

The test that I took was developed and administered by Birkman and Associates, 3040 Post Oak Boulevard, Houston, TX 77056. Two other standard tests are the Strong-Campbell Interest Inventory and the Kuder Occupational Interest Survey, both of which should be available to professional counselors and consultants. (Testing by schools and government employment agencies is usually free of charge.)

TESTS THAT MEASURE REASONING ABILITY

I do not like the term "intelligence" test, sometimes called mental alertness tests or measures of verbal and numerical comprehension. Whatever they are called, these tests attempt to measure your ability to read, understand, and reason.

Typically, the tests are timed and are usually a mix of questions that emphasize verbal abilities (the use of words) and numerical abilities (the use of numbers). Most questions are pretty simple but a little tricky, requiring you to think. There may be more questions than the average person can answer during the time limit, so your score will be based on the number of correct answers.

As with virtually all tests, your score is only significant as compared with the population. Your score, then, will indicate how you did compared with everyone else.

Your raw score, the actual number right, is meaningless. It must be converted to a relative score, usually a percentile. A percentile score is a number from 0–100 that tells you how you did compared with everyone else who has taken the test. If your score is 80, that means you did better than about 80 percent of the others, and about 20 percent did better than you. A 99 means only 1 percent did better than you; a 50 is average.

Some of these test scores can be converted into that sometimes dreaded and ambiguous reference, an I.Q. (Intelligence Quotient) score. But whether you call it an I.Q. or something else, it is the relative score as compared with others that makes the difference.

Many books have been written about whether these types of scores have any meaningful accuracy. I will not attempt to enter that debate here, but I will give you some principles that you can use to assess your own such test results, so you won't get too conceited if you did very well or too discouraged if you did not do well.

If you scored well, it means you are probably a good reader and probably very good at verbal and/or numerical skills, depending on how high your score was.

If you did not score well, it *may not* mean the opposite of the above. It *may* mean any of the following:

> You tightened up for some reason on this particular test and you might do well on a retake.

> You are mentally very sharp but you are a slow reader, for many possible reasons. You can improve this.

You did poorly on either the verbal or the numerical part, not both, meaning you may be very strong on one and weak on the other. If possible, ask the test monitor for a breakdown.

Please remember that these tests measure only a very narrow definition of mental alertness. You may have exceptional reasoning ability but did not score well because the reading is so important to taking the test. Do not let a low score cause you to have low self-esteem. You may be unusually bright, and your mental abilities will manifest themselves in other ways.

Nevertheless, it is important to remember that reading, verbal, and numerical skills are usually important in most, if not all, administratively oriented jobs. If you scored low, this may tell you that such work is not for you and that you are being guided in a different direction.

But again, make any such judgment cautiously, not just based on a single test score. I know one man who scored horribly on one of the mental alertness tests who has been performing admirably for several years as a top executive of a large corporation.

Test-taking ability can strongly affect these scores. I have taken so many tests in my life that I can add many points to my score by technique alone, which does not mean that I am smarter than someone who has not had similar experience.

Your inner tempo can have an effect, since these tests are usually timed, and you are under pressure to answer as many questions as possible. Some folks just move with a slow but deliberate speed, getting superior results when given the time. People seem to live in different time dimensions.

We *are* "fearfully and wonderfully made," as the Bible says, and each is unique. Human attempts to classify and categorize so often miss the mark.

PERSONALITY TESTS

This is one of the most controversial forms of psychological and vocational testing. These tests attempt to analyze your personality and then predict whether you would be successful in certain vocations. Many of them have various categories of personality traits, and you are rated in each of these categories. These categories vary markedly from test to test with surprisingly little similarity. They may include such traits as sociability, intuitiveness, perceptiveness, extroversion, introversion, persuasiveness, energy, structure, flexibility, adaptability, and so on. There is also much variance in results. You may look at three different results for the same person and you would think there were three different people!

A psychologist making the same observation explained this aptly. Our personalities are multifaceted, like prisms. One particular test will reflect our natures from one angle, another at a different angle. It is all the same person but viewed in different lights. A wise observation, but there is one other factor: Sometimes personality tests are wrong.

I have personally struggled with this type of test more than any other. I have seen it amazingly right; I have seen it amazingly wrong. I have seen it used and misused.

Statistical data suggests that some of these tests may be as high as 80 percent accurate, which is outstanding. But remember, this is a "statistical average." You are not an average but a specific. If it is accurate for you, then it is 100 percent accurate as far as you are concerned. If it is not right for you, then it is 0 percent accurate. Accuracy of 80 percent means it will be right for eight in ten of the people tested and wrong for two. Will you be one of the eight or one of the unfortunate two? How will you know?

That's the $64,000 question. As a manager I have wrestled with it for a long time, but I think I finally have the answer, thanks to one of the sensitive counselors at Birkman and Associates. I took her thoughts on the subject and combined them with some of my own to come up with the Bramlett Theory.

If you are trying to decide whether a particular personality test result really describes you, *here is the key:*

> Pray. Agree with the Lord to approach this honestly. Ask for His help. Study the test results. Do not jump to conclusions, either to agree or disagree. Meditate on the matter. It may take a few hours, maybe days. Gradually, the truth will emerge. *You will bear witness to what is you and what is not you.* What appears as truth, hold onto; what appears not to be you, reject.

Isn't this the way God's guidance works? Let external devices and circumstances confirm or disavow your inner conviction. Where confirmed, be strengthened in your resolve to be what God wants you to be.

There are many different personality tests. One of the popular ones is the Worthington-Hurst, which requires the testee to complete a battery of sentences. Another popular one is the Myers-Briggs, which can help you determine which of many different types and combinations of types best describe your personality and which can be used for vocational counseling and guidance.

APTITUDE AND SKILLS TESTING

Some tests attempt to show whether you have potential skills or aptitude to do various jobs, such as manual, mechanical, or clerical work. Others measure your actual skills, such as your typing speed, although that is not considered a psychological test.

You may have a strong aptitude or potential in an area you do not realize. If you are in contact with a counselor or vocational guidance office, inquire as to what they can offer you in aptitude testing. It is well worth your while.

WHERE TO GET VOCATIONAL TESTING

If you are in school, try your guidance office. Some state employment agencies and Job Service Centers also offer vocational testing. You can also look in the Yellow Pages under Vocational Guidance or Psychologists.

RECOMMENDED READING

How to Pass Employment Tests, Arco Editorial Board, Arco Publishing, Inc., NY, 1983.

Essentials of Psychological Testing, Fourth Edition, by Lee J. Cronbach, Harper and Row Publishers, NY, 1984.

PART III
Preparing Yourself

Chapter 5 ————————
HOW TO SET
VOCATIONAL GOALS

Someone once made the profound observation, "If you don't know where you are going, any road will get you there."

That was the story of my life. After my freshman year at college, I made a drastic change in my major and even then felt unsure. It just seemed like a more interesting subject than the last one. I had not the foggiest idea what I would ever do with the liberal-arts education I was getting. Upon graduation, I accepted a U.S. Air Force ROTC commission as a second lieutenant and decided to give it a try.

My misdirection continued. I reported to the processing base in San Antonio, Texas. Based on my college major, I tried to get into the personnel or intelligence fields, but both were closed at the time. So, I made a profound decision, based on a well-planned and rational strategy for using my gifts and maximizing job satisfaction. I said to my superiors, "Okay, then, since my wife is pregnant, give me the occupation with the longest school available, so we will be settled when the baby arrives."

If you think you've got vocational problems, forget it! That strategy sent me to a forty-three week school in telecommunications and electronics and dictated my occupational efforts, home locations, birthplaces of my children, and their education for years after.

This is an example of the most haphazard kind of planning. Still, a great principle can be learned: In spite of my carelessness, the Lord was in it all. Were those intervening years wasted? No, but only because the Lord is the Great Economist. He redeems all things.

You see, we were "chosen in Him before the foundation of the world" (Eph. 1:4). He knows the end from the beginning (Isa. 46:10). Sometimes you do not know where you are headed, but He does. When planning and goal setting, always remember:

> Commit your works to the Lord, and your plans will be established (Prov. 16:3).

Have you only recently accepted the Lord, asking Him to take control of your life? Are you concerned about those seemingly wasted years? Well, I have good news. One of the Lord's most amazing and endearing traits is to redeem the past and shape it for His glory. If you have received Him, you are now on course. If you have committed your life and works to Him, your plans will be established.

Keeping in mind our earlier thoughts about divine guidance, let's look at some of the practical ways God can help you determine the new course you're about to take.

PLANNING

First, you can set goals and accomplish short-, medium-, and long-range planning. What are the differences and why these three categories?

A long-range goal is where you ultimately want to be in your vocation, a place where, after an appropriate period of training and experience, you would be most fully using the talents that God has given you. A medium-range goal is the intermediate step or steps needed to get you there. Short-range planning is what you have to do now to eat.

Let's discuss each of these.

LONG-RANGE PLANNING

Long-range planning cannot be defined in terms of a certain number of years. One person's long-range goals may be achievable in five years, and another person's in twenty. I'm not talking about a place of rest or retirement (postvocational) or necessarily a place of perfect tranquility or even financial security. It is a place where your gifts and talents are honed and refined by preparation, training, and experience, and where you have reached a point of optimal fruitfulness in your calling.

The problem Christians often have is in confusing this with worldly rewards of ever-increasing personal status, title, recognition, and material possessions. Your long-range place may *result* in some or all of these things. They are not evil in themselves, and our Father is generous to His children. But your long-range place may *not* result in these things. Consequently, they should not be the object of your affections and efforts but the incidental side effects of maximizing your God-given potential.

My thoughts turn again to the apostle Paul who, before his dramatic conversion, was held in great esteem by the prevailing value system and was probably peaking in his vocational pursuits. But later, after he had really entered into God's ultimate plan for his life, he testified:

> Whatever gain I had, I counted as loss for the sake of Christ . . . I have suffered the loss of all things, and count them as refuse, in order that I may gain Christ (Phil. 3:7–8 RSV).

Paul went upward and onward in a different way than people usually think of. But look at the lasting fruit of his life. Had he remained seeking the world's recognition and status, you would have never heard of him.

My point is that planning for the Christian is different than for others. The result may be the same; the motivation is different.

Goal-setting is easy for some and difficult for others. If you simply cannot do it after prayer and consideration, set it aside for a while and don't worry about it. You might be surprised how your mind will clear on the matter after you lay it to rest for a few nights.

For some, there is within a mysterious, compelling desire to "be" a certain thing someday. Those people are like a hound dog after a scent. They go after it relentlessly and usually make it.

If you are one of these, your long-range goal-setting is relatively easy. Sometimes, for His own reasons, the Father will plant such strong guidance within a person that the person seems to "know" that he or she wants to be a nurse, doctor, lawyer, domestic engineer (housewife), or what-have-you. Your goal may be drawing you like a magnet.

If not, let's look at some steps that can help establish your long-range goals.

1. Review the gifts and talents that God has given you.

2. Prayerfully take a fresh look within yourself for what may be a God-given desire. Consider an occupational area, a type of work, or a specific job. As thoughts come to your mind, be uninhibited; let them flow freely, and write them down. Judge them later.

3. Compare Steps 1 and 2 for compatibility. Give special attention to compatible items. For example, in Step 1, you may have listed a real talent for comprehending and using numbers. In Step 2, you may have found that a career as an accountant has always held a fascination for you. This indicates a probable direction.

4. From the results of Step 3, list as many possible occupational responsibilities as you can where that

talent and interest can be used. Scan the appendixes to this book for help. A trip to your nearest library and a little research are also worth the effort.

5. Look at your list and see if you can picture yourself at any of these positions in the long-range future, perhaps in ten or twenty years. Would any of them satisfy your heart's desire? If so, put a big circle around it.

6. If you emerged with only one item in Step 5, let that be your long-range goal. If you had two or more items, you should prayerfully choose one as a primary goal and then prioritize any remaining as secondary goals or backups.

MEDIUM-RANGE PLANNING

You now have a long-range vocational goal. Your medium-range goals should include whatever steps, in terms of training and experience, that are necessary to achieve that end. For example, if your long-range goal is to become a general accountant and be in business for yourself, there are certain prerequisites to meeting this goal, such as:

Earning a bachelor's or master's degree in accounting.

Taking and passing your Certified Public Accountant (CPA) examination.

Acquiring a certain number of years of experience in a public accounting firm.

These, then, would be specific medium-range goals. Multiple steps obviously must involve some sequence, so arranging them on a projected time line is also desirable. In the above example, if you are just starting your accounting education, the above steps alone could carry you ten or more years into the future.

Specific medium-range goals, such as the above, should be further analyzed and expanded. For example, for item number 1, decide when and where you want to get your college education. Where are the good schools for this subject? Do you want to stay close to home or are you free to go elsewhere? You are now ready to do some detailed planning.

Appendix D may help you determine the prerequisites for selecting vocational goals and jobs. If the type of job you seek is not contained in this selected list, refer to the *Occupational Outlook Handbook,* published by the U.S. Department of Labor, Bureau of Labor Statistics, available in your local public library or from the Superintendent of Documents, U.S. Government Printing Office, Washington, DC 20402.

SHORT-RANGE PLANNING

This is normally associated with meeting today's needs. Sometimes you have to "take what you can get" for the moment to buy time as you get on track with medium-range goals en route to long-range goals.

At first glance there seems to be not very much planning required for the short range, and to some extent that is true. It is best, however, that even short range decisions be made with one eye on the future.

For instance, it is often possible to find immediate employment in a position related to your medium- and long-range goals. If you are hoping to become an accountant but presently lack the formal education, you might find your short-range employment in an accounting-related area. Consider anything that would put you around the accounting function of a company or an accounting firm itself so you can begin to hear and learn the language.

Every occupation, no matter what it is, has an esoteric language spoken only by the people in it. Some say that most specialized education is, in a sense, devoted to learning the vocabulary. Concepts themselves are often relatively simple; it's the language they are couched in that has to be learned.

In the above example, getting a job as a clerk or a helper in an accounting office is a great way to begin. I know one young man who had just graduated with a liberal arts degree and entered the job market. For the lack of anything better, he took a job in an accounting office as a clerk typist. They hired him because he had had one accounting course in college; besides, he was a fair typist because he had taken a high school typing course and had practice in doing term papers.

The young man started taking accounting courses at night at a nearby university, soon completed several night courses, and was promoted to an accounting position. He continued taking accounting courses at night and within two years had worked his way up to the position of budget manager of the corporation. I also know that his workdays often ran twelve to sixteen hours. Two years later, he applied and was accepted at Harvard Business School and became a successful management consultant in Boston with one of the most prestigious firms in the nation.

This is an interesting case because not all goals were clear at the outset. Initially, the goal of his first job was survival, but it was soon transformed into job improvement. A graduate education then became his intermediate goal. His longer-range but still intermediate goal was to contribute in the area of business management, which is what he is now doing. I do not know what his long-range goals are now, but next time I see him I plan to ask. I am particularly interested in this case; he is my oldest son.

This case demonstrates that goal-setting is dynamic and that not all goals can always be clear-cut. You do the best you can with the sanctified intelligence that you have, but trust the Lord for the results and the necessary course corrections.

If you believe you have a calling to full-time Christian work in your vocation, give first priority to Christian organizations as you proceed in your short-range planning and even temporary summer jobs, if available. It is worth a try. There are just about as many occupational specialties used in Christian organizations as there are in secular work. It takes many people in many specialties to keep a ministry going. You will find that there are positions in administration, data processing and computers, technical, and engineering as well as accounting and financial areas, public relations, media, marketing, and art.

COURSE CORRECTIONS

Now that you have made your plans, be prepared to discard them all. Do not be rigidly locked into any direction. Be prepared for course corrections along the way. Some, at least, will be inevitable. It has been said that a wise man has the right to change his mind, and probably an unwise man never changes his mind.

Be prepared for change and the necessity of altering your course—maybe frequently. Every time you alter it, go full speed until you reach your goal or are redirected. One mark of the flow of God's Spirit is *change*. He is dynamic, always creating, always moving forward. You want to stay in tune and flow with Him.

Commit your works to Him, and your plans will be established in the knowledge that all things, planned or unplanned, will work together for your good because you love Him and are "called according to His purpose" (Rom. 8:28).

Chapter 6 _____
HOW TO PREPARE
YOURSELF
EDUCATIONALLY

By now, you have spent time analyzing your gifts and talents, and you have spent some time establishing your vocational goals. The next thing to consider is preparing to accomplish these goals.

It may be that you are already sufficiently prepared, at least for your short- and maybe medium-range goals. If so, you are that much ahead of the game. You may fall into one of the many categories: in high school, thinking about the future; just out of high school; just out of college; or maybe you have been in the job market for a long time and are reassessing your situation and contemplating a new direction. Whatever your category, further preparation for the future is important.

Let's face it, sometimes opportunity or achievement may just happen—but very rarely. Achievement usually comes only after hard work and preparation. To the old saying that genius is as much perspiration as inspiration, I would add a third ingredient: preparation.

WHETHER TO GO TO COLLEGE

You may be debating whether to go to college, to take night courses, or to study for a higher educational degree. It may or may not be for you.

Consider this: Only about 20 percent of all jobs require a

college education. The remaining 80 percent are skilled jobs that can be learned in other ways, such as technical or on-the-job training.

One might argue that to rise in management in these positions a college degree would be necessary, but that is not always true. It might help, it certainly will not hurt, but it is not always necessary. One can usually rise to first-line management and beyond without a degree. More important are your *technical* and *interpersonal* skills. Supervisory skills can be acquired through practice, self-study, and company-offered courses and seminars. Some employers stress the need for a degree, but many are just interested in results and performance.

Nevertheless, a college degree is sometimes desirable or even mandatory, especially in certain professional areas. And it may be that you function well in an academic environment. You *want* more formal education for its own sake and for what it does for you. College offers much more than learning a trade or preparation for a vocation. With it comes improved communications ability, increased knowledge of your culture, government, business environment, and physical environment.

More important is this question: Do you *need* a college education for where you are headed?

My sons represent the gamut. My oldest, Jim, loved school. He got a bachelor's degree, worked for four years, then went back for a master's degree. He is now in his niche. My next son, Steve, is just as bright but technically oriented and wanted to get into a skilled profession. All of his training has been on the job, and he has progressed rapidly in electronics. College would have been a waste of his time and my money. My youngest son, Scott, has set vocational goals that will be enhanced by a degree, which he has obtained.

All three analyzed their situations, aspirations, and goals; all three are comfortable with their decisions.

I'm sure you will do the same.

CHRISTIAN VERSUS SECULAR EDUCATION

If you decide to go to college, should you go to a Christian or a secular school? Let's look at the pros and cons.

Few people know that fully 104 of the first 119 colleges founded in the United States were Christian, dedicated to the idea that God is the basis of all knowledge. Harvard, founded by the Puritans, had in its college laws that each student should consider " . . . the main end of his life and studies to know God and Jesus Christ . . . and therefore to lay Christ in the bottom as the only foundation for all sound knowledge and learning." Yale, Columbia, and Princeton had similar Christian roots; that has changed radically, however.

Charles Malik, past president of the United Nations General Assembly, once asked Cyrus Vance, then Secretary of State, "Do you know what is wrong with your country?" The secretary responded in the negative. "I'll tell you," said Malik. "You have taken Jesus Christ out of your universities."

The chief disadvantage, then, of a secular institution is that you will spend several years being fed knowledge without God or the Bible as a presupposition. Sometimes, biblical truths about origins, human nature, morality, and God are even ridiculed as superstition. There is no conflict with God and truth, but there is often conflict between God and man's contemporary perceptions of truth.

You are warned to "See to it that no one takes you captive through philosophy and empty deceit, according to

the tradition of men . . . rather than according to Christ"
(Col. 2:8).

Often, though, secular institutions do offer distinct
advantages, including better facilities, better research
opportunities, more qualified staffs, and a broader curriculum. Not unimportant is the prestige of holding a degree
from a particular institution, possibly enhancing opportunities for you in the future and also your effectiveness for the
Lord.

In this question of Christian versus secular education,
there are opposing arguments: One says that Christians
should be trained only in Christian environments and with
a Bible-oriented, or at least respected, curriculum. The
graduate should then go and take the world for Christ.

The other argument says that graduates of Christian
schools sometimes have difficulty getting high posts in the
world's systems. Their chances of exerting meaningful
influence are reduced; therefore, it is best to get your
education in the top secular universities after or concurrent
with a firm grounding in the Word of God.

I believe there is a place for both. I am convinced that
God, who is bigger than we often conceive Him to be, does
it both ways. One of these directions will be right for you.
The Lord will show you the way.

CHRISTIAN COLLEGES
AND UNIVERSITIES

For information on Christian colleges, contact one of the
following: Christian College Coalition, 329 Eighth Street,
N.E., Washington, D.C. 20002; Christian College Consor-
tium, 6 Pine Tree Drive, Suite 180, St. Paul, MN 55112;
American Association of Bible Colleges, P.O. Box 1523,
Fayetteville, AR 72702. Then contact the specific college

directly and ask them to send you a catalog. Compare their offerings with your vocational goals, financial situation, geographical preferences, and other factors of interest to you. Also check with your church for additional colleges or graduate schools that may be funded by your denomination.

If you are looking for a truly Christian educational institution, the key is whether the school's posture is to honor Jesus Christ as Lord and the Bible as His Word. You will have to discern this in your selection process.

Be cautious on this point with any school you consider. There are some schools that have a loose denominational affiliation and are subsidized by church member donations but in the name of academic freedom have drifted from the precepts on which they were founded. Academic freedom is often a guise for teaching antibiblical material.

OTHER TYPES OF SCHOOLING

Colleges and universities are not the only way to obtain formal education and, in some instances, are not necessarily the best way. In some cases, preparation can best be met with shorter and more specialized or technical training.

Technical and specialized schools operate in most larger communities. The range of subjects is wide in scope. One way to find them in your community is to look in the Yellow Pages of your telephone directory, or you may wish to contact the National Association of Trade and Technical Schools (NATTS). Single copies of two of their publications, *Handbook of Accredited Private Trade and Technical Schools,* and *How to Choose a Career and a Career School,* can be obtained from NATTS at 2251 Wisconsin Ave., N.W., Suite 200, Washington, DC 20007.

The National Home Study Council also supplies information about home-study programs. They distribute the *Directory of Accredited Home Study Schools* (free) and *There's a School in Your Mailbox* (a slight charge). You can request these from the National Home Study Council, 1601 18th Street, N.W., Washington, DC 20009.

PART IV
Finding a Job

Chapter 7

HOW TO FIND JOB OPENINGS

The big question is: "Where can I find job openings?" The purpose of this chapter is to give you plenty of ideas. However, first we need to discuss and analyze the job market in general. Then we'll give you lots of places where you might find an opening.

As a Christian job seeker, there are certain things about the potential job market that you should consider. An important marketing principle is that whenever you have a product to sell, you analyze the potential market. Determine through research what you can about your potential customers: who they are, where they are, how they think, what they want.

It is no less true for the Christian job seeker. The product is *you*. Your potential customers are your potential employers. You must market yourself; a job search is a selling campaign. All of your efforts, telephone calls, letters, resumés, and interviews are part of your marketing campaign.

Still, there is a special consideration and dimension for the Christian that does not apply to anyone else. Beyond a cold market analysis, ask yourself if you feel drawn toward a particular ministry or organization. This is what happened to me when I first entered full-time Christian service. I felt almost a magnetism toward a certain organization. I proceeded in that direction, and it was later confirmed clearly that that is where I was supposed to be.

Such an inner witness takes priority over all techniques, even though you may not have any such leadings now. Until or unless you do hear a strong inner voice, proceed with your marketing strategy.

DEFINE YOUR PRODUCT

Review what we covered in previous chapters about your gifts and talents. Which one or ones do you want to market, to use in pursuing a vocation?

In industry, market research helps a company to determine what the characteristics of a product should be, such as shape, size, color.

Just so, you should review your present product. Review your gifts and talents, your interest, your training and experience, and any particular calling you may have discerned, your perception of what God's will for your life may be. If you have not already done so, *write it all down*. Take paper and pencil and put these down in vertical lists, so you can look at them, add to them, or change them. This will also help you to meditate on them.

The sum total of what you have just done from this exercise is *you,* your product.

Now let's take a look at the market.

JOB-MARKET CONSIDERATIONS

Your potential job market is going to depend, of course, on the specific product you are offering. If your talents are very specialized, your potential market will be narrow. If your talents are general, your market will be wide and will include a large number of potential employers.

For example, if your specific talent is in aviation, your

potential Christian market is relatively small because not too many ministries have an airplane. Still, some do because it is either necessary for their work, such as resupplying missionaries in isolated areas, or, in some cases, it is a cost-effective alternative to commercial travel. If your talent is in electronics, your market is much larger because there are scores of ministries that use electronics in their work, especially the radio and television ministries. If your gifts are administrative, your market is almost unlimited because administrative skills are needed virtually everywhere.

So, as you analyze your potential market—what types of ministries or companies can use your talent—it will narrow the list of possibilities for you.

GEOGRAPHICAL CONSIDERATIONS

Do you prefer a state or specific region of the country? Do you feel a definite calling to work overseas? Let this help you narrow your market further. Of course, the less you are concerned with geographical considerations, the wider your potential market.

TYPE OF MINISTRY

Can you focus on a particular type of ministry that fits your talent and heart's desire? If so, that will narrow your market even further.

There are all kinds of Christian organizations and ministries. Do you lean toward the purely one-on-one evangelical ministry? A social service ministry that helps needy people? A publications or broadcasting ministry? Maybe a ministry devoted to youth is your calling? Maybe to the elderly? The world is full of needs, and there is probably a ministry that focuses on just about each one of them. This is the wonderful characteristic of the body of

Christ: being wherever believers are, ministering, caring, loving, sharing the Good News. That is why Jesus said, "Greater works . . . shall he do; because I go to the Father" (John 14:12).

DOCTRINAL CONSIDERATIONS

I usually do not like to mention doctrine because it is sometimes divisive, but it is a reality Christians have to deal with and it can be a factor in your job search.

Let us hope that you have learned how to be comfortable with believers everywhere, regardless of some points of disagreement on biblical interpretation. It is really liberating just to love and appreciate all other believers. Our fellowship is in Him, not in doctrine.

Nevertheless, Christians are diverse for traditional, historical, or sociological reasons. No one seems to have a corner on all the truth, though most think they do at times. On some points of doctrine there can be no compromise: the deity of Jesus Christ, the efficacy of His blood, and salvation by grace through faith. But there are other points on which Christians perennially disagree, and if any of these are critically important to you, it will help narrow your job market. For example, if you believe strongly that the supernatural gifts of the Holy Spirit ended when the last apostle died and that anyone manifesting them today is crazy, deceived, or demon-possessed, then you would be most out-of-place and unhappy in a ministry that believes otherwise.

Do not seek employment anywhere unless you can, in your heart and with the light the Lord has given you, accept that ministry or company as it is, without a critical, judgmental, or superior attitude.

PROFIT VERSUS NONPROFIT

It may surprise you to learn that some organizations deeply involved in the work of the Lord are actually commercial, profit-making enterprises. This does not make them any less spiritual or less fruitful for the kingdom. Making a profit is not a sin; operating on donations is not necessarily saintly. It's what you do with both that counts.

If it is important for your own definition of spirituality to work in a nonprofit ministry, it is best to be true to yourself and narrow your potential job market accordingly. If not, your market is obviously wider. For example, many commercial enterprises are purely Christian endeavors, including broadcast stations, publishers, and film producers.

The key is to examine the fruit. Do not harshly judge a company that is concerned with profit performance, which is necessary for survival in a tough, economic world. Consider that investors deserve a return on their capital; what they do with the return is between the Lord and them.

SALARY VERSUS RAISING YOUR OWN SUPPORT

What you can expect in terms of remuneration in the Christian marketplace varies widely, both in *philosophy* of remuneration and an organization's *ability* to pay.

Some ministries believe that a Christian vocation should be a sacrifice in every respect and that if the Lord did not have a place to lay his head, then why should we? Therefore, wages are minimal, at or near subsistence level. A major advantage of this type of philosophy is that commitment is virtually assured from those who embark upon such a ministry.

Others believe that "a laborer is worthy of his hire" and are concerned about not "oppressing" or putting a "yoke" (see Isa. 58) on their employees, and they offer wages that are more competitive with the commercial job market.

Some believe in and would like to offer competitive wages but do not have the financial ability to do so. This also may be a matter of prioritizing. A new project may be deemed more important than a needed salary increase.

Then, there are hybrids of the above, paying top salaries for hard-to-get skilled people but keeping a tight lid on the lesser skilled. This is more of a truly commercial philosophy of paying "what the traffic will bear."

Still another approach is to require the committed employee to raise his own support from church, friends, or sponsoring organizations. This is a valid form of missionary endeavor and gives sponsors the opportunity of sharing both the responsibilities and the spiritual rewards of the mission outreach.

My purpose in reviewing these approaches is not to judge or evaluate. Moreover, I'd like to caution you about your evaluation: Do not let money make the decision for you. You obviously should not opt for the highest salary or serve the Lord for mercenary reasons. Neither should you become masochistic, seeking a low wage because that's the most spiritual thing to do.

The goal is to be where the Lord wants you. It may be a place of high or low financial reward, but wherever, it will be the place of greatest happiness and fruit.

To give you a feeling for average salaries for selected jobs in the United States, listings from the Department of Labor, Bureau of Labor Statistics, are included in appendixes D and E. A listing of many Christian organizations and ministries is included as appendix F.

SPECIFIC CAREER INFORMATION

Appendix D is especially included to give you a broad cross-section of selected jobs that might be applicable to both Christian and secular organizations and helpful information about these jobs, including: nature of the work, working conditions, training and other qualifications needed, possible earnings, and sources of additional information.

WHERE TO GET A JOB

Christian Employment. If you are aiming for Christian work, you may already know where you want to apply. If not, appendix F contains the names of over 2,000 potential Christian employers. If any appeal to you, even if you don't know whether they have any openings, it wouldn't hurt to contact them, just in case.

Other employment. If you are considering the general job market, consider the following for job information and potential sources of job openings:

State employment services offices
Civil Service announcements (federal, state, local)
Classified ads
    Local and out-of-town newspapers
    Professional journals
    Trade magazines
Labor unions
Professional associations (state and local chapters)
Libraries and community centers
Women's counseling and employment programs
Youth programs
School or college placement services
Employment agencies and career consultants
Employers
Parents, friends, and neighbors (Using all the influence and referrals at your disposal—sometimes called "networking"—it's smart.)

Public Employment Service. The State employment service, sometimes called the Job Service, operates in coordination with the Labor Department's U.S. Employment Service. Its 2,000 local offices, also known as employment service centers, help job seekers locate employment and employers find qualified workers at no cost. To find the office nearest you, look in the state government telephone listings under "Job Service" or "Employment."

If you go to one of these centers, an interviewer will determine if you are "job ready" or if counseling and testing services would be helpful before you begin your job search. You may examine the Job Bank, a computerized listing of public and private sector job openings that is updated daily. Select openings that interest you, then get with a counselor who can give you more information and set up an interview for you.

These centers can provide a wealth of free information and services, including aptitude testing and counseling to help you choose a career.

Special Groups. You may be entitled to special consideration. By law veterans, for example, are entitled to priority at state employment service centers. If you are economically disadvantaged or face barriers to employment, you may find help through the Job Training Partnership Act, with information available through the service centers.

Youth Programs. Summer Youth Programs provide summer jobs in city, county, and state government agencies for low-income youth. Students, school dropouts, or graduates entering the labor market who are between 16 and 21 years of age are eligible. In addition, the Job Corps, with more than 100 centers throughout the United States, helps young people learn skills and obtain education.

Classified ads. "Help wanted" newspaper ads list hundreds of jobs. Realize, however, that not all job openings are listed there. Also, be aware that classified ads commonly do not give some important information. Many offer little or no description of the job, working conditions, pay, or benefits. Some do not even identify the employer. Here are some tips for using these ads:

— Don't rely solely on them. Follow other leads as well.
— Answer ads promptly. Check them every day as early as possible.
— Beware of "no experience necessary" ads. They often signal poor working conditions, low pay, or commission-only work.

Federal Jobs. For information on Federal jobs only, contact the Federal Job Information Center, 1900 East St., N.W., Washington, D.C. 20415, or call (202) 653-8468.

A PARTING WORD

Remember—if you spend as much time in pursuit of a job as you would on the job if you had one (i.e., eight hours a day), your chances of getting a job are much higher. Too many people take a totally relaxed attitude and seek a job only halfheartedly, starting late in the day, ending early, with plenty of time off in between.

Let your aggressiveness and time spent in searching for a job be proportional to your need for one. A person who doesn't put forth the effort shouldn't complain if he doesn't get a job!

But that's not you. You are taking the time to read this book; therefore, I believe you will diligently apply its principles.

Chapter 8

HOW TO USE PLACEMENT ORGANIZATIONS

Government agencies were described in the preceding chapter. This chapter will primarily discuss nongovernment and Christian agencies. Few Christians seeking full-time work with a Christian organization consider using a placement organization. Yet, these organizations can be helpful, believe it or not.

Some Christian organizations *do* seek help through placement services. This is especially true for certain positions that are difficult to fill, including entry-level and executive positions. For example, as a personnel director, I occasionally had need for clerical help, and, even though the organization received several hundred applications per month, I could not always find qualified people. I had to go to a private placement organization.

Keep in mind that a Christian organization that is *less* visible to the public generally has fewer applicants and is *more* likely to use placement organizations. For example, a Christian broadcasting organization is very visible and may get hundreds of unsolicited resumés each month. The mass media attract attention and are less likely to have to search for employees. Conversely, ministries that operate out of the public eye, accomplishing one-on-one ministry, do not attract as much attention.

There is nothing wrong with using a placement organization, but if you are already drawn to a particular ministry or type of work, why not just communicate directly? Still, each situation is different, and there may be good reasons for your feeling the need to use a placement firm. Let's examine how these organizations can help you.

TYPES OF PLACEMENT ORGANIZATIONS

There are both government and private organizations that specialize in helping people find jobs.

PRIVATE PLACEMENT FIRMS

There are several different types of private agencies: Some only handle clerical and blue-collar jobs; some specialize in middle management and professional areas; others handle only executive and upper management. They differ greatly as to who pays the bill for their services— you or the employer—and how much.

Traditional Employment Agencies. The employment agency with which most people are familiar deals mostly with clerical and blue-collar positions. There is much competition between the various agencies, and they usually do not offer exclusive listings. Some require payment by the job seeker in the form of a significant percentage of the initial salary. This can really hurt if you are just starting out to work. Some are paid by the employer. There are some hybrid arrangements with pay coming from both. Some of these agencies only get paid when there is a hire, so the pressure on them is intense to get interviews, often resulting in a waste of your time. Placement is often not as selective as it should be.

You might benefit from using this type of agency, which sometimes handles positions for Christian organizations; however, try to avoid a fee being imposed on you instead of the employer. If there is a high fee, you would probably be better off without their help, doing your own job hunting. Also, try to avoid any exclusive arrangement that would restrict your own continued searching or the use of other agencies.

Contingency Agencies. Contingency-type agencies generally deal with the next higher level on the job ladder; for example, professional positions in accounting, engineering, data processing, sales, and the like, with annual incomes from approximately $20,000 to $50,000. The fee for this service is usually paid by the employer and may be as much as 30 percent of the first-year salary. Many are plugged into a national network of job openings, so you might want to use one of these as long as it does not cost you anything.

Executive Search Firms. These agencies deal only with the very high executive and upper management positions, the top of the job ladder. Fees for this type of recruiting may be as high as 40 percent of the annual salary for the position plus expenses, whether or not their search is successful. And the expenses, such as travel, can be enormous. Many companies place a high value on their services for filling certain executive positions because a right or wrong decision about a high-level employee can save, make, or cost a large company millions of dollars.

If this is your league, in very large cities you might find these listed in the Yellow Pages. Also, try the *Wall Street Journal* or write the Association of Executive Recruiting Consultants, Inc., 30 Rockefeller Plaza, New York, NY 10020.

CHRISTIAN PLACEMENT SERVICES

One very fine organization you should consider is Intercristo, a nonprofit, Christian organization dedicated to providing placement services for Christians on a worldwide basis.

Intercristo uses a computer-matching approach. They have a very large data bank of jobs available with Christian ministries and with companies that are headed by Christians and who want only Christian employees.

They only charge you a small administrative fee to enter your personal data into the computer and do a search for you. The computer will try to match your interests and skills with those of many potential employers.

You simply fill out a form, disclosing essential information about yourself, such as your interests, education, and experience; the computer searches for a position to match. You will be given a print-out of jobs available for which you qualify, along with the names, addresses, and telephone numbers of the potential employers—all you need for further inquiry. Your information will also be sent to the potential employer for his information.

You can contact Intercristo by calling (800) 426-1342 (recording), or (800) 426-1343. Their address is P.O. Box 33487, Seattle, WA 98133.

The Christian Ministries Management Association maintains certain job listings. They can be contacted at P.O. Box 4638, Diamond Bar, CA 91765, (714) 861-8861.

If you are interested in the mission field, contact the missions function of your church or denomination, or one of the following:

Global Opportunities, 1600 Elizabeth Street, Pasadena, CA 91104; Tent Makers, International, P.O. Box 33826, Seattle, WA 98133; the Association of International Missions Service (AIMS), P.O.Box 64534, Virginia Beach, VA 23464. Also see missions organizations listed in appendix F.

Chapter 9
HOW TO CONTACT EMPLOYERS

This chapter will tell you how to make your initial contacts with potential employers. First, however, before we do, let's consider something very important to you as you contact them—your mental attitude and self-image. How you see yourself will affect how they will see you.

You are a product and you are marketing or selling yourself. As with all marketplaces, there are competing products. Your potential customers are going to say, "Should I buy him or that other person I'm considering?" The employer will be greatly influenced by how the applicants are wrapped or packaged, that is, how they present themselves and how they appear during the critical stages of consideration. I want you to consider this marketing principle of packaging as it pertains to you and your efforts. Product packaging is a very important subject and, where tangible goods are concerned, is one that commands much time and attention from the marketing experts. Packaging is designed for attractiveness and shelf appeal, to make the product almost shout, "Take me."

Your wrapping—how you appear to a potential employer—is very important, and I do not mean just your physical appearance. I'm also referring to the inner you— the real you—that part that you want to be most appealing to a prospective employer.

YOUR SELF-IMAGE

What *do* you think about yourself? I have known people whose self-image has defeated them before they ever started looking for a job. It is very important to cover this subject, especially within a Christian context.

My concern here is not with those who are overflowing with self-confidence, although I would suggest that you substitute "His-confidence." My concern is with any reader who may be suffering from a poor self-image, low self-esteem, a lack of confidence, or an inferiority complex. There are many causes of this, such as how you were treated as a child, unhappy experiences in school, or maybe some hard times you have had later in life.

Through prayer, the Lord may allow the root cause, whatever it is, to come to the surface, so it can be recognized. Recognition is a major step toward healing. When you get these things out of the recesses of your mind, they are usually much smaller than you thought and you see them in a new perspective.

Once you gain this perspective, the second step is possible. You can have assurance that you are accepted by God because of Jesus, the Savior, and what He has done for you. In this light, you discover your only possible identity: Without Him, you are truly nothing; with Him, you are truly everything. If you have given yourself to Him, He accepts you.

> Therefore having been justified [acquitted, found not guilty, a legal term] by faith, you have peace with God through our Lord Jesus Christ (Rom. 5:1).

Peace with God. When the Father looks at you, He sees you clothed in the righteousness of His Son. You no longer have to feel guilty, because you are one of His and you were bought with a price. He approves of you.

Once you get this revelation in your heart, you can be set

free to be the happy, peaceful, and confident creature that your Father wants you to be. It will enhance your love and affection toward the Lord because of a greater appreciation of what He has done for you, which will affect your whole being. *It will affect you vocationally,* as an outworking of a new inner reality.

Once you are rooted in the knowledge of "the love of Christ which surpasses all knowledge," you can be "filled with all the fullness of God" (Eph. 3:17–19 RSV). This knowledge is vital to your vocational aspirations, for this power at work within us is "able to do far more abundantly than all you ask or think" (v. 20).

In summary, let your heart's image of yourself be molded by a clear understanding of your special place in the Savior and by a knowledge of His power working in you. *As you think in your heart about these things, so will you be.* And so will you appear.

Now with some spiritual preliminaries out of the way, let's look at some practical tips on how to present yourself to a potential employer.

IN PERSON, BY TELEPHONE, OR BY MAIL?

Let's say you have picked out one or more organizations that appeal to you. Further, you believe you have talents that could be used. How do you do it? Do you drop by in person first? Do you call first? Or do you mail them a resumé? Maybe there is another alternative.

Geography is a major consideration. If the potential employer is a thousand miles away, it isn't practical to travel that far at this stage. Surprisingly, however, some people do. As a former personnel director, I saw many instances when people came from long distances unannounced and with no appointment. Some had spent their last cent to get there, and when they arrived, they had no money for food and shelter. Often, they would say "the Lord told me to come and you would have a job for me." Unfortunately in every case I can think of but one, there was never such an opening. Naturally, we were gracious and loving, though to be so was a burden to the ministry.

What I'm saying is this, if God truly has a place for you with a given ministry, it will be easier—and less taxing on everyone—if you write or call first. Just showing up does not necessarily demonstrate your faith to a potential employer.

Decrying them as too bureaucratic, rigid, or legalistic, some people are critical of Christian organizations that have standard personnel procedures, yet good, sound (and flexible) personnel practices are wise. More often than not, I have seen their violation result in disaster. Adherence to them can save an organization from many problems. Keep this in mind as you are dealing with organizations and faced with their procedures.

Remember, your ability to hear from God is only half of the equation. I once had dramatic spiritual insight that the Lord had prepared a job for me in a certain place, but I withheld the information during the interview, not wanting to use it as spiritual leverage. If it were truly of God, I reasoned, they would hire me. Besides, I wanted to test it further, to see if it was really of God. I was hired.

I recommend you use the same principles. I must admit that whenever I feel someone using his divine guidance as leverage, I am automatically defensive. Instead of applying this sort of pressure, simply believe that God is big enough to bring the right applicant to the right job at the right time. When you walk in for a scheduled interview, you may be that right person.

Several years ago when my personnel assistant decided to go to seminary, I was forced to find a replacement for him. I checked the files of resumés that had been received over the previous couple of years. One resumé looked good to me. The fellow had over twenty years of personnel experience. He seemed to be spiritually motivated. But his resumé had been on file for about six months, and chances were that he had found a job. But I decided to call him and confirm his availability.

Sam was astounded at my call. He had just voluntarily resigned from his previous position that very week as an act of obedience to what he thought the Lord was saying. He had no other job offer or possibility. He was just trusting the Lord would provide something. He had even felt led to put his house up for sale, even though he had no idea he would be leaving the area.

The timing of my telephone call was an amazing and dramatic confirmation of God's faithfulness. After going through our rigorous screening procedures, Sam joined the ministry shortly thereafter and became one of the most dedicated and faithful employees. The Lord was surely working on both sides of that arrangement—the need and also the provision.

APPLYING BY MAIL

If you are applying to an organization some distance from you, in another city or state, I recommend:

Prepare a good resumé.

Telephone in advance, just to let them know that you are sending them your resumé. This will put you in their minds and on the alert for your correspondence. It might help; it cannot hurt. Of course, if they are immediately excited and invite you for an interview, then go. This is not likely, however, and they will probably be polite and encourage you to go ahead and send your resumé.

Mail your resumé with a warm, friendly, but professional cover letter. (See the next chapter about this subject.)

I recommend you follow the above procedure whenever you are a significant distance from the potential employer. An in-person visit is always best but rarely worth the cost from a long distance.

APPLYING IN PERSON

When would you apply in person? Whenever the distance is reasonable, such as within a fifty-mile radius.

Even when you apply in person, do not expect an immediate interview. Be prepared, but you may not get it. They will probably want to have time to review your resumé and get back with you, if they see a possibility.

But by applying in person, at least you have established a *presence* and an *impression*. Then whenever they see your resumé, they will think of that charming, friendly, impressive, and well-groomed person who brought it in. That is you, isn't it?

Whenever you make any kind of contact with a potential employer, do not make the fatal mistake of thinking he is just a good old, regular guy (or gal) who won't mind if you look or act a little sloppy. After all, the main thing is your spiritual commitment. No need to bother with worldly appearances. Right?

Wrong! Your physical appearance is critically important. Believe it or not, your external appearance almost always reflects an inward attitude that even correlates with work performance and habits. With everyone, neatness makes an impression, as does the lack of it.

SPECIAL CONSIDERATIONS

APPLYING TO A NON-CHRISTIAN COMPANY

Your calling may not be to a Christian organization but to a secular profession and company. This is no less worthy, a point that cannot be emphasized too strongly. As mentioned earlier, what is truly spiritual is to be where the Lord wants you, and a secular career can be as much a calling as working in a Christian ministry or company. God wants His people to be salt and light throughout the world.

I assume you have a commitment to the Lord, or you would probably not be reading this book. But with this commitment, what should your approach be when applying to a secular organization? First, I strongly suggest that you don't apply carrying a big black Bible and wearing a six-inch cross dangling at your neck. And don't greet the personnel director with, "Praise the Lord, brother!" You just might scare him to death. In your contacts with the world, you need to be as wise as a serpent and as harmless as a dove. You share your faith as the Spirit gives opportunity, but it is sometimes counterproductive to wear it on your sleeve.

If asked, never be reluctant to mention your faith and commitment, but let the Spirit be in control. If not asked, or unless the Spirit really gives an opening, save it. Do not be unwise and jeopardize a job opportunity and thereby maybe miss God's best for you.

If, during recruiting or later on the job, you detect a conflict of principle—something that the company does or wants you to do that you believe to be ungodly and wrong—pray about how to approach the matter and ask for wisdom. The incident may shatter your relationship with the company; nevertheless, it is also possible that if handled with *love* and *wisdom,* you might be an agent of change and have a vital influence on individual lives. Isn't that what it's all about? "We are ambassadors for Christ, God making His appeal through us" (2 Cor. 5:20 RSV).

APPLYING TO A CHRISTIAN ORGANIZATION

Although discussed previously, now you need to consider your approach to the specific Christian organization to which you are presenting yourself. God's people come in lots of flavors, with varieties of opinion about behavior and appearance. Do some checking, maybe with a telephone call or two, and find out what peculiarities there may be that you should know. Some companies have rules against smoking; others have rules about weight, dress, and appearance—or strong feelings on some fine points of doctrine.

None of these may ever be a factor for you, yet either for you or for your prospective employer it is always best to be prepared and not to be surprised.

In conclusion, here are some practical pointers as you proceed with your job hunting whether Christian or secular:

DO proceed with a firm conviction that God loves you, is with you, and is helping you.

DO let that conviction give you a strong confidence.

DO exhibit to potential employers a commitment and enthusiasm to serve unselfishly and be effective in whatever God has for you.

DO proceed with your resumé and letter writing, painting a positive and professional image of yourself.

DO have a resumé that will be noteworthy in content, style, format, and accuracy.

DO appear at interviews with your "best foot for-ward," properly dressed and well-groomed.

DO be positive and confident at all times.

DO find out what you can about any ministry or organization to which you apply, so you will be (and will appear to be) well-informed.

DO NOT approach your job hunting with a complacent or lackadaisical attitude. *It deserves your best effort.*

Chapter 10

HOW TO PREPARE
A RESUMÉ

Your resumé is truly a self-portrait. You prepare it, and the subject is you. You are saying, loud and clear, "This is me!" Your resumé is your advertisement.

I am amazed at how some people portray themselves. Some people are just careless. Be careful when preparing your resumé because it is one of the most important things you will do in your job-hunting process. Extra time in preparation will pay later.

Technically, you do not need a resumé. Every company has application forms you can use to paint your portrait, and some companies require you to fill out an application form whether or not you have a resumé. But using an application form without a resumé lacks *class*. It's like painting your portrait using paint-by-numbers instead of with the skilled hand of a creative artist. You deserve a resumé.

If you don't take time to prepare it correctly, however, you would be better-off without it because your resumé is often the first and most critical impression given to a potential employer. Look at your resumé from the employer's viewpoint. If your resumé is sloppy, you are sloppy. If it is too verbose, you are probably too verbose. If it is too short, you probably have little to offer. If it is full of mistakes, you are probably a mistake. If it is not well organized, you are probably not well organized. If it is full of baloney, well, guess what?

Really, what else can he think? After all, he only has your resumé, maybe one or two sheets of paper, and he has to form a judgment, usually a quick one because of other pressing matters. And remember, he has never had the pleasure of meeting you and knowing what a charming, bright, and impressive person you are. He doesn't know that you were just too busy to do a really super job on your resumé and you assumed that he would understand. He doesn't understand because he is much busier.

When you give or send your resumé, it is assumed that you are saying, "Hey, this is my best shot." Before you make that shot, let's look at some ways you can communicate in the most effective manner.

First, let's size up your audience. Your resumé will probably go to a very busy personnel administrator. He needs to fill a job with the best person, with the least amount of effort because there are a million other things that are waiting to be done. Your resumé is one of scores of papers to reach his desk that day. Some of them are other resumés. (I have personally reviewed as many as eight hundred resumés in a single month, one hundred once at one sitting.)

Your resumé comes to the top of the stack. You are actually there by proxy. Now is your big chance. You finally have his attention. Through your resumé, you say to him, "Look at me!"

If your resumé is poorly done, his immediate reaction will be, "Ugh. Anyone who does such a poor job here will have poor work habits." He will hasten to dispose of it, giving it a quick glance, then assigning a brief code, so his secretary will know to send a nice rejection letter.

If, however, you have taken the time and done good work, his reaction will be, "Hmm. Anyone who would do a nice job like this must be worth considering. I'll look at it closely."

That first glance at your communication is critical, and it

probably takes only five to ten seconds. This is where you really want to attract attention.

THE ATTENTION-GETTER

Your best attention-getter is not the resumé but a cover letter. A good cover letter is absolutely essential. In fact, I consider it as important as the resumé attached, and it baffles me that so many people do not use one. No matter how good a resumé is, receiving it in the mail without a cover letter is like receiving a cold fish wrapped in a newspaper.

The cover letter adds a little warmth and personality to the necessarily formal resumé and is simply a brief introduction and statement of interest and availability. In Christian employment it is also the perfect place to let them know immediately that you are a Christian and share the organization's values and goals. A good cover letter can actually be magnetizing, drawing the reader to give attention to your resumé. Therefore, do not use a form letter. A personalized letter has a much greater effect. Two to four short paragraphs are usually best, never more than a page.

To whom do you address it? Normally, address it to the personnel director. If it is a small ministry or company, address it to the president or whatever title the leader may have, and use his name with the title. If you do not already know this information, call and ask.

The cover letter, as well as the resumé, should be typed clearly and with no obvious mistakes, even if you have to pay to have it typed and especially if you are seeking a management-level job.

A sample letter is included. Use words such as these if they apply to you; otherwise, use your own words. Be real, be positive, and be upbeat.

Sample Cover Letter:
Your street number
City, State, Zip
Date, Area code, and telephone number

Mr. Hiram Firum
Personnel Director
Especially Anointed Christian Ministries, Inc.
Anytown, USA

Dear Mr. Firum:

I have always loved Especially Anointed Christian Ministries and have wanted to be a part of it. I want to thank all of you for being such a blessing to me.

Since I am graduating soon, I have been seeking the Lord's will for my life. I definitely feel a call to be in full-time Christian work. It would be a great privilege and blessing if this could be with your ministry.

Enclosed is a copy of my resumé. The Lord has gifted me in (your talent), and I know that with His help I could be an asset to your organization. I want to be a part of what you are doing and use my gifts to help further your wonderful work.

I am anxious to meet you and look forward to hearing from you at your earliest convenience.

Sincerely,

Nita Job

A final suggestion. There must be a book somewhere that tells letter and resumé writers to exude so much confidence that they come across as egomaniacs. I've read too many of their resumés. Confidence is good, but extreme self-exaltation is not good. Don't succumb to the temptation and say something like this:

"I am confident that my talents can solve your problems in no time." (Reader's reaction: *He doesn't even know what our problems are! It sounds like he would be another problem.*)

A little humility is healthy. Also, be careful what type of person you describe yourself to be.

"I am a strong manager, able to get optimal results from people with minimal costs." (Reaction: *Sounds like an unpopular slave driver. He would probably cause people problems.*)

"I am people-oriented and have unusual skills at relating with fellow employees and subordinates." (Reaction: *Sounds like a goof-off, who wastes time talking all day.*)

"I can help the organization reassess its goals and direction to make a larger impact, and I have some great new ideas." (Reaction: *Sounds like a know-it-all, who would give the boss a hard time. Who needs it?*)

THE RESUMÉ

The resumé should be a brief summary of yourself, not an autobiography. It should have a certain structure, allowing for some variance, but not too much. There are two main types of resumés, the chronological and the functional. See samples included.

THE CHRONOLOGICAL RESUMÉ

This is the most popularly used resumé, so personnel people are very familiar with it. In this resumé, employment experience is listed in reverse chronological order, with most recent work listed first. It is a concise, orderly record of work experience; a disadvantage is that it will

reveal shortcomings in experience and gaps in employment. I recommend this for your primary consideration,
however, because a sharp interviewer will be suspicious
and see your attempts to use format to hide lack of
experience.

THE FUNCTIONAL RESUMÉ

This format does not contain employment dates but
instead emphasizes qualifications, skills, and accomplishments. It stresses a specific ability you are trying to
market. This is not a bad format for a student just
graduating who has had no work experience. But for
anyone else, the interviewer will ask himself, *What has he
done, when and where? And why is he trying to hide it?*

You can combine the above two types of resumés, giving
both a chronological work history and also functional
emphases, but length may be a problem. Again, if you have
only a student background and a little work history, a
combination might be best for you. The functional part can
emphasize some of the strengths you have exhibited in
school activities, such as school or campus organizations;
your work history can include summer or part-time jobs
you have had.

PARTS OF A RESUMÉ

There are several categories of information that are
essential to every resumé, but do not necessarily have to
be in the order given below.

Personal Identification. Your name, address, and telephone number should appear at the top of the first page in
the center or at the margin.

Objective. Write your employment objective in one brief
sentence. If applicable, use the position, title, or type of

responsibility of the job being sought, but do not make this more specific than you really want it to be, or it will box you out of other position possibilities. Also, consider wording your objective differently for resumés sent to different companies.

Education. List degrees earned, when and where. If you have a college degree, do not show high school information; if you have no degree, do indicate same. Show school honors, awards, and (if superior) your grade point average. Also, show significant additional schooling, such as non-degree work, technical training, special seminars, and structured self-study.

Employment Experience. Show employment experience in reverse chronological order (latest one first). List company and job titles held, with a brief description of responsibilities and major accomplishments. Also, consider these points, if significant:

Show to whom you reported, if impressive, such as to the president or top executive.

How many people were you responsible for?

How big a budget were you responsible for?

Show significant promotions.

Military Experience. If applicable, show military service time, branch of service, specialty, and highest rank held. Also, include any present reserve activity or obligations.

Personal. There are some things you are not legally required to divulge, and some would urge you not to do so. I recommend, however, that you be totally open. I would tell age, marital and family status, and health status. If any of these are not important to an employer, such as your age, it will not hurt. If it is important, he is going to find out anyway. The government may say it is not necessary, but the government is not hiring you.

Community/Civic Involvements. List any organizations, offices held, dates, and achievements.

Professional Affiliations. List membership in professional organizations.

Special Skills. List any special skills, such as foreign languages or licenses held.

Interests and Activities. List hobbies and avocations (or combine under *Personal*).

References. At this point, just say the standard, "Available upon request."

All this and brief too? Yes. It may take some practice and a few rewrites, but you can do it. To say a lot in a few words is an art, and your prospective employer may recognize your talent here.

STEPS IN PREPARING A RESUMÉ

It is best to start by doing a thorough self-analysis, using the major points of a resumé. Take full inventory of yourself in rough form before you start writing your resumé. List everything point-by-point with dates at every relevant point, which will be the raw material for your resumé. Next, decide upon a resumé format that suits you best.

WRITING YOUR FIRST DRAFT

Brief, action-oriented wording is essential, not long, drawn-out phrases, full sentences, or the pronoun "I." Use past tense *action verbs* and short phrases in describing your experience. For example, say, "Operated computer terminals," instead of saying, "I was responsible for the operation of computer terminals."

Avoid the use of abbreviations where possible. Be consistent in your format, order of information, tense of verbs and style.

Do the best you can on your first draft but remember, it is *only* a draft. Type it or have it typed, so it can be properly critiqued.

CRITIQUE YOUR FIRST DRAFT

It would be wise to get some help from others to review what you have done, especially if they are familiar with the type of work you are applying for or if they are accustomed to reviewing resumés. The impression of others is very important. You may not use all their suggestions but you need their reactions to these questions:

Does it appear neat?

Does it appear orderly?

Is it easy to read?

Does it convey the message you want?

Is the format efficient and attractive?

THE FINAL DRAFT

Incorporate all relevant feedback and begin writing your final draft. Continually try to improve the wording, making every word meaningful. Attractively use all space on each page.

Here are some additional tips for your final product:

Keep length to one or two pages.

Use only one side of the page.

Don't use language from official job descriptions.

Don't state details of employment more than ten years past.

Don't include salary history, picture of yourself, or attachments of official documents.

Don't include a covering sheet (this does not mean cover letter, which is recommended).

Always have it typed on a professional typewriter in good condition. I suggest a professional service, but ask for a sample of their work for inspection first.

If you really want to go first class, have it typeset and printed.

Use only high-quality paper. The greatest resumé on cheap paper loses its effect. Consider tinted paper.

Have it reproduced only by a high-quality, offset method. This is not expensive, and it will look much better.

(CHRONOLOGICAL FORMAT FOR RESUMÉ OF RECENT GRADUATE)

Name
Address
Telephone Number

OBJECTIVE

Position as programmer, with opportunities for growth and increased responsibility.

EDUCATION

B.S. in Computer Science, June 1991, Colonial State University, Tidewater, Virginia.

Highlights: GPA 3.4/4.0, Dean's List; Chairman, Computer Club; Omicron Delta Kappa, leadership fraternity; Cadet Major, Air Force ROTC; Earned expenses through part-time employment.

Computer languages learned: FORTRAN, COBOL, BASIC, AND APL.

EMPLOYMENT EXPERIENCE

Computer Consultant, Colonial State University, 1989–1991. Consultant for the university while attending as full-time student. Aided students in hardware and software applications.

Assistant Manager, Pizza Den, Inc., Tidewater, Va., 1988–1991. Assisted in the management of restaurant. Hired, trained, scheduled, and supervised evening shift. Responsible for four people. Reported to manager. Part-time, approximately 20 hours per week.

MILITARY STATUS

Second lieutenant, U.S. Air Force Reserve. No active duty commitment.

PERSONAL

Birthdate: November 19, 1969. Single. Health excellent. Special interests: sports, music. Church basketball team. Study guitar. Participate in Bible study group.

COMMUNITY ACTIVITY

Member, Jaycees; Assistant Scoutmaster, Boy Scouts of America.

PROFESSIONAL AFFILIATIONS

Member, Computer Software Association.

SPECIAL SKILLS

French language, fluent. FAA Private Pilot's License.

REFERENCES

Available upon request.

(FUNCTIONAL RESUMÉ FORMAT FOR SAME PERSON)

Name
Address
Telephone Number

OBJECTIVE

Position as programmer, with opportunities for growth and increased responsibilities.

EXPERIENCE

Programming
Extensive experience in academic environment of programming using languages of FORTRAN, COBOL, BASIC, and APL.

Teaching
Classroom experience for two years, teaching students various hardware and software applications.

Management
Responsible for personnel selection, hiring, training, scheduling, and insuring operational effectiveness under high pressure environment.

Public Relations
Maintained outstanding relations with public in difficult retail marketing situation. Improved customer satisfaction, resulting in increased gross revenue and profit for corporation.

EDUCATION

B.S. in Computer Science, Colonial State University, 1991. GPA 3.4/4.0, Deans List. Chairman, Computer Club. Omicron Delta Kappa, leadership fraternity. Cadet Major, Air Force ROTC.

MILITARY STATUS

Second lieutenant, U. S. Air Force Reserve. No active duty commitment.

PERSONAL

Birthdate: November 19, 1969. Single. Health excellent. Special interests: sports, music. Church basketball team. Study guitar. Participate in Bible study group. Fluent French. FAA Private Pilot's License.

COMMUNITY ACTIVITY

Member, Jaycees; Assistant Scoutmaster, Boy Scouts of America.

PROFESSIONAL AFFILIATIONS

Member, Computer Software Association.

REFERENCES

Available upon request.

(COMBINED FUNCTIONAL-CHRONOLOGICAL FORMAT)

Name
Address
Telephone Number

OBJECTIVE

Position as a programmer, with opportunities for growth and increased responsibilities.

EDUCATION

B. S. in Computer Science, June 1991, Colonial State University, Tidewater, Virginia. Highlights: GPA 3.4/4.0, Dean's List. Chairman, Computer Club. Omicron Delta Kappa. Cadet Major, Air Force ROTC.

AREAS OF EXPERIENCE

Programming and Teaching.
Extensive experience in academic environment of programming with FORTRAN, COBOL, BASIC, and APL. Two years of classroom experience teaching hardware and software applications.

Management and Public Relations.
Have managed people, hired, scheduled and insured operational effectiveness of a high pressure business. Maintained outstanding relations with public in difficult retail marketing situation. Helped improve company profitability while improving customer satisfaction.

EMPLOYMENT HISTORY

Computer Consultant, Colonial State University, 1989–1991. Consultant for the university while attending as a full-time student. Aided students in hardware and software applications.

Assistant Manager, Pizza Den, Inc., 1988–1991 (part-time). Assisted in management of restaurant. Hired, scheduled, supervised evening shift. Responsible for four people.

PROFESSIONAL AFFILIATIONS

Member, Computer Software Association.

COMMUNITY ACTIVITY

Member, Jaycees. Assistant Scoutmaster, Boy Scouts of America.

PERSONAL

Birthdate: November 19, 1969. Single. Health excellent. Special interests: sports, music, Bible study. Fluent French.

MILITARY STATUS

Second Lieutenant, USAF Reserve. No duty commitment.

REFERENCES

Available upon request.

AT LAST, YOU ARE FINISHED!

Put your cover letter on top of your resumé and mail or take it to your prospective employers.

Folding is acceptable, but it is better if you do not fold. Buy a large envelope for mailing to avoid folding. It will appear neater when reviewed.

Congratulations on finishing your resumé. You put a lot of hard work in on it but it was worth it. You will be glad you did.

In job hunting, you need to stand out to an employer every chance you get. The resumé is the best place to start.

You can expect an interview soon. Let's get into that subject so you can be well-prepared.

Chapter 11 _____
HOW TO BE INTERVIEWED

You have done such a magnificent job on your resumé, an interview is inevitable. You've probably imagined what it's going to be like when you meet the interviewer. Maybe you've gone so far as to pick out the clothes you'll wear. You've had them cleaned, and now they are hanging in your closet, ready to wear.

It will probably surprise you to learn that for your first interview you may not need your clothes at all. In fact, your pajamas will do just fine. How's that? The reason is that your first interview may be by telephone.

THE TELEPHONE INTERVIEW

When you speak of an interview, usually your first thoughts are of a face-to-face encounter with someone in the personnel department. This is usually the case, but you may first experience a telephone interview.

To save time and as part of the screening process, an employer may telephone you before inviting you for a personal visit, especially if you do not live in the same city. With a telephone interview the employer decreases the risk of spending money to bring you there only to find you do not fit the position. Even if you *are* in the same city, you may first receive a telephone interview before the employer moves to the next step. Be prepared for this eventuality.

You should keep in mind that an employer wants to accomplish one or more of the following objectives over the telephone:

He wants to see if you are still available, especially if there has been a significant time lapse since your previous contact.

He wants to get a feel for your personality, to discern if you sound pleasant and rational.

He wants to get clarification or elaboration on questions he may have had regarding your resumé or application.

A Christian employer may want to find out where you stand spiritually, and sometimes your doctrinal stance. For example, an evangelical employer will usually prefer, even require, that you have been born again by faith in the Lord Jesus Christ and that you believe the Bible to be the Word of God. To some, various points of doctrine may be important. In case you may be wondering, it is proper and not illegal for religious organizations to discriminate on religious grounds; therefore, there are no problems with this type of questioning. One exception is FCC licensed radio and television stations where, according to one notable court case, religious criteria can only apply to certain job positions, those that influence program content.

He may ask if you can come for a personal visit and if you want to set up an appointment.

He may want to obtain references and check them before he spends additional time and money, especially if you live out of town.

The best way to handle the telephone interview, as with all communications, is with courtesy and honesty. In explanations, try not to say too little, which might cause him to be suspicious—or too much, which might make you appear overly talkative.

THE WALK-IN APPLICANT

Some people, referring to those who "pop in" with no previous communications or appointment, are termed "walk-in" applicants. It is not a bad idea to hand-deliver your resumé instead of sending it through the mail. If you do hand-deliver it, you will be a walk-in.

Walk-in applicants may or may not be interviewed immediately. It depends on the organization, how busy they are, how well they are staffed, and how needy they are for a new employee. They may need you so badly that they interview you when you come—but don't expect it. Chances are that a walk-in candidate will not be interviewed. The typical organization, especially if it is very visible, receives so many applications that it is just impossible to interview everyone. Employers have to be selective, based on sheer volume alone.

You will probably be treated very courteously and told something like, "Thank you very much for coming. After this is reviewed if we see any possible openings for you, we'll be in touch with you right away."

Sometimes an alert receptionist or secretary may be trained to make a cursory review and assessment of the applicant and spot that occasional pearl with unusually impressive credentials or experience that can fill a need. In such cases the receptionist may check to see if someone is available to meet you. If someone is available and agrees with the receptionist's judgment, you have an interview.

Present yourself to the receptionist as friendly, eager, and courteous but not too familiar. Mix friendliness with a certain air of professionalism. Be *cautiously* assertive, pointing out how much it means for you to get an interview. Most of the Christians in this business are just old softies anyhow and do not like to disappoint people. You might get your interview.

If you are visiting from out of town, make sure the receptionist knows this. You should not unexpectedly appear from out of town and demand an appointment. It is presumptuous and discourteous to expect people to drop what they're doing to accommodate your poor planning. Still, they may do it for you because of their compassion and to take advantage of your availability.

Be respectful of the receptionist's time but do not be like this applicant:

> *Extreme Applicant Number One* walks in, tersely asks for an application, sits down, fills it out, drops it on the appropriate table or desk, then walks out without saying a word. (Reaction: *What's wrong with this one? Mad about something?*)

Be friendly but not as friendly as this applicant:

> *Extreme Applicant Number Two* is excessively chatty and wastes an hour of the receptionist's time, acting like a long-lost friend. (Reaction: *Doesn't he know I have work to do? This is probably what he would do on the job!*)

PREPARATION FOR THE INTERVIEW

No matter how you arrive at an interview, you should be prepared. It is critically important that you know the exact time and place of the interview, the interviewer's full name (the correct pronunciation), and his or her title.

You should also find out some specific facts about the company or ministry, such as what it does, where its major offices are, a little about its history and future plans. If you cannot find this out anywhere else, telephone the company and ask someone beforehand, preferably someone in the public relations department. If applying to a secular firm, you may be able to get information in your local library in reference books such as these: *Dunn and Bradstreet Reference Book, Standard and Poor's Corporation Records, Moody's Manuals, Fitch Corporation Manuals,* or *MacRae's Bluebook.*

THE BIG MOMENT

This is it! Your big moment has arrived. You're about to see the personnel director, an assistant, or possibly a department manager where there is an opening. You will be escorted or called in and introduced to the interviewer. Your first major challenge will be to avoid tripping or falling as you enter the office.

You have only been in the presence of the interviewer a few seconds and you have already made a big impression (whether or not you tripped). How? By your appearance. Of course, you have groomed yourself and dressed properly.

What is proper? Well, not necessarily a pinstriped suit for a man or an evening gown for a woman. Dress appropriately or somewhat better for the job. If you are seeking an office job, a coat and tie is recommended for the male—for the female a smart dress or suit. If you are color blind or have notoriously poor taste, get someone to help you decide what to wear. Clashing or unharmonious colors can communicate negatively, even subconsciously, and hurt your image.

If you are seeking a non-office job, such as one with a manual skill, a coat and tie is not necessary, although it will not detract from your appearance. But whatever you do, be neat and clean. Experienced employers know that there is a correlation between an unkempt appearance and sloppy work habits, because appearance represents a frame of mind. Also, they assume that any thinking person will look his best for an interview. If your best is bad, what will you look like on the job?

Women should not overdo the make-up. Some Christian employers may not like it at all, but that would be rare. In most cases, modesty is the rule in all matters of appearance.

The interviewer will ask you to be seated and will initiate some small talk. Let the interviewer take the initiative in steering the conversation. You may have a great deal you need to say, but wait for the right moment. Timing is important.

The initial small talk is to break the ice and help you relax. So relax. Be yourself. The interviewer will sense your naturalness and appreciate it. Believe me, pretentiousness is obvious and always counterproductive, communicating not only falseness but insecurity.

It will take the interviewer just a few moments to get down to business. He will probably ask you several questions. Below are some you should be prepared to discuss, though not necessarily in the order given.

ABOUT YOUR FAITH

In a Christian organization, an astute interviewer will somehow ask about your faith, though how it is done may vary with the situation. Nevertheless, it is important for such an organization to know where your Christian position is. The approach might be something subtle, "Why are you interested in working for a Christian organization?" It might be more direct, "How long have you known the Lord?" The important thing for you at this point is to know where you stand with your faith and that you have a positive stand. Be able to articulate it to some degree.

If you are not sure what you believe, come to grips with it before the interview. It's much more important to you than the job is, but the Lord may be using the situation to cause you to examine certain things.

ABOUT YOUR EXPERIENCE

The interviewer will probably want to know more than what is in your resumé. Be honest and answer all questions; still, if there is any area of weakness in your experience, be careful about volunteering it. Point out your strengths and accomplishments.

The employer wants a "can do" person. Radiate confidence, not conceit—there's a big difference. Confidence can contain humility, an "I can do all things through Christ" attitude. A word of caution: Do not say you can do something you cannot do. "If you have a horse," an old farmer once said, "don't say you have a cow. If you do, somebody will tell you to milk it someday."

ABOUT YOUR REFERENCES

You will probably be asked for personal and professional references, the latter only if you have a work record. The interviewer may ask, "Will any of your references give you anything other than a good report?" A sharp personnel department will diligently check references, including your former bosses whether or not you included them as references. Surprisingly, some companies are lax on this.

If you had a problem in the past and it was not your fault, it is best to mention it now and tell your story. Otherwise, they may find it out without the benefit of your explanation, then jump to a conclusion.

Unless you are Public Enemy Number One, your personal references should be no problem. After all, you picked them and surely you picked people who are *very objective* and will testify that you walk on water! In case you do not know it, it is considered a courtesy to request permission before you use someone as a reference.

ABOUT SALARY

The interviewer may want to know your salary expectations and ask, "What kind of salary do you feel is necessary for you now?"

This is a touchy one. At this point, be a little vague. If you come back too high, you may box yourself out of a job. Even though you might work for less, they may fear you would be unhappy and not stay long. If your expectations are too low, you may be volunteering to work for even less than they are willing to pay, giving them an unnecessary bargain.

Counter with something like this: "Well, I do have some responsibilities and would trust that any position would pay a fair salary. Are your salaries competitive?" You might also ask, "What is the salary range for this job?" You and the interviewer can maneuver on this one, and a possible starting range will emerge.

OTHER QUESTIONS YOU MAY BE ASKED

You may be asked many open-ended questions just to see how you react and how you think. They are interested in your whole person, not just in whether you can perform certain tasks. Why? Because your whole person comes on board when they hire you. Companies buy into much more than a task performer when they hire someone. They will have to relate to you eight or more hours a day and need to be able to trust you as a member of their team. They will invest a great deal of time and money in you, including fringe benefits, and the government will tax them heavily with FICA and unemployment taxes because of you. They want you to be the *right* person.

To help you prepare, here are some types of questions you may expect:

How did you hear about us?

Why would you like to work for this company?

What did you like best about your previous job?

What did you like least?

What is your primary skill or ability?

What do you think you can do for this company?

What are your long-range goals?

Are you willing to relocate?

What do you know about our company?

What have you learned from some of the jobs you've held?

What is your major weakness? (Be careful here or you will hurt your cause.) If you can do it truthfully, turn it around positively. You might say, "Well, I'm too conscientious about my job and tend to work too hard." That will be music to their ears!

QUESTIONS YOU CAN ASK

You should be given the opportunity to ask questions. If not, try to seize the opportunity. You'll seem a little dull if you don't ask anything. Besides, there are some important things you need to know.

Could you tell me about this position? (If you are applying for a specific job.)

Could you tell me what you have available?

What do you see as the future for this organization?

Does the company encourage growth and promotion from within?

What opportunity is there for increased responsibilities?

What kind of training and development program do you have?

Why is this position open right now? Did someone hold it before?

What kind of fringe benefits do you have? (Medical insurance, vacation, paid holidays?)

How is the company's financial situation? (The interviewer may not know unless it is near disaster, in which case the response would reveal a problem. Some Christian organizations remain at or near financial disaster and keep on going. It could mean possible layoffs or minimal salary increases in the future.)

GENERAL GUIDELINES

Here are a few final and general guidelines that will help you have a successful interview.

Avoid controversial subjects and remarks, from which there is little to gain and much to lose. The interviewer may hold an opposing view and naturally would think you have faulty reasoning.

Be positive. Avoid critical remarks as much as possible, even if a former employer may have treated you unfairly. Why? A good interviewer knows there are usually two sides to a story and may suspect your former employer had good reason. A critical remark can boomerang.

Try to focus on the needs of the organization and how you can meet them. If you can find out what the job need is, give emphasis to that part of your skill, training, or experience.

Don't get too touchy about your rights if questions are asked that you are not legally required to answer. This will be an immediate turnoff, and you will be labeled as a potential troublemaker. Such questions may be asked harmlessly, and, in my experience, will not be used to discriminate against you.

My advice to all interviewees is to answer all questions. What have you got to hide? There is happiness in being comfortable with yourself and what you are and in being transparent with others.

IN CONCLUSION

Your interview is over. You may have a job offer. If you do, shout, "Hallelujah!" Feel free to skip the next chapter on follow-up, but be *sure* to read the last three chapters.

If you do not have an immediate job offer, be sure to find out the next step before you leave. Are you supposed to do anything? Is the interviewer going to set up another interview or call you? You might say, "Well, where do things stand now?"

Be sure to express your appreciation and thanks to the interviewer and also to the receptionist or other clerical personnel who may have assisted you.

Chapter 12 _____
HOW TO FOLLOW UP

You have sent in your resumé with a nice cover letter. You may have even been interviewed. Days have gone by, maybe weeks. You've heard nothing. Naturally, you are anxious to hear something. You felt so good about everything, and your interview seemed to go well. You just knew you would have a job by now. What do you do?

Here are some reasons why you may not have heard yet:

Some organizations move slowly. They don't want to rush because they want to make the right choice.

They want you, but the budget is tight. The particular slot for you is not in the budget, and hiring will be delayed until they have the money.

The personnel people are swamped and haven't been able to take further necessary steps, such as conducting reference checks.

Your references are out of town or, for some reason, unavailable.

They received your resumé by mail but have been too busy to reply.

They like you but want to look at as many applicants as possible before they make a hiring decision.

There is no job opening, and they have been too busy to tell you. This should not happen, but sometimes the sheer volume of recruiting and applications keeps them from paying all the courtesies normally desired.

These are just some of the many reasons you may not have heard, but it does seem time to do something about it.

WHAT YOU SHOULD DO

FOLLOWING UP A MAILED RESUMÉ

If you are dealing through the mail, I hope you followed the advice of a previous chapter and preceded the mailing with a telephone call to introduce yourself and let them know your resumé is on its way. Whether you did or not, if you have not heard anything in two weeks, call again. Two weeks allows time for mail delays, intra-organizational mail distribution, and processing.

In your follow-up call, ask for, by name, the person you talked with the first time. Thank that person for watching out for your resumé and ask if he or she has seen it yet. If the answer is no, it may have been lost. This is unlikely, but unless it can be found right away, send another to make sure one does get there.

If they say it has been received, politely ask for the status of your application: "How does it look right now?" It would be best if you were talking with the personnel director or whoever does the recruiting and screening, but talk with whomever you can.

Be friendly, courteous, gentle and *just a little* pushy, but not too much. Even though personnel people are busy and really do not care for the interruptions and the bother (they're human too), if you are polite, a little aggressiveness can help. That's because you make an impression, and their sensitivity to your expectations can sometimes, even subconsciously, cause them to want to help you. There is a tendency in all of us to want to respond to people's expectations, and it's especially true for Christians, who are prone to want to be helpful.

Pursue this line until you are satisfied that you are being properly considered.

FOLLOWING UP AN INTERVIEW

Let's assume there was a degree of interest in you, and for that reason you were given an interview. You haven't heard anything in several days. Here's what to do:

First, sit down and reflect on your interview. Try to remember what was said to you about a follow-up or a notice about the decision. Make some notes to have available as you follow up.

Telephone the person who interviewed you. If he or she is unavailable, ask for a return call. If your call is not returned, call back again. But always be courteous and polite. If you are politely persistent, you will probably get through. Ask if the position you interviewed for has been filled.

The answer may be yes, which closes the door. If they are still considering and the door is ajar, ask if there is anything you can do to help things along. For example, ask if you can speak directly with the person who will need your services. If that person is not available, ask, "Well, you don't mind if I contact him, do you? Could you give me his name and phone number?"

Always be searching for another avenue to explore such as the one I've just suggested, something to keep your case active and drawing the company's attention, if not in one department then in another. Most companies have so much paperwork that it is easy for them to fall victim to the "out of sight, out of mind" syndrome. In follow-up, the adage that says that "the squeaky wheel gets the grease" is often true.

FOLLOWING UP A REJECTION

No one likes a rejection of any kind. It's one of the worst things that can happen to us, a real stab in the old ego.

After you recover from the initial shock, everything gets back into perspective. It's really not all that bad. Besides, you didn't really want to work at that place if the Lord didn't want you there. The question is what should you do now? Should you follow up with this company any more or just forget it?

Before you decide, review the events to date. Ask yourself if you gave it your best. If so, let it go for now, but if three months go by and you are still waiting for the Lord to open a door, inquire again with a personal telephone call or visit. Keep inquiring periodically. It's possible that a vacancy may occur that didn't exist the first time around, and by keeping your name on the front burner, you may get a chance at it.

WRITTEN FOLLOW-UP

Even though I place so much value on the personalized telephone call, make it a practice to follow up a telephone call with a nice, brief letter, beginning like this:

"This is a follow-up to our telephone conversation of (date). I really appreciate your taking the time to talk with me. Your personal interest is sincerely appreciated."

This is a good place for me to reiterate a major principle: According to the Word of God, He is the one who opens doors that no man can close and closes doors that no man can open. *Never* be discouraged at closed doors because our wonderful heavenly Father always has something better for us. I know it is true because His Word says it; I have seen it happen many times.

Accordingly, do not try to knock the door down with all the force of your personality and cunning. If God closes the door, you do not want to go in. Move on. Greater things are waiting.

Chapter 13 _____
HOW TO CHANGE
CAREERS

Maybe you remember the old television sitcom in which a harried corporate executive in a high-pressure big-city job gets fed up with the "rat race." To the consternation of his employer and his wife, he resigns, sells his home, and moves to an idyllic country location that has cows, pigs, and, we find later, bad plumbing, a broken tractor, and rural neighbors who think he is peculiar. Outlandish as it may seem, this is a fantasy held by many people as they reach a certain *season* in life: They desire *change*.

Could this be you? Have you been pursuing a certain career for some time, only to find you are bored? Are you thirty, forty, fifty or more years of age and feel a growing dissatisfaction with what you are doing?

You discover that your heart really isn't in your work. You no longer look forward to going to work in the mornings or whenever. In fact, you dread it. At the office you find yourself daydreaming about being somewhere else and doing something else. What's going on? A midlife crisis? Is it you and your attitude?

Perhaps God is stirring up a "holy discontent," as some call it, to cause you to move on to another place He has for you.

Some people seem to find a niche early in life and are happy ever after; others are discontented. For many people, discontentment with their job status quo is a real problem and needs to be recognized. More than that, it needs to be solved.

As Christians we must first rely on an all-wise and all-loving Master who oversees every aspect of our lives. Therefore, we can view *all* circumstances as wonderful opportunities that our Father has given for our growth, direction, and blessing. If you find yourself dissatisfied with your work, consider *a change in your situation,* or *a change in how you view your situation.* We will consider both.

The possibility of a career change at any time in life is a very important decision and should not be treated lightly because of the investment in your present career: an investment of time, energy, and dedication, then a harvest of experience, seniority, pay, and prestige. It's possible, of course, that you have made the investment above but have not acquired the dividends that should have come to you, such as fair pay or promotion. That may be the root of your problem. Nevertheless, you are in a career crisis that needs to be faced prayerfully, wisely, and systematically.

The classic approach to problem-solving involves several steps, which we will work through.

ANALYZING THE SITUATION

A big question is facing you: *Is God leading you to make a significant career change?*

The symptoms you are experiencing also present other possibilities. *Consider them carefully.*

Basically, you're in the right occupation, but your present job has lost its challenge or has become a dead end. Rather than a career change, a transfer within the same company or maybe to another company will give you the challenge and renewed interest you need.

You are in the right occupation, but your dissatisfaction is coming from a demoralizing climate, a company philosophy, or management style that has a negative impact on you. What you really need is a new employer. It just may be that the environment is at fault, and a total career change is not in order.

You don't feel appreciated. No one ever compliments your efforts or recognizes you. This does not necessarily mean you are seeking self-glory. Even the most sacrificial people need approval or at least the knowledge that their superiors are pleased with them. If you know that you're effective in what you're doing, however, don't let ego needs destroy your efforts. Some employers are dreadfully negligent in this area of human relations, too often caught up in their own affairs. A Christian's "meat" is to do the Father's will and, if necessary, you can survive without the accolades of men.

You have succumbed to bad working habits—maybe even laziness—and feel your present responsibilities are a threat to your preferred work style. You want to escape to greater ease and comfort. Be careful, for this can be an unconscious desire. You'd better get your battery recharged and be thankful for what you have.

An in-law is giving you a hard time, and you transfer your bad feelings to your job. No offense to in-laws, but personal problems can spill over and affect entire lives, even on the job. As you analyze your situation, evaluate your whole life to give yourself the widest possible perspective.

For whatever reason, you have developed a negative attitude. You may have caught it from someone else, and you are probably infecting others. A negative attitude produces negative words that produce negative actions (toward others) and reactions (toward us). Before you know it, you are a sourpuss, and everything about your job is wrong, so wrong that you really do need a change. Unfortunately, unless you deal with the problem now, it will follow you.

Let's assume that none of the above applies to you, which puts you back to the original question.

Is God leading you to make a significant career change?
God sometimes calls people to make radical leaps of faith into the unknown, and He may be calling you. Do not do anything rash that would endanger your present income until you have assurance that God is leading. You may have family responsibilities; you may be locked into a budget bracket based on a child's educational need or a family member's health. Remember, when you take that leap of faith, you are taking them with you.

You may be willing to sacrifice by assuming an austere lifestyle, at least until "things work out" and you reestablish yourself. But does your family feel the same way? God is interested in their needs and emotional well-being, as well as yours. And they look to you as God's provision for them. Strongly consider a loss or a significant reduction of income for a period of time as you make the transition from one career to another.

Second, consider the amount of experience, credibility, and expertise you have in your present career, purchased with the price of sacrifice, sweat, and tears. It should not be cast aside on a whim, but only after prayerful deliberation.

Third, ask yourself whether your present career is

making use of the basic gifts and talents that God has given you. Or is your career just the result of opportunistic job openings in the past. Did you get where you are by occupational osmosis? *Are you optimizing your gifts in your present career?* This is a key question. A yes answer will cast doubt on the wisdom of a career change; a no answer will tend to confirm it.

A theory of some Christian vocational counselors is that most people are in opportunistic jobs for which they are ill-equipped and not called, thereby causing a lack of job satisfaction, fulfillment, and productivity. I believe this is true to some extent but not to the degree that some claim. In God's sovereignty I believe He can also bring good out of what appear to us as only opportunistic jobs. He provides the opportunities!

CONSIDERING AND SELECTING A SOLUTION

The foregoing appears slanted toward dissuading you from making a career change. The slant is intentional—not to dissuade, but to ensure that you cautiously consider all these factors before you make up your mind. If you have gone through the above steps and after prayerful consideration are convinced that a career change is what God wants for you, the questions are now simple: What? Where? And in applying your solution, when?

Parts I, II, and III to this book are as applicable to you as they are to someone who has never held a job before. You are on the verge of blazing a new trail for yourself in parts unknown. You need to reevaluate God's calling and will for your life. You need to take a deliberate, serious, and systematic look at yourself, at who and what you are. You need the self-assessment exercise in part II. And at this critical stage in your life, I strongly recommend professional vocational guidance and testing. It can help you find the *real you* who wants to come out and be expressed. A small investment in professional advice is well worth the expense. These steps will help you establish *what* you are going to do.

Now you have to discover the *where*. Your task is no different from anyone else's in seeking employment. You need to analyze the job market, decide whether to use a placement organization, and develop a strategy for presenting yourself to a potential employer.

Perhaps you plan on being self-employed. Then, you are not seeking a job; you are creating one. This can be an exciting challenge for anyone. America was made by entrepreneurial and industrious people who struck out on their own. Such an adventure has both risks and rewards. There are books about this, and you would be wise to read one or two. Success will largely depend on good planning, adequate capitalization and controls, and hard work. For the first year at least, it is best to overestimate your expenses and underestimate your income, because it often works out that way. Many new businesses go under because of unrealistic cash-flow projections; others who estimate conservatively often find themselves pleasantly surprised.

If you seek employment, decide in what kind of an organization you want to work and where you want to live, if that is important. This is a new life you are making for yourself, so make it as pleasant as possible.

If you have always had a desire to live in a certain place—a state, city, or section of the country—then consider it. Why not? There may be constraints against it, confining you to a certain location; otherwise, broaden your horizons. After all, the world is your Father's orchard, and you are His child.

Sometimes, you just get into a rut and need a change to

make the world look a little brighter. Everyone seems to need some kind of change now and then. It is very interesting that the Bible compares us to sheep, and sheep are prone to follow the same path over and over. They graze the same fields even after the food is inadequate, and pollute the same ground until their well-being is threatened. The wise and loving shepherd always leads his sheep into new and better paths and pastures. It is the same with our Good Shepherd. He knows when we have overgrazed our location and are in need of a new life.

The fringe benefits of being a believer are simply incredible. The Lord is our Shepherd . . . He restores our soul . . . He leads us . . . His rod and staff comfort us . . . goodness and mercy follow us all the days of our lives. These promises are for you occupationally as well as for all areas of your life.

As you decide on the *what* and the *where,* do it prayerfully. Although I have discussed the systematic approach, do not be so systematic as to restrict the Spirit's leading. In the final analysis, life is subjective, not objective. Give proper emphasis to the desires of your heart and assume that your intent is to please God and be in His will.

MAKING THE CHANGE

You have made your decision. You have decided on a new direction. You have picked a new career; you have done some vocational planning, and you are itching to get on with it. It's time to move ahead. Your heart is already separated from what you are doing, and you want to move as soon as possible. There is one final word of advice about the *when.*

Timing is important. Make events work in your favor, not against you. Manage events and do not, by acting impulsively or rashly, let them manage you. Stay with your present employment until you have done all your planning. If at all possible, obtain any necessary retraining or get additional education while still employed and drawing an income.

If you work it properly, you can make a smooth transition from one career right into the other. Patience will always pay off. If you feel that you "just can't take it anymore," it's not true. You can take it until the time is optimal for you. Make a rational, Spirit-led decision.

Many factors affect your timing, such as retraining needs, job search, present employer's vesting or benefit accrual plan, children's school year, spouse's employment, seasonal housing market considerations, anticipated extraordinary expenses, and current indebtedness. There are others. All possible factors must be considered when selecting an optimal time to make your change.

One last word: Conditions will never be *perfect*. Discernment is important here. Sometimes, all you can do is optimize the conditions as best you can, then take a bold step and trust God to see you through. He will.

Proceed with boldness and confidence. Never look back to question your decision; look forward to new and greater things in the Lord. You have the promise of your loving Creator who says:

> Do not fear, for I am with you;
> Do not anxiously look about you, for I am your God.
> I will strengthen you, surely I will help you,
> Surely I will uphold you with My righteous right hand (Isa. 41:10).

RECOMMENDED READING

Starting Over, Allen A. Swenson, A and W Publishers, Inc., New York, NY, 1978.

PART V
Now That You Are Hired

Chapter 14

HOW TO MAKE YOUR NEW EMPLOYER GLAD THAT HE HIRED YOU

Congratulations on your new job! It may be your first or your twenty-first. Nevertheless, it is a new start for you. You are about to enter a whole new world that will occupy most of your waking hours and give you a whole new circle of relationships.

In your new position you want to do well not only for the sake of doing your best but also to learn and grow as well as make a favorable impression on your company, especially when future promotions and pay raises are considered. Also, if you leave this company, it's essential that you are given a good reference. Good or bad, your record always follows you.

This is the time to consider what will help you begin work and do well in your new job.

YOUR RELATIONSHIPS

Your relationships take top priority with God. And practically, how you relate to others is of utmost importance to your success. Studies have shown that the leading single reason people get fired from their jobs is not incompetence but failure to get along with others.

You may think this is not important if you are going to work for True Paradise Christian Ministries, since everyone there must be so spiritual and loving. Invariably, however, there will be a *porcupine* personality around, which will rattle your cage. I call them "grace testers" because they test the level of the grace and love in your life.

If you are going to work in a Christian organization, plan to be a positive and edifying influence. One of the best ways you can do this is to guard your tongue. Some of the most spiritual people still have trouble with that little, fiery member that the Bible talks about in James 3. Remember, God did not lead you there to be a critic.

In any organization there are two things that can tempt you to complain and criticize.

The first is something going contrary to your opinion. In some way, however slight, your ego is offended. Then what happens? Something inside called Self (which you thought was crucified) experiences a temporary resurrection. Self's weapon is only about three inches long but so powerful that the Bible compares it to a spark, which can set an entire forest ablaze—the tongue.

Such a situation often results in complaining and criticism of others, even to the point of slander. Sometimes this comes out harshly, or it can be cloaked in the most spiritual terms that prompt others to think you are exceedingly wise and saintly in your insightful analysis as to what really should have been done!

The second situation is when we may not personally be affected by something, but someone else is. We are affected by such a situation because the negative feelings it generates are contagious.

It is strange yet true: Both positive and negative attitudes are contagious. If a fellow employee is beefing about something, there is a tendency in everyone to be a good Joe and agree. But if you do, your own spirit is affected, and you are likely to spread the contagion by passing it along.

Conversely, a good positive word is also contagious. Did

you know that little old you, whoever you are, can enter a group and set the tone and attitude of the whole gathering by an uplifting and positive word or a negative one? That's why Scripture says:

> Keep thy heart with all diligence: for out of it are the issues [forces] of life (Prov. 4:23 KJV, definition mine).

It's not easy to avoid saying the wrong things and to say the right things always. Yet, by giving this subject attention in the workplace and elsewhere and with God's help, you can heed the words of this important Scripture:

> Let no unwholesome word proceed from your mouth, but only such a word as is good for edification according to the need of the moment, that it may give grace to those who hear (Eph. 4:29).

TEMPTATIONS

Those of you who may be working in non-Christian organizations face a special problem. You will often be faced with temptations to do things that grieve the Holy Spirit and hinder your spiritual walk. You will know, too, that refusing to do certain things will damage your relationship with your peers, even your boss.

Let me advise you from years of experience in secular work. If you maintain your position with love, wisdom, and tact, you probably will *not* offend them but will gain their admiration and respect. You can either come across as a self-righteous, finger-pointing fanatic and lose your effectiveness with them, or you can tactfully decline any questionable activities. Let your peers and your boss experience the life of Christ in you in everyday matters, and they will know why you are declining to do certain things. They may thereby sense the "sweet fragrance of the Spirit" in your life and be attracted by it.

For example, I was the commander of an organization in the United States Air Force when I first committed my life fully to Christ. It was customary for the commander to give a Christmas party at which alcoholic beverages were expected. I made the decision to give the party without alcohol. There were complaints among some who had heard about my plans; one young officer and his wife were downright angry. I felt the pressure and was very apprehensive as the day approached. I prayed beforehand for the Lord to help make it a blessing. The party day dawned.

That evening everyone came, some begrudgingly, but there was a mysterious warmth present that I had never before experienced at a party. Everyone sang carols about the Savior so heartily and with such feeling that I was dumbfounded. Most didn't even know Him. They all left the party feeling wonderful, and the next day the couple who had been so angry called to say it was the best Christmas party they'd ever attended.

They had savored the sweet fragrance of the Savior. May those in darkness always experience that from our presence in their lives. What a privilege to be able to touch someone's life with, perhaps, an eternal result. Is there anything more important?

YOUR ATTITUDE

The attitude of a Christian in any organization should be that of a servant.

This goes against the world's teaching, which instructs us to gain mastery over others, even through deception and manipulation. If you don't believe this, check some of the latest books on how to get ahead and be successful.

Once upon a time Someone was starting to put together a worldwide organization. It became obvious very early that

His staff was already vying for positions of leadership. This Leader was very wise. In fact, He was the wisest leader ever. He told them, in effect, "Listen fellows. That's the way the world does it. But that's not the way it works in this organization. Around here, if any of you want to be great, you must become a servant." In case that quotation seems familiar, it's Bramlett's paraphrase of Matthew 20:26-27.

The Lord did not say that it's wrong to be great. What He did say is that the route to *true* greatness is in becoming a servant. The Savior went on to tell us that if we humble ourselves, we will be exalted (and vice versa). That's a pretty good promise, one worth believing.

How do you translate this into a hard-nosed job situation? Easily. Make up your mind that your purpose in being there is not just to claim a paycheck on Fridays but genuinely and faithfully to serve the needs of people who may be touched by your work. No matter what or where your work is, you cannot do a job without its affecting others. Whether or not you come in contact with people is irrelevant; what you do still directly affects either the public or those in another department.

Here's another attitude necessary for success: *You need to have a team attitude.* Every group of two or more engaged in a common purpose is a team—your family, your civic organization, your Sunday school, and your department. If one member acts without regard to the others, the team effort is damaged and the team can even be destroyed.

An independent attitude is usually just another manifestation of that old nemesis, Self, and can be called what it is—*selfishness.* A team attitude, on the other hand, is a manifestation of *unselfishness,* with the common good as its goal.

Have you ever seen a basketball player with the ball near his goal *not* take a shot but pass off to a teammate who is in a better position to make the shot? That's team spirit and unselfishness. The first player stood to improve his statistics by taking and making the shot and drawing the cheers of the crowd, but points for the team were more important. That kind of basketball player is recognized as great by those who really know the sport, and he is in greater demand by the college and professional scouts.

Since you have these attitudes, your new boss is really starting to feel glad that he hired you. Nonetheless, you need to be concerned with only one other thing.

YOUR PERFORMANCE

Unfortunately, you can be the greatest man or woman in the world with a positive attitude and a servant's heart and still miss the mark.

I hate to mention performance here at the end of the chapter and spoil all the fun, but it's not without importance. Some folks place this too far down on their list of priorities and opt for more fellowship and fun. They usually don't last very long.

The *bottom line* is that you were hired because there was an important function to be performed, so important that the company agreed that it was worth it to invest in you. That investment is not only your salary but also the many added costs, such as social security taxes, unemployment taxes, fringe benefits, and training. You not only owe it to the Lord to perform well, you also owe it to the company. In addition, you owe it to yourself, your self-esteem, and your future.

Here are some valuable tips on how to do this and to have your new boss say to himself, *Hey! This new person is super. What wisdom I displayed in hiring him!*

136

TRAINING

If your new job has a formal training program, enter it and learn as much and as fast as you can. If you are forced to learn on your own, find out what you need to study and start immediately. Read publications applicable to your job; ask appropriate questions; stick around after hours, studying, learning, asking, doing. Make it obvious that your goal is excellence and that you want to know everything there is to know about your position and the jobs affecting yours.

I cannot emphasize too much—*Learn.*

Learning will enhance your performance, your self-confidence, your standing in your company's eye, and your future.

NEVER SAY NEVER

Eagerly take on responsibility and more work. There is a limit to how much you can take, but until you establish yourself as a performer, do as much as you can. Never tell your boss you can't do something. Find a way; make a way; at least, *try.* Let your boss know early that you have a *can do* attitude and that you can be relied upon to get the job done. You will become invaluable and respected.

Never say or imply, "That's not in my job description." If you are worried about sticking to your job description, you are starting off on the wrong foot. Most job descriptions are not very accurate. My advice is to do what's on the job description, not be bound by it. With your sterling performance and budding promise, they will soon be writing a new one for you, much more to your pleasure and suitable for your obvious talents.

OVERKILL

Do your job so well and so thoroughly that it will be much more than was really expected of you. Yes, it will take some extra time and effort but it will be worth it, especially on your first few assignments. Those initial assignments are critical in the impression you make and the pattern you set for yourself.

In the military they have medals and citations for performance above and beyond the call of duty. Your company may not give you a medal for your work, but they may give you other more practical forms of recognition, perhaps a pay raise.

THE NEED FOR ENTHUSIASM

Here's a big warning, maybe one of the most important in this book:

> *Never* think about your work as that yucky, old place you have to go between periods of time off. If you do, it will invariably show in your face, attitude, and performance.

Instead, *radiate enthusiasm.* Sometimes, you may have to force yourself to do it, but *do* it. Later, it will be natural and affect your performance significantly. You will do more and be happier doing it; so will everyone else.

Chapter 15 _____

HOW TO ADJUST
TO A CHRISTIAN
WORKPLACE

Working in a full-time Christian vocation can be the most glorious and rewarding vocational experience of a lifetime; it can also be one of the most difficult experiences. Since becoming a committed Christian, I have suffered two major disappointments: I discovered that other Christians are not yet perfect; I discovered that I am not yet perfect either.

At first I perceived in other Christians nothing but outward love, joy, peace, and holiness, so I decided that that was how it was for them all the time. All I had to do was "be one of them" and I would reach perfection on earth too. My problems would be over.

The problem was that I never reached perfection—and when I got to know those other *perfect* Christians, I learned that they hadn't reached it either.

In the meantime we learned to tolerate one another. It dawned on me at one point that if loving each other were an automatic result of being born again, then the Bible would not have to remind us to do so.

I say this to warn you that none of your fellow employees at True Paradise Christian Ministries, or wherever you are, is likely to be perfect. You will find yourself in a crucible with others, and sometimes rough edges will grate together. In my Christian work I have yet to meet anyone who already has his glorified body. All are still in process.

But before you get disappointed, let me tell you the good news. There is a big and wonderful difference in a Christian vocational environment—the Spirit. People in God's work really experience the power of His Spirit. As the apostle Paul said:

> We have this treasure in earthen vessels, *to show that the transcendent power belongs to God and not to us* (2 Cor. 4:7 RSV, italics mine).

That's it! We are just the earthen vessels. All the fruit of our efforts is not really caused by us at all—it is His transcendent power operating through us.

This is that mystery of "Christ in you," which Paul talks about (Col. 1:27). It's an example of his profound proclamation, "It is no longer I who live, but Christ. . . . " (Gal. 2:20). So when great things happen through your work and ministry, who gets the glory? Not you, but He.

Another big difference in a Christian organization is that the Holy Spirit is at work in a special way in departmental matters and relationships. Though our lower nature may sometimes manifest itself, a spirit of reconciliation and forgiveness prevails. With co-workers praying for and with one another, friction is usually short-lived; wounds are quickly healed.

Sometimes there are exceptions. Certain people may carry hurt or hard feelings. Rare incidents of this give you opportunities to demonstrate longsuffering, love, and grace in a way that only the Lord can do through you. You can "bear one another's burdens and thus fulfill the law of Christ" (Gal. 6:2).

HARD WORK

"Boy, I can't wait to go to work with True Paradise Christian Ministries, Inc. Good ol' Reverend Blessum is so sweet, kind, and spiritual. I'll bet it's a ball working for him. I'll bet he goes around blessing the employees all day.''

Do you think this way? If so, forget it. Reverend Blessum may be putting in sixteen-hour days of hard labor under the pressure of his ministry, running the organization, responding to the public, and trying to raise enough money to pay all the bills, including your salary.

Part of your job will be to help support him and bear his burden. You will be expected to produce, not only just to do your job but also to make improvements and be innovative. No matter what your job or where you are in the organization, you can expect difficult, demanding work. It probably won't be easy.

Did Jesus promise an easy time? No, but He did promise He would be with us. When you undertake the Lord's work, remember, He didn't promise you a rose garden.

Be prepared with the correct mental attitude when you start, and you will have the problem in hand.

SPIRITUAL WARFARE

This is the least desirable subject to discuss but a necessary one. I don't like to give the Devil any credit because he is already a defeated foe; nevertheless, a reality. You can remember and heed the Spirit's warning.

> For our struggle is not against flesh and blood, but against the rulers, against the powers, against the world forces of this darkness, against the spiritual forces of wickedness in the heavenly places (Eph. 6:12).

You know who the winner is; but meanwhile you are in a wrestling match. This is true in your personal life whether or not you are in a full-time Christian vocation, but it is especially true in the special work of the Lord.

If the organization is moving in the Spirit, you *will* be in spiritual warfare. You, your department, your family, and everyone may experience buffeting and attack, especially at your weak spots. Don't be surprised. Satan wants to discourage you and dull your effectiveness. True to his biblical description, he wants to "steal, kill, and destroy" the work of the Lord. The enemy may attack one person with discouragement; another with financial loss or gain; another with sickness; another with greed or lustful temptations.

More important, I want to remind you that the enemy's attacks can all be thwarted and defeated very simply. You really need not fear because God has given us the answer. Our solution is found in Ephesians 6.

> *Be strong* in the Lord and the strength of his might . . . (and) *put on* the whole armor of God, that you may be able to *stand* against the wiles of the devil (vv. 10–11 RSV, italics mine).

Therefore, you continually "put on" the Son by letting Him be Lord of your everyday situations, remembering that you are "in Him" and that He is with you.

I love the words of Martin Luther in his soul-stirring hymn "A Mighty Fortress is Our God."

> . . . Our ancient foe doth seek to work us woe; his craft and power are great; and armed with cruel hate. . . .

Despite this dire threat, the third verse rings with our sure victory.

> We tremble not for him; His rage we can endure, For lo! his doom is sure; one little word shall fell him.

Chapter 16 _____
HOW TO BE HAPPY AT WORK

Have you ever noticed a person who is obviously very happy with his work—the smile, the sense of peace? It just seems that some people find their perfect niche, and you cannot imagine anyone doing the job better.

Have you ever seen the opposite—a sourpuss who is obviously very unhappy with his work? You know something is wrong: Maybe he's just having a bad day; maybe he's in the wrong place, using the wrong skills. But more than likely, he just doesn't know how to be happy at work.

I can think of examples of both.

Tina knows how to be happy at work. She's a receptionist and switchboard operator for a large organization. Over the telephone or in person, she radiates joy. She has been offered other positions within the company, some of which would have paid more money and held more potential for growth. Yet, she has always turned them down, feeling that God had her exactly in the right place, where she could be a special blessing to people in the way she knew best.

I can understand that. It would not seem right for Tina not to be there. She fits. She touches hundreds of lives daily, each of which cannot help but feel a little better after her touch. She is what I call one of God's "sunbeams." Her light might shine somewhere else but be under a bushel.

I have known others who were dealing with the public

and had the opposite effect. Paulette seemed to irritate everyone. She dealt with the public all day, and just about everyone was given the feeling that they were imposing on her. Her attitude seemed to say, "Why are you bothering me? Don't you know I'm too busy to help you? Do it yourself." Although she didn't actually say it, that was her nonverbal message.

After a while, people would call her only as a last resort, then with much apprehension. Paulette was actually a very intelligent young person, and I don't believe she meant to be rude. In other ways she could be very thoughtful and loving. Of course, there is no excuse for rudeness. But with her, it seemed less a case of bad manners and more the wrong attitude about her job. The message she communicated to people was "I'm not really happy about my work. Why are you bothering me?"

What's the cause of happiness or unhappiness with work? First, you must be careful about saying it's always one thing or another; nevertheless, you can observe some important principles. If you apply them, no matter where you are—even in a job that's not right for you—you can be happy.

A NECESSARY TOIL

Aside from the fact that work is necessary to supply you food and shelter, it's also a means of fulfillment, of expressing yourself to other people. And though you do not always think of it this way, it's also a means of serving others. In some form or another, we all manufacture, sell, or administer products or services for other people. People other than Christians often find fulfillment in their work. How much more should God's people be in the niche for which they were created and be happy and fulfilled in it?

It is God's gift to man that everyone should . . . take pleasure in all his toil (Eccl. 3:13 RSV).

HOW TO TAKE PLEASURE IN YOUR TOIL

One of the best ways to enjoy your work is to be in the right job, using the gifts and talents God has given you. This should be your aim. But whether or not you are in a perfect job for you, there are ways in which you can look forward to getting up in the morning and going to work, feeling fulfilled about where you're spending your waking hours. Below are three ways that will really help you.

HAVE A HEALTHY ATTITUDE TOWARD WORK

As human beings, work is our lot. God has ordained it, and all His ways are perfect. He is Love and always looking out after your best interests. Accept work generally, not just as something necessary to buy groceries and pay rent but as a means to do that for which God created you.

RESOLVE TO GIVE IT YOUR BEST SHOT

Whatever your hand finds to do, do it with all your might (Eccl. 9:10 RSV).

Whatever you do, whether in word or deed, do all in the name of the Lord Jesus, giving thanks. . . . (Col. 3:17).

Did you understand these verses? Combining these means that wherever you are and whatever you are doing, you should do it with all your might in the name of the Lord, then give thanks. *This is a true prescription for happiness and success in the workplace.* It also means that

145

even though you may not be in God's best job for you now, whatever you are doing, you should do it with all your might in the name of the Lord.

RESOLVE TO BE A BLESSING TO OTHERS

Your job may seem isolated and remote. You may be like Joe Lugwrench on the assembly line, who does nothing but install bolt number 47 all day. But have you ever thought about how many people, or things, depend upon bolt number 47 functioning properly? At the very least, Joe's work has an effect on the installers of bolt number 46 behind him and number 48 ahead of him!

The point is you *affect* people. Chances are you affect them much more than you realize. Regardless of your actual job, your attitude and demeanor at work greatly affect those around you. It's a fact that *emotions and attitudes are contagious.* If you act positively, those around you will also tend to act positively; if you are negative, you will soon be surrounded by negative people.

Here is an awesome thought: If you don't like the attitudes of some of those around you, consider that they may be a mirror image of you—a reaction to your own attitudes. Oppositely, if you are blessed with a happy workplace and positive fellow workers, it may be that your light is shining more than you know.

To be happy and to enjoy your work, *make a decision and resolve to be a blessing to everyone you touch, directly and indirectly.* You will then be a true ambassador for Christ.

My prayer is that the Father will richly bless you vocationally, that you will be happy in your work and a source of happiness and blessing to those around you.

Appendixes

Appendix A
"QUICK GET-A-JOB CHECKLIST"

This checklist is provided as a quick summary, reminder, and tool. It is strongly recommended that you use it—it will help you get a job.

DATE ITEM ACCOMPLISHED   **ACTION**

1. _____ Pray.

2. _____ Determine God's vocational *calling* and *will* for your life. (Chapters 1, 2, and Appendix B.) Do in conjunction with Item 3, below.

    a. _____ Decide that God's will is really what you want.

    b. _____ Tell Him in prayer.

    c. _____ Seek in His Word, in your spirit, through counsel, through circumstances, through your sanctified desires.

3. _____ Determine your God-given gifts and talents. (Chapter 3.)

    a. _____ Use self-assessment.

    b. _____ Consider professional testing and counsel.

    RESULTS. Primary gift/s: _____ Others: _____

4. _____ Do vocational planning. (Chapters 5, 6.)

    a. _____ Set long-range goals.

    b. _____ Set medium- and short-range goals.

    c. _____ Plan and pursue any education and training needed.

5. _____ Analyze job market and review sources of jobs. (Chapter 7.)

6. _____ Consider using a placement organization. (Chapter 8.)

7. _____ Establish proper self-image and review approaches before contacting potential employers. (Chapter 9.)

8. _____ Prepare a good resumé. (Chapter 10.)

9. _____ Prepare for interviews. (Chapter 11.)

10. _____ Contact potential employers. (Chapters 7 and 9.)

11. _____ Follow up contacts. (Chapter 12.)

12. _____ Thank God for your new job, whatever it may be. Serve Him and others with gladness, doing it with all your might, heartily as unto the Lord.

Appendix B

HOW TO KNOW THE WILL OF GOD FOR YOUR LIFE

By
Dr. Bill Bright, President
Campus Crusade for Christ International

The following pages contain Dr. Bill Bright's special insights on how to find God's will and are used with his personal permission and encouragement. We are indebted to Dr. Bright for allowing us to include these valuable principles.

The information is also included in his book, *Come Help Change the World*, copyright 1979, revised 1985, Campus Crusade for Christ, Inc., published by Here's Life Publishers, P.O. Box 1576, San Bernardino, CA 92402.

I encourage you to read Dr. Bright's book. In it, he tells about a letter he received from one of America's leading theologians, who wrote:

> "I am at Wheaton College where I am to speak at chapel tomorrow. I arrived late last night tired and eager to rest. However, before I went to sleep I decided to read the first chapter of your book, *Come Help Change the World*, which I had just acquired. It is now 2 A.M. and I have just finished reading the first eight chapters. I have gotten down on my knees to rededicate my life to the Lord Jesus Christ. Thank you for writing this book. It touched my life."

Though not actually written to Paul Brown, the following letter contains the basic counsel which Dr. Bright gives students and adults concerning "How to know the will of God for your life."

Mr. Paul V. Brown
The Graduate House
University of California
Los Angeles, California 90024

Re: How to know the will of God for your life
according to the "sound-mind principle" of Scripture

Dear Paul:

Thank you for your recent letter sharing some of the exciting experiences which you are having in your new and adventuresome life with Christ.

When I read that part of your letter in which you expressed the desire to invest your life fully for Christ, I paused to give thanks to the Lord, first, for His great love and faithful direction of the lives of all who will trust Him, and second, for your response to His love and your willingness to trust Him with every detail of your life.

It is at this crucial point that many Christians deprive themselves of the full, abundant and purposeful life which the Lord Jesus promised in John 10:10. Failing to comprehend the true character and nature of God, His absolute love, grace, wisdom, power and holiness, many Christians have foolishly chosen to live according to their own plans rather than consider and do the will of God. Some have such a distorted view of God that they think of Him as a tyrant whom one must either appease or experience His wrath, as those who worship a pagan god. Since they are afraid of Him, they cannot love and trust Him. This is sometimes true of individuals who have transferred to God their fear of an earthly father who may have been overly strict, unduly demanding, or even tyrannical.

152

In all fairness I should say that there are many sincere Christians who want to do the will of God but do not know how to go about discovering His will for their lives.

A choice young college graduate came recently for counsel concerning God's will for his life. "How can I know what God wants me to do?" he asked. Briefly I explained the safest approach to knowing the will of God—to follow what I have chosen to call the "sound-mind principle" of Scripture. In less than an hour, by following the suggestions contained in this letter, this young man discovered what he had been seeking for years. He knew not only the work which God wanted him to do, but the very organization with which he was to be affiliated.

Now you may ask, "What is the 'sound-mind principle' of Scripture?" In 2 Timothy 1:7 we are told that "God has not given us the spirit of fear, but of power, and of love and of a sound mind." The sound mind referred to in this verse means a well-balanced mind, a mind that is under the control of the Holy Spirit, "remade" according to Romans 12:1, 2: "Therefore, my brothers, I implore you by God's mercies to offer your very selves to Him, a living sacrifice, dedicated and fit for His acceptance, the worship offered by mind and heart. Adapt yourselves no longer to the pattern of the present world, but let your minds be remade and your whole nature thus transformed. Then you will be able to discern the will of God and to know it is good, acceptable, and perfect" (NEB).

There is a vast difference between the inclination of the natural or carnal man to use "common sense" and that of the spiritual man to follow the sound mind principle. One, for understanding, depends upon the wisdom of man without benefit of God's wisdom and power; the other, having the mind of Christ, receives wisdom and guidance from God moment by moment through faith.

Are your decisions as a Christian based upon unpredictable emotions and chance circumstances, the common sense of the natural man? Or do you make your decisions according to the sound mind principle of Scripture?

Through the years, as I have counseled with many Christians, the question most frequently asked has been, "How can I know the will of God for my life?" Inevitably, the majority of Christians who come for counsel are looking for some dramatic or cataclysmic revelation from God by which they will know God's plan. Without minimizing the importance of feelings, which Jesus promised in John 14:21 as a result of obedience, more emphasis needs to be placed upon the importance of the sound mind which God has given. Multitudes of sincere Christians are wasting their lives, immobile and impotent, as they wait for some unusual or dramatic word from God.

The Scripture assures us that "God has not given us a spirit of fear, but of power, and of love, and of a sound mind." Thus, a Christian who has yielded his life fully to Christ can be assured of sanctified reasoning, and a balanced, disciplined mind. Also, God has promised to give His children wisdom according to James 1:5–7. Further, we can know with settled and absolute assurance that when we pray according to the will of God, He will always hear and grant our petitions (1 John 5:14, 15). Since the Christian is to live by faith, and faith comes through an understanding of the Word of God, it is impossible to over-emphasize the importance of the Scripture in the lives of those who would know and do the will of God.

If you would like to know the will of God for your life according to the sound mind principle of Scripture, may I suggest that you follow this bit of logic: Consider these questions. First, "Why did Jesus come?" He came "to seek and save the lost" (Luke 19:10). Then, "What is the greatest experience of your life?" If you are a Christian, your answer quite obviously will be, "Coming to know Christ personally as my Saviour and Lord." Finally, "What is the greatest thing that you can do to help others?" The answer is again obvious, "Introducing them to Christ."

154

Jesus came to seek and to save the lost, and every Christian is under divine orders to be a faithful witness for Christ. Jesus said, "Herein is my Father glorified, that ye bear much fruit; so shall ye be my disciples" (John 15:8, KJ). It logically follows that the most important thing I can possibly do as a Christian is to allow the Lord Jesus Christ in all of His resurrection power to have complete, unhindered control of my life. Otherwise He cannot continue seeking and saving the lost through me.

Thus, every sincere Christian will want to make his God-given time, talents and treasure available to Christ so that his fullest potential will be realized for Him. For one Christian, this talent which God has given him may be prophetic preaching, evangelism or teaching; for another, it may be business; for another, the ministry or missions; for another, homemaking, as expressed in Romans 12:5; 1 Corinthians 12; 1 Corinthians 14; Ephesians 4; and other Scriptures.

Chart 1

Campus Crusade		Teaching		Church Ministry		Business or Profession	
Pro	Con	Pro	Con	Pro	Con	Pro	Con

As you evaluate the talents that God has given you in relation to your training, personality, and other qualities, may I suggest that you take a sheet of paper and make a list of the most logical ways through which your life can be used to accomplish the most for the glory of God. With the desire to put His will above all else, list the pros and cons of each opportunity. Where or how, according to the sound mind principle, can the Lord Jesus Christ through your yielded life accomplish the most in continuing His great ministry of "seeking and saving the lost"? Like my young friend, you will find that such a procedure will inevitably result in positive actions leading to God's perfect will for your life. But note a word of caution. The sound mind principle is not valid unless certain factors exist:

1. There must be no unconfessed sin in your life; following 1 John 1:9 takes care of that: "If we confess our sins, God is faithful and just to forgive us our sins and to cleanse us from all unrighteousness."

2. Your life must be fully dedicated to Christ according to Romans 12:1, 2, and you must be filled with the Holy Spirit in obedience to the command of Ephesians 5:18. As in the case of our salvation, we are filled and controlled by the Spirit through faith.

3. In order to know the will of God, you must walk in the Spirit (abide in Christ) moment by moment. You place your faith in the trustworthiness of God with the confidence that the Lord is directing and will continue to direct your life according to His promise that the "steps of a righteous man are ordered of the Lord." For, "As you have therefore received Christ Jesus the Lord, so walk in Him." How? By faith, by placing your complete trust in Him. Now, you must go on walking by faith. Remember, "that which is not of faith is sin," and "the just shall live by faith," and "without faith it is impossible to please God." Faith is the catalyst for all our Christian relationships.

The counsel of others should be prayerfully considered, especially that of mature, dedicated Christians who know the Word of God and are able to relate the proper use of Scripture to your need. However, care should be taken not to make the counsel of others a "crutch." Although God often speaks to us through other Christians, we are admonished to place our trust in Him. In Psalm 37 we are told to delight ourselves in the Lord and He will give us the desires of our hearts, to commit our ways unto the Lord, to trust Him and He will bring it to pass. Also, in Proverbs

3 we are told, "Trust in the Lord with all thine heart; and not unto thine own understanding. In all thy ways acknowledge Him, and He shall direct thy paths."

God never contradicts Himself. He never leads us to do anything contrary to the commands of His Word; for according to Philippians 2:13, "It is God who is at work within you, giving you the will and the power to achieve His purpose" (Phillips).

Through the centuries sincere religious men have suggested spiritual formulas for discovering the will of God. Some are valid; others are unscriptural and misleading. For example, a young seminary graduate came to see me. He was investigating various possibilities of Christian service and had come to discuss the ministry of Campus Crusade for Christ. Applying the sound mind principle approach to his quest, I asked him, "In what way do you expect God to reveal His place of service for you?"

He replied, "I am following the 'closed door' policy. A few months ago I began to investigate several opportunities for Christian service. The Lord has now closed the door on all but two, one of which is Campus Crusade for Christ. If the door to accept a call to a particular church closes, I shall know that God wants me in Campus Crusade."

Many sincere Christians follow this illogical and unscriptural method, often with most unsatisfactory and frustrating consequences. Don't misunderstand. God may and often does close doors in the life of an active, Spirit-controlled Christian. This was true in the experience of the apostle Paul. As recorded in Acts 16:6–11, he was forbidden by the Spirit to go into Bithynia because God wanted him in Macedonia. My reference to "closed door" policies does not preclude such experiences, but refers to a careless hit-or-miss attitude without the careful evaluation of all the issues.

This approach is illogical because it allows elements of chance to influence a decision rather than a careful, intelligent evaluation

157

of all the factors involved. It is unscriptural in that it fails to employ the God-given faculties of reason that are controlled by the Holy Spirit.

Further, the closed door policy is in error because it seeks God's will through the process of elimination rather than seeking God's best first. It should be understood that true faith is established on the basis of fact. Therefore, vital faith in God is emphasized rather than minimized through employing Spirit-controlled reason. In making decisions some sincere Christians rely almost entirely upon impressions, or hunches, fearful that if they use their mental faculties they will not exercise adequate faith and thus will grieve the Holy Spirit.

There are those who assume that a door has been closed simply because of difficulties that have been encountered. Yet, experience has taught and Scripture confirms that God's richest blessings often follow periods of greatest testing. This might include financial needs, loss of health, objection of loved ones and criticism of fellow Christians. God's blessing is promised, however, only to those who are obedient, who keep on trying, who demonstrate their faith in God's faithfulness. The apparent defeat of the cross was followed by the victory of the resurrection.

An acceptable consideration for discussing God's will contains four basic factors somewhat similar to the sound mind principle. God's will is revealed in (1) the authority of Scripture, (2) providential circumstances, (3) conviction based upon reason, and (4) impressions of the Holy Spirit upon our minds. However, such an appraisal is safer with a mature Christian than with a new or carnal Christian, and there is always danger of misunderstanding impressions.

You must know the source of leading before responding to it. To the inexperienced, what appears to be the leading of God may not be from Him at all but from "the rulers of darkness of this world." Satan and his helpers often disguise themselves as "angels of light" by performing "miracles, signs," by "foretelling events," etc. The enemy of our souls is a master counterfeiter.

Remember, just as the turning of the steering wheel of an automobile does not alter its direction unless it is moving, so God cannot direct our lives unless we are moving for Him. I challenge you to begin employing the sound mind principle today in all your relationships. Apply it to the investment of your time, your talents and your treasure; for this principle applies to everything you do in this life. Every Christian should take spiritual inventory regularly by asking himself these questions: Is my time being invested in such a way that the largest possible number of people is being introduced to Christ? Are my talents being invested to the full to the end that the largest possible number of people is being introduced to Christ? Is my money, my treasure, being invested in such a way as to introduce the greatest number of people to Christ?

Every Christian is admonished to be a good steward of his God-given time, talents and treasure. Therefore, these investments must not be dictated by tradition, habit or emotions. Every investment of time, talent, and treasure, unless otherwise directed by the Holy Spirit, should be determined by the sound mind principle of Scripture according to 2 Timothy 1:7.

Regarding the questions asked by your girlfriend, the same principle applies to her. How does this sound mind principle apply in the case of a secretary, a homemaker, an invalid, or one who, because of circumstances beyond her control, does not have direct contact with men and women who are in need of Christ?

First, each Christian must be a witness for Christ. This is simply an act of obedience for which one need not possess the gift of evangelism. If normal day-to-day contacts do not provide opportunities to witness for Christ, an obedient Christian will make opportunities through personal contacts, church calling, letter writing, etc. Two of the most radiant, effective and fruitful Christians whom I have known were bed-ridden invalids who, though in constant pain, bore a powerful witness for Christ to all—stranger and friend alike. "That which is most in our hearts will be most on our lips" was demonstrated in their lives.

Second, a careful evaluation should be given to determine if God may not have a better position for one. Again, the sound mind principle applies. For example, a secretary in a secular organization may have less opportunity to make her life count for the Lord. It may be that God wants to use one's talents in a Christian organization. (I happen to know that there is a great scarcity of qualified secretarial help in many Christian organizations, including Campus Crusade for Christ.) One should be very careful, however, not to run from what appears to be a difficult assignment. A careful appraisal of one's present responsibilities, with this new understanding of God's leading, may well reveal a great potential for Christ.

Quite obviously, members of an office staff do not have as much contact with men and women who are in need of our Savior as those who are actually working on the campus or conducting evangelistic meetings. However, according to the sound mind principle, if these staff members' lives are fully dedicated to Christ, they can make a vital contribution to the effectiveness of any Christian ministry. By relieving others who have the gift of evangelism without the talent for business or secretarial responsibilities, the overall ministry for Christ in such an organization is strengthened greatly. In this way, they can more fully utilize their talents in helping to seek and save the lost.

For example, a dedicated member of the secretarial staff of the world-wide ministry of Campus Crusade for Christ is just as vital to the success of this campus strategy as those who are working on the campus. My own personal ministry has been greatly increased by the dedicated efforts of several secretaries who are more concerned about winning students to Christ than their own personal pleasure.

One further word of explanation must be given. It is true that God still reveals His will to some men and women in dramatic ways, but this should be considered the exception rather than the rule. God still leads men today as He has through the centuries. Philip, the deacon, was holding a successful campaign in Samaria. The sound mind principle would have directed him to continue his campaign. However, God overruled by a special revelation, and Philip was led by the Holy Spirit to preach for Christ to the Ethiopian eunuch. According to tradition, God used the Ethiopian eunuch to communicate the message of our living Lord to his own country.

Living according to the sound mind principle allows for such dramatic leadings of God, but we are not to wait for such revelations before we start moving for Christ. Faith must have an object. A Christian's faith is built upon the authority of God's Word supported by historical fact and not upon any shallow emotional experience. However, a Christian's trust in God's will revealed in His Word will result in the decisions which are made by following the sound mind principle. The confirmation may come in various ways according to many factors, including the personality of the individual involved. Usually, the confirmation is a quiet, peaceful assurance that you are doing what God wants you to do, with expectancy that God will use you to bear "much fruit."

As any sincere Christian gives himself to a diligent study of the Scripture and allows a loving, all-wise, sovereign God and Father to control his life, feelings will inevitably result. Thus, the end result of a life that is lived according to the sound mind principle is the most joyful, abundant, and fruitful life of all. Expect the Lord Jesus Christ to draw men to Himself through you. As you begin each day, acknowledge the fact that you belong to Him. Thank Him for the fact that He lives within you. Invite Him to use your mind to think His thoughts, your heart to express His love, your lips to speak His truth. Ask Jesus to be at home in your life and to walk around in your body in order that He may continue seeking and saving souls through you.

It is my sincere prayer, Paul, that you may know this kind of life, that you may fully appropriate all that God has given to you as your rightful heritage in Christ. I shall look forward to hearing more from you concerning your personal application of the sound mind principle.

Warmly in Christ,

Bill Bright

Appendix C
REAL-LIFE EMPLOYMENT SITUATIONS

CASE HISTORIES

Do you want to know how some people get into full-time Christian work? The examples below are from situations with which I am familiar and give testimony that there is a power beyond you and me in charge of all this. The Lord is truly the Personnel Director, and the rest of us in the personnel field just help Him out sometimes, if that's possible. Sometimes we even hinder Him, but He still does what He wants to do, as you will see.

These cases are included to help you understand that if God wants you in a particular organization or job, no person can stop you. If He doesn't, no person can help you.

CASE 1

Ella applied for a job one day after her college graduation. After reviewing her qualifications and all of our vacancies, I advised her there was nothing available at the time, but we would surely keep her in mind. I was impressed with her and had a feeling that she was supposed to have a job but I could see absolutely nothing for her. We terminated the interview and parted. As far as she was concerned, she had heard the final and authoritative word from the personnel director himself. I left for a meeting down the hall.

I returned from the meeting thirty minutes later, and guess what? Ella had been hired. How could that be if the director had said no? Well, there was a Higher Director who had said yes. After I had left, Ella was talking to my secretary, and during the conversation, previously unknown information about a vacancy became available to my assistant. Ella had gotten the job because God wanted her there. That first job was an entry clerical position, but Ella has since progressed to be the head of a major department and has been a continual blessing to everyone. And she was hired in spite of me.

CASE 2

Speaking of "in spite of me," this is a good example. One day a young man came to volunteer as a telephone counselor, not an employment situation. He seemed a little young, so I asked his age, to which he replied, "Seventeen." I explained that our policy had always required a counselor to be at least eighteen, largely because of the number of calls that require a degree of experience and maturity. I told him I appreciated his offer, but our rule prevented us from using him. I was about to learn a lesson about rules and grace.

I invited him to sit in the counseling center at a vacant position to observe what was going on, assuming it might be interesting to him. I took the phone off the hook so that it would not ring and would give a busy signal to the caller.

After he had been sitting there just a few moments, *the telephone rang.* Puzzled, our young friend picked up the handset and put it to his ear, not knowing what, if anything, to expect.

Believe it or not, the caller was another seventeen-year-old, and our young friend turned out to be the perfect person for the job.

Ever since then, I have had no trouble believing in the

impossible or trusting in God's sovereign power. We have the privilege of being co-workers with Him, but it is comforting to know that if our frailty causes us to fail, He will still accomplish His purpose.

CASE 3

At one time I had to travel to recruit representatives in certain major cities. Usually I knew no one in the cities I visited and relied solely on prayer and one or two referrals as initial contacts. On different occasions in two different cities I had made a contact or two, but absolutely nothing was happening. I had no prospects for the job, important work needed to be done, and my time was rapidly running out. As some say, I was between a rock and a hard place. Have you ever been there? It's no fun.

In both situations, I had been forced to my knees on the floor of my hotel room. I remember it vividly. In both situations, precisely when I was on my knees praying, the phone rang. Frankly, I was a little bothered that the phone had interrupted me.

I know this will sound too good to be true, but in one case, the caller was the one chosen for the job; in the other, the caller quickly led me to the right person. The timing was simply incredible.

Would they have called if I had not prayed? I doubt it. I do know for certain that my respect for the power of prayer was dramatically increased, as well as my dependence on God to provide in times of need. From then on, I have been careful to take no chances. *The kneeling position is a reliable place to get answers.*

CASE 4

In Case 1, I gave you an example of a situation in which I perceived no job availability for a person, but God had a different idea. The opposite has also happened to me.

Mike was one of the sharpest fellows I had ever met. He had excellent administrative skills, outstanding experience and education, and was very personable. He had it all. In fact, I couldn't think of a single negative.

Mike had been trying to become employed with the Christian ministry I represented for several years, but the door never opened. As personnel director, I tried my best to get him on staff, but my best was not enough. No one had any negatives about him. It just could not be made to happen because it was not the will of Him who closes doors no man can open.

CASE 5

My middle son was just finishing high school and looking for a job. He would be available in about two weeks. He did not have a trade but was adept at electronics from hobby work. Though not adept enough to be called a technician, he was prepared for a minimum-wage entry position somewhere.

Being a personnel director, I was always a "straight arrow" in not allowing relations or acquaintances to affect my hiring decisions. I was a "company man" through and through. Therefore, I was really reluctant to help my son get a job where I worked. Frankly, I feared the accusation of nepotism or favoritism even though I could have gotten away with it as others sometimes did. My pride too was probably a factor.

But God had other plans, my pride notwithstanding. Again, the timing was incredible. Just when Steve started looking for a job, the head of the engineering department expressed a desperate need for four young men who would be willing to work for minimum wage, preferably knowing a little about electronics. As only temporary positions with minimum-wage pay, they would be very difficult to fill. His immediate need became my immediate recruiting problem.

Where could I find four such people so quickly? I was trapped.

You've guessed the solution. Steve, out of necessity, was one of the four. It was our Father's plan to bless Steve and our family.

Steve's performance not only led to his acquiring a permanent job and increased responsibilities but also to his meeting a wonderful girl, Ruth, who became my daughter-in-law. I'm so glad that it is not I, but God who is managing our lives.

CASE 6

By now, you are probably wondering what I was doing there as personnel director. Sometimes I wondered that too, but occasionally I saw evidence that maybe I was in the right place.

In reviewing the mail one day I noticed the resumé of a pilot. He had felt led to make his services available, assuming that we had a corporate airplane. We didn't, so I sent him a courteous reply to that effect but saved his resumé for future reference in case we needed him.

Just a short time later, the president of the company asked me to look for a pilot because the organization had just purchased an airplane. The pilot applicant was soon hired and at the controls. Once again the timing was amazing. Of course, you know Who is really at the controls.

CASE 7

Andy had recently had an experience with the Lord. In a radical act of commitment, he decided to forsake his high-salaried, executive position and offer his services to the Lord's work by sending us a resumé. He did not realize, however, that our large volume of mail often caused a two-week, maybe longer, delay in responses. Even then, there were internal and built-in delays that were unavoidable.

A long time had elapsed, and he had not heard anything. His boss knew that he might lose Andy soon because of his commitment and application. But Andy could not keep his boss dangling any longer. He had to make a decision, and, not having heard from us, assumed that it was not the Lord's will. He was within two or three minutes of walking into his boss's office and reaffirming his commitment to the company.

Just before he walked out of his office, the telephone rang. Guess who was on the other end of the line? Yes, yours truly calling to express our interest in him and wanting to set up a serious interview, just in the nick of time. A few more seconds, and it would have been too late.

How did I know to call at that very moment instead of, for instance, the next day? I didn't know. That's what is amazing about being led of the Spirit. It's natural. You don't have to strain to be spiritual; He works through you just the way you are.

At that time we did not know, but God knew, that we would soon be losing a key manager and that without Andy, the organization would have had a serious problem. My awareness of God's omniscience and sovereignty is increased whenever I witness it this way.

Can you doubt that He will take care of your life, with no less efficiency and adequate timing? Trust Him.

CASE 8

Linda had been a secretary for several years and had just moved to the city from a small town. She and her husband rented an apartment near one of our office complexes in the suburbs. She decided she wanted a job in a Christian company, if possible, but didn't know the city or where there might be such a thing. She had never even heard of our ministry.

She decided to look in the Yellow Pages for a Christian organization and saw our name listed. Though she didn't know anything about us, we immediately appealed to her because our office was directly across the street from her apartment. Of course, she didn't know that our personnel office had a desperate need for a secretary.

Linda walked in, applied for the job, was interviewed, checked out, and within hours was hired. In addition, she had a need, and one of our volunteer prayer counselors prayed for her in my office. She was instantly and dramatically touched by the Lord with an answered prayer. Linda was truly called for that job, and she became one of the most efficient secretaries I have ever known.

CASE 9

This is about me, but don't stop reading. You will enjoy this. Once I reached a place in my own search for God's vocational direction where I had to step out in faith, so the Holy Spirit, the rudder of my life, could do some steering. With all the discernment I could muster, I picked out what I thought was the will of the Lord. Then with all the courage I could muster, I sent my resumé to the ministry I had selected.

Days, weeks went by. No response. My personal situation was dictating that something happen soon, and I was becoming a little frantic. Had I missed the Lord's guidance? Had I really blown it?

My concern reached a climax one morning. I awakened very early. I went to my usual morning prayer location and decided I was really going to get serious with the Lord. I needed an answer desperately. I prayed fervently for about an hour, pounding heaven's gates, pleading for a breakthrough. I finally sensed my prayer had been heard. I said my amen, got up, and went about the rest of my morning routine.

I happened to stay home that day. About five hours after my prayer ended, the telephone rang. It was a dear elderly lady from across town, whom I had met only one time. Constance was one of those rare people called into a deep intercessory prayer ministry. For some reason (obviously the Spirit's promptings), she had felt she should pray for me ever since we met. But she did not know about my vocational desires or that I had sent a resumé to a certain ministry.

Constance immediately began to reveal a most intriguing story. The preceding day, she had been reading her Bible when suddenly she experienced the sense of the Lord's presence in her room. She did not see anything but heard what she described as an audible voice saying, "Jim's going to (the name of the ministry where I had applied)."

For some reason she chose to call to tell me not that day but the next. Frankly, I didn't know what to make of it. I believed in such things, but it was a heavy message. Could it really have been the Lord? And a voice? We chatted a moment; I thanked her, and she hung up.

Would you believe that thirty minutes later the postman brought me a letter from the president of the ministry where I had applied, asking me to come over to talk about a job? I noticed that the postmark was the same day Constance had received the message.

Needless to say, a job quickly evolved, and I was where God intended. I sometimes hesitate to tell that story because I sense some people's question, "Why doesn't He give me such strong confirmation?" I can't say why it happens. I suspect that in my case it may have had something to do with the weakness of my faith and the testings to come. This strong confirmation helped see me through them.

If you have prayed and asked Him to take over your life,

you may rest in the confidence that He has everything under control and on schedule. You are His child; you have only to watch as He unveils His steps before you. What an exciting life you have ahead!

Appendix D
DESCRIPTION AND QUALIFICATIONS NEEDED FOR SELECTED OCCUPATIONS

This appendix gives vital information about selected occupations, including

a description of the work,

training and other qualifications needed,

typical earnings (otherwise found in appendix E),

sources of additional information.

There are actually many thousands of different types of occupations, depending on how they are classified. The purpose of this appendix is to give you some representative information on different occupations, covering a wide range of categories. This selection may not include the exact occupation you are considering, but you may find one that is close, giving you an approximate picture of your specific interest. The source of most of this information is the *Occupational Outlook Handbook,* 1990–91 Edition, published by the U.S. Department of Labor, Bureau of Labor Statistics. In selecting the following occupations, possible applicability to Christian organizations was a factor.

Many of the potential salaries for these positions are listed in appendix E.

INDEX OF OCCUPATIONS

ACCOUNTANTS AND AUDITORS

NATURE OF THE WORK

Managers must have up-to-date financial information to make important decisions. Accountants and auditors prepare and analyze financial reports that furnish this kind of information. Three major fields are public, management, and government accounting. Public accountants have their own businesses or work for accounting firms. Management accountants handle the financial records of their company. Government accountants and auditors examine the records of government agencies and audit private businesses and individuals whose dealings are subject to government regulations. Most work in offices and have structured work hours, although in some cases extra-long hours are needed, such as with tax accountants during income-tax season.

TRAINING AND OTHER QUALIFICATIONS NEEDED

Training is available at colleges, universities, accounting and business schools, and correspondence schools. Most firms require at least a bachelor's degree in accounting or a related field. Many require a master's degree, and firms are increasingly requiring a knowledge of computer applications in accounting and auditing. Previous experience in accounting or auditing can help an applicant. Many colleges offer students an opportunity to gain experience through summer or part-time internship programs, conducted by public accounting or business firms.

SOURCES OF ADDITIONAL INFORMATION

American Institute of Certified Public Accountants, 1211 Avenue of the Americas, New York, NY 10036.

National Association of Accountants, 10 Paragon Drive, Montvale, NJ 07645.

Institute of Internal Auditors, 249 Maitland Avenue, Altamonte Springs, FL 32701.

For information on educational institutions offering a specialization in accounting, contact the American Assembly of Collegiate Schools of Business, 605 Old Dallas Road, Suite 220, St. Louis, MO 63141.

ACCOUNTING CLERKS AND BOOKKEEPERS

NATURE OF THE WORK

Every business needs systematic and up-to-date records of accounts and business transactions. Bookkeepers and accounting clerks maintain these records in journals, ledgers, or other accounting forms. They also prepare periodic financial statements, showing all money received and paid out. Duties vary with the size and type of business. Most use calculating machines; many use check-writing and bookkeeping machines. In a small firm, one general bookkeeper may handle all the bookkeeping; in large firms, the work may be very specialized with an accounting clerk, for example, just handling accounts receivable (money owed to the company), or accounts payable (money owed by the company), payroll, or other functions. These would work under the direction of a head bookkeeper or accountant. Working conditions are typical for an office. Workers must sit for long hours, working with numerical information.

TRAINING AND OTHER QUALIFICATIONS NEEDED

High school graduates who have taken business arithmetic, bookkeeping, and principles of accounting meet the minimum requirements for most bookkeeping jobs. Many employers prefer those who have completed courses at business schools or community colleges. Many such programs are available in most cities. The ability to use bookkeeping machines and computers is also an asset. Bookkeepers and accounting clerks need to be good using numbers and doing detailed work for long periods of time. Small mistakes can be very serious, so carefulness and accuracy are very important.

SOURCES OF ADDITIONAL INFORMATION

For schools in your area, check your local Yellow Pages.
Many state employment offices can provide information on job opportunities in your area.

ACTORS AND ACTRESSES

NATURE OF THE WORK

Actors and actresses entertain and communicate with people through their interpretation of dramatic roles. They rely on facial and verbal expression as well as body motions for their creative effort. Acting requires persistence, practice, and hard work, in addition to special talent. Only a few become stars in their profession; more become well known in lesser and supporting roles; still more struggle for a toehold in their profession, with pick-up parts wherever they can. Employment for actors is characteristically unsteady, so many take temporary jobs, often as waiters and waitresses, while waiting on their next part. Beginning actors usually start with bit parts, where they may speak only a few lines. If successful, they progress to larger roles. Some actors move into acting-related jobs, such as drama coaches or directors, or possibly teaching.

TRAINING AND OTHER QUALIFICATIONS NEEDED

Aspiring actors should take part in high school and college plays as much as possible, in local little theater, or in other drama activities. Some people enter the field with no formal training, but some formal training or acting experience is usually considered necessary. Training in the dramatic arts can be obtained at specialized schools in New York and Los Angeles or in about 620 colleges and universities in the United States.

EARNINGS

Acting jobs surveyed in off-Broadway productions earned as little as $280 per week, whereas Broadway productions paid a minimum of about $800 per week. Motion picture and television actors and actresses earned a minimum daily rate of $398, or $1,385 for a five-day week. The Actors Equity Association, which represents about 30,000 actors, reported that about 23,000 of their members had no earnings in the year surveyed, and 4,500 of them made less than $2,500. Only 675 earned more than $35,000.

SOURCES OF ADDITIONAL INFORMATION

American Theater Association, 1000 Vermont Avenue N.W., Washington, DC 20005.

Theater Communications Group, Inc., 355 Lexington Avenue, New York, NY 10017.

AIR-CONDITIONING, REFRIGERATION, AND HEATING MECHANICS

NATURE OF THE WORK

Almost all homes and buildings have some sort of climate control to allow heat in the winter and cooling in the summer or both. Installing and maintaining these systems is a highly technical specialty. Some mechanics specialize in one of the functions, such as heating or air conditioning; others are competent in all areas. These systems require more than just a single machine and may involve fans, compressors, condensers, evaporators, control devices, ducting, and pipes. Many companies with large buildings hire their own technicians to take care of their systems; others may contract the work to an outside firm. The work can be strenuous and may involve outside exposure in both hot and cold weather. Mechanics sometimes must work in awkward and cramped positions. They are exposed to occasional hazards, such as high voltage and burns.

TRAINING AND OTHER QUALIFICATIONS NEEDED

Most mechanics start as helpers and acquire their skills after several years of experience in assisting and observing. Formal training is available in many high schools and, of course, vocational schools in most areas. Training is not always required to get a job, but it helps. A mechanical aptitude is a necessity.

EARNINGS

The average weekly salary for those surveyed and not self-employed was $414.

SOURCES OF ADDITIONAL INFORMATION

National Association of Plumbing, Heating and Cooling Contractors, P.O. Box 6808, Falls Church, VA 22046.

For additional information, contact local contractors or the state employment office.

ATTORNEYS

NATURE OF THE WORK

Attorneys, or lawyers, act as both advocates and advisors. As advocates, they represent opposing parties in criminal and civil trials by presenting arguments that support their side in a court of law. As advisors, lawyers counsel their clients as to their legal rights and obligations and suggest particular courses of action in business or personal matters. In common with all is the interpretation of the law and its application in a specific situation, often requiring much research. Many practice independently in their own business; many others are employed by the government or by private companies. There is much specialization, such as in communications law, tax law, international law, etc. Some use their law background in fields such as journalism, management consulting, lobbying, and political office. Most of the work is in offices and courtrooms with frequent travel to attend meetings, gather evidence, and appear before courts and other bodies.

TRAINING AND OTHER
QUALIFICATIONS NEEDED

This is a highly regulated occupation with its practice needing state approval, usually by passing its bar examination. Applicants must take a written examination to pass the bar, although some states drop this requirement for graduates of their own law schools. In most states, a bar applicant must have had three years of college and be a graduate from a law school approved by the American Bar Association or appropriate state authorities.

SOURCE OF ADDITIONAL INFORMATION

Information Services, American Bar Association, 750 North Lake Shore Drive, Chicago, IL 60611.

BROADCAST TECHNICIANS

NATURE OF THE WORK

Broadcast technicians operate and maintain the electronic equipment used to record and transmit radio and television programs. They work with microphones, sound and videotape recorders, light and sound effects, television cameras, transmitters, and other equipment. In small stations, they perform a variety of duties; one person may perform most or all the technical duties. In large facilities, tasks are more specialized; there are transmitter operators, maintenance technicians, audio-control engineers, video-control engineers, lighting technicians, recording technicians. The terms "operator," "engineer," and "technician" are often used interchangeably; although within a particular company there may be very distinct definitions pertaining to responsibility. Most work locations are indoors and in very pleasant surroundings. Work, though, sometimes involves long hours and the pressures of broadcast deadlines.

TRAINING AND OTHER QUALIFICATIONS NEEDED

Some of these positions require a license or permit from the Federal Communications Commission; other positions require a written examination. Many available schools help train people for these examinations. High school students who hope to pursue this occupation would be helped if they take as many mathematics courses as possible as well as physics and electronics, if available. Technical school, community college, and regular college training is an advantage. The more you can learn, the better you will be.

EARNINGS

Average earnings for technicians surveyed at radio stations were $21,600; at television stations, between $20,300 and $61,500. Earnings are higher at the larger stations in the larger cities, up to twice as much as for the smaller stations in smaller cities.

SOURCES OF ADDITIONAL INFORMATION

For information about permits and licenses, contact the Federal Communications Commission, 1919 M Street N.W., Washington, DC 20554.

For information on careers, contact the National Association of Broadcasters, 1771 N Street N.W., Washington, DC 20036.

For a list of schools that offer programs or courses in broadcasting, contact the Broadcast Education Association, National Association of Broadcasters, 1771 N Street N.W., Washington, DC 20036.

COLLEGE CAREER-PLANNING AND PLACEMENT COUNSELORS

NATURE OF THE WORK

Career-planning and placement counselors help bridge the gap between education and work by assisting students and alumni in all phases of career planning and job search. They encourage students to examine their interests, abilities, values, and goals and assist them in exploring career alternatives. They help arrange internships, field placements, or part-time or summer employment. They must keep abreast of labor-market information, including salaries, training requirements, and job prospects. They help students find jobs by arranging interviews and campus visits by potential employers. They also may advise school administrators about curriculum and course content.

TRAINING AND OTHER QUALIFICATIONS NEEDED

There is no educational program that specifically prepares people for college career-planning and placement work. Applicants are usually sought with a master's degree in counseling, in college-student personnel work, or in behavioral science. Some people enter the field after gaining broad experience in business, government, or education.

EARNINGS

According to a survey, the average salary of school counselors was about $27,600; salaries vary with the size, level, and locality of the school.

SOURCE OF ADDITIONAL INFORMATION

American Association for Counseling and Development, 5999 Stevenson Avenue, Alexandria, VA 22304.

COLLEGE AND UNIVERSITY FACULTY

NATURE OF THE WORK

Faculty members provide instruction in particular fields of study to meet the needs of the students. Many conduct several courses within the same field. Some specialize in undergraduate studies; some in graduate studies; some in both, using various methods to present their information. Some lecture to both small and extremely large classes; some work primarily in laboratories; some may use closed-circuit television, computers, and other aids. They must keep up with developments in their field by reading current literature, attending professional activities, and conducting research. Publishing books and articles is also considered very important in the profession. Faculty members work with student organizations, school administration, and the community too. Though they may work long hours, they usually have flexible schedules and are not continuously in a particular office or location.

TRAINING AND OTHER QUALIFICATIONS NEEDED

A master's degree is a minimum requirement and is satisfactory in some colleges in some fields; competition is so keen for academic positions, however, that a doctoral degree is often necessary for consideration. Doctoral programs usually require three to five years of study beyond a bachelor's degree.

EARNINGS

Earnings vary greatly depending on faculty rank and the type of institution. A survey showed salaries for full-time faculty members with nine-month contracts to average from $23,600 for instructors to $50,420 for full professors, with an average of $31,000.

SOURCE OF ADDITIONAL INFORMATION

American Association of University Professors, One Dupont Circle N.W., Suite 500, Washington, DC 20036.

COMPUTER-OPERATING PERSONNEL

NATURE OF THE WORK

Computer-operating personnel perform various operating duties with computers, consisting of entering data and instructions, operating the computer, and retrieving the results. Data and instructions to be put into the computer are called input, and results from the computer are called output. Information input is handled by keypunch operators who operate a machine similar to a typewriter that punches holes in cards that are later read by the computer. This may be done by data-entry or data-typist personnel directly into the computer electronically through a special keyboard. Once the information is entered, console operators then manipulate the computer controls to make it do whatever function is required. The output sometimes is already in the necessary form to be used, although in some cases other operators perform this function. Finally, tape librarians classify and catalog all material, programs, listings, and test data. Work is usually in a physically comfortable environment, although some equipment may be noisy. Also, some companies run odd-hour shifts because of workload and to maximize utilization of the equipment.

TRAINING AND OTHER QUALIFICATIONS NEEDED

A college education is not required for this field, but some training is necessary to enter unless an employer will be willing to train you. Sometimes an employer will take someone who can type and train him or her in data entry, a closely related function; or a bookkeeping machine operator may be transferred to operate the computer after some on-the-job training. In most cases, however, training should first be obtained from one of the many sources available, such as high school, a private computer school, a community college, or a vocational school.

SOURCE OF ADDITIONAL INFORMATION

Association for Computer Operations Management, 742 East Chapman Avenue, Orange, CA 92666.

COMPUTER PROGRAMMERS

NATURE OF THE WORK

Because computers cannot think for themselves, computer programmers must write detailed instructions called programs that list in a logical order the steps the machine must follow to organize data, solve a problem, or do some other task. Programmers usually work from descriptions prepared by systems analysts who have carefully studied the task that the computer system is going to perform. In some companies particularly smaller ones, there may be no systems analyst and both jobs are done by a programmer-analyst. Programmer work varies with the type of task, whether it is scientific or business related, for example. The programmer codes instructions into the computer, then tests what he has done, and finally prepares instruction sheets for the computer operator who will run the program and operate the computer. Working conditions are usually pleasant. The work, however, might be very demanding sometimes. Hours may be regular or, in some cases, require much overtime.

TRAINING AND OTHER QUALIFICATIONS NEEDED

Because employers' needs vary, there are no universal training requirements. Most programmers are college graduates; others have only taken special courses to supplement their experience in other areas, such as accounting and inventory control. Computer programming is taught in vocational schools, community colleges, and other public and private schools, including high schools and home-study courses. Employers look for people who can think logically and are capable of performing exacting work. The job calls for patience, persistence, and the ability to work with extreme accuracy under pressure. Ingenuity and imagination are important to problem solving.

SOURCE OF ADDITIONAL INFORMATION

The Institute for Certification of Computer Professionals, 2200 East Devon Avenue, Suite 268, Des Plaines, IL 60018.

CONSTRUCTION OCCUPATIONS

NATURE OF THE WORK

Construction craft workers represent the largest group of skilled workers in the nation's labor force. They represent good opportunities for young people who do not want to go to college but want to learn a trade. Once the trade is learned, jobs are available throughout the country. In addition, it is easy to form your own business as an independent contractor in these crafts. Workers in these fields build, repair, and modernize buildings of all types. Construction work may be divided into three categories: structural, finishing, and mechanical. Structural includes such specialties as bricklaying and carpentry; finishing includes painting and plastering. All of these jobs require physical exertion and good health and strength. The work is often outdoors and sometimes hazardous.

TRAINING AND OTHER QUALIFICATIONS NEEDED

Many acquire these skills as a laborer or helper. Many also learn through a formal apprenticeship program, which is probably the best way because of the structured training program that includes both on-the-job and classroom training. Obviously, those entering these fields should enjoy and be adept at working with their hands.

EARNINGS

The following represents average weekly rates for selected construction occupations:

Electrician	$478
Plumber/Pipefitter	461

Bricklayer	448
Carpenter	381
Painter	328

SOURCES OF ADDITIONAL INFORMATION

AFL-CIO, Building and Construction Trades Department, 815 16th Street N.W., Washington, DC 20006.

Associated General Contractors of America, Inc., 1957 E Street N.W., Washington, DC 20006.

National Association of Homebuilders, 15th and M Streets N.W., Washington, DC 20005.

Contact the local state employment office, state apprenticeship agency, or office of the Department of Labor.

ENGINEERS

NATURE OF THE WORK

Engineers apply the theories and principles of science and mathematics to practical, technical problems. Often their work is the link between a scientific discovery and its application. They design machinery, equipment, systems, and processes for efficient and economical performance. Many engineers work in testing, production, operations, or maintenance. They can work in administration, management, or technically oriented sales. Engineers specialize in most scientific areas, such as aerospace, agriculture, chemical, electrical, civil, industrial, mechanical, metallurgical, and petroleum. Though some travel or work outdoors, most work inside at a desk the majority of the time.

Work time will vary because some will need to devote much overtime on priority projects with no overtime pay.

TRAINING AND OTHER QUALIFICATIONS NEEDED

A bachelor's degree in engineering is usually acceptable for beginning positions, and in some cases, a degree in a natural science or mathematics is also acceptable. Experienced technicians with some engineering education are often able to advance into engineering positions. Some two-year programs and an associate degree in engineering technology may give adequate preparation for practical design and production work in some companies.

SOURCE OF ADDITIONAL INFORMATION

JETS-Guidance, 1420 King Street, Suite 405, Alexandria, VA 22314.

LEGAL ASSISTANTS

NATURE OF THE WORK

Legal assistants, sometimes called paralegals or legal technicians, normally work directly under the supervision of a lawyer. The lawyer always takes final responsibility for the legal assistant's work; a legal assistant, however, is allowed to perform all the functions of a lawyer other than accepting clients, setting legal fees, giving legal advice, or presenting a case. The law is presently being tested in at least one state where a paralegal has been operating independently for years, saving people vast sums of money on legal fees and claiming to give service just as well as a lawyer. If the courts continue to allow this, the practice

190

will undoubtedly spread and change the complexion of the entire legal industry and give new opportunities for the paralegal profession. The actual duties of most legal assistants vary greatly, depending whether it is a private practice, corporate, or governmental legal work.

TRAINING AND OTHER QUALIFICATIONS NEEDED

Some employers just require a high school diploma and train their legal assistants on the job; others train experienced legal personnel, such as legal secretaries, for the job. Increasingly, employers are requiring formal legal assistant training. Some of the training available is completed in an intensive several-week period. Most legal assistant training programs can be completed in two years, although there are some four-year programs.

EARNINGS

According to one survey, non-government legal assistants had an average salary of $24,900. Government paralegals averaged $29,200.

SOURCES OF ADDITIONAL INFORMATION

American Bar Association, Standing Committee on Legal Assistants, 750 North Lake Shore Drive, Chicago, IL 60611.

National Association of Legal Assistants, Inc., 1601 South Main Street, Suite 300, Tulsa, OK 74119.

LIBRARIANS

NATURE OF THE WORK

Librarians make information available to people. They serve as a link between the public and the millions of sources of information by selecting and organizing materials and making them accessible. Their work is divided into two basic functions: user services and technical services. Librarians in user services, such as reference and children's librarians, work directly with the users to help them find the information they need. Librarians in technical services, such as acquisitions librarians and catalogers, are primarily concerned with acquiring and preparing materials for use. Libraries can be busy, demanding, and even stressful places to work. While the atmosphere is usually pleasant, the job may require much standing, stooping, bending, and reaching.

TRAINING AND OTHER QUALIFICATIONS NEEDED

In most public, academic, and special libraries, a master's degree in library science is necessary to obtain an entry position. Many schools offer such degrees. This may not be necessary for public school libraries, where state certification requirements vary widely. Most states require that school librarians be certified as teachers, so a library degree is not always necessary. Because school libraries have become learning resource centers, they are staffed by personnel with a variety of educational backgrounds. Many are media professionals because of the increased emphasis on audio-visual and other media resources.

EARNINGS

Salaries vary with type of library, its size and geographical location, and the person's qualifications. In the latest survey available, starting salaries ranged from an average of $21,531 in public libraries to $25,183 in school libraries. The median salary for experienced librarians in colleges and universities was $22,454 and in the federal government, it was $34,282.

SOURCE OF ADDITIONAL INFORMATION

American Library Association, 50 East Huron Street, Chicago, IL 60611.

MARKET-RESEARCH ANALYSTS

NATURE OF THE WORK

Market-research analysts analyze the buying public's wants and needs, thus providing the information upon which major marketing decisions can be made. All kinds of activities—profit, nonprofit, and government—have to make marketing decisions constantly, such as when and how to put a product or service on the market, to solicit the public to contribute to charity, to recruit in the armed forces, just to name a few. Market-research analysts plan, design, and implement surveys as well as analyze their results. They are often concerned about discovering the preferences and buying habits of people. Their job is to find out everything possible about the market. For example, market research will tell a television station the approximate number of people watching at different hours of the day, their sex, ages, how long they watch, as well as other things. Accordingly, advertisers base their decisions on commercials. Market-research analysts usually work in offices, either as a member of a team or alone using calculators, preparing statistical charts, and analyzing data. Long hours are not unusual.

TRAINING AND OTHER QUALIFICATIONS NEEDED

Although a bachelor's degree is usually sufficient for trainees, a graduate education is necessary for many specialized positions in market research and also for later advancement. A major study in marketing is essential, especially in undergraduate work. A sizeable number of market researchers have graduate degrees in business administration and other fields. Study and/or experience in statistics and quantitative-research methods is very important in this field; thus, sociologists, economists, and others who have such a background often qualify for market-research positions.

EARNINGS

A recent survey showed beginning salaries with a bachelor's degree to be about $24,400 annually. The average salary for all analysts was about $35,000.

SOURCE OF ADDITIONAL INFORMATION

American Marketing Association, 250 Wacker Drive, Chicago, IL 60606.

MUSICIANS

NATURE OF THE WORK

Professional musicians are found in all forms of music, and there are many: classical, gospel, country, rock, jazz, just to name a few. They play all kinds of instruments and in all kinds of situations. Many play engagements in nightclubs, restaurants, parties, concerts, weddings, and other special events. Classical musicians play in symphony, opera, ballet, and theater orchestras. Some play in churches. A few well-known musicians give their own concerts, appear as soloists with symphony orchestras, and make recordings. Musicians often work at night and on weekends, spending much time in practice and rehearsal as well as travel. Many musicians only find part-time employment and must supplement their income with other types of jobs.

TRAINING AND OTHER QUALIFICATIONS NEEDED

Study usually begins at an early age; though talent may be discovered and developed at any age. Intensive training is needed to be a competent musician, even with the greatest natural talent. Training may be with a private tutor or in one of the many conservatories or college music programs. About 500 colleges, universities, and music conservatories offer bachelor's or higher degrees in music.

EARNINGS

Earnings vary too greatly to generalize. However, minimum salaries surveyed in major, large-budget symphony orchestras in 1989 averaged from $685 to $1,065 weekly.

SOURCES OF ADDITIONAL INFORMATION

American Federation of Musicians (AFL-CIO), 1500 Broadway, New York, NY 10036.

National Association of Schools of Music, 11250 Roger Bacon Drive, Reston, VA 22090. (Ask for brochure entitled *Careers in Music.*)

PERSONNEL SPECIALISTS

NATURE OF THE WORK

Personnel specialists interview, select, and recommend applicants to fill job openings. They keep informed about rules and regulations concerning employment and oversee the implementation of policies governing hiring and advancement. They handle wage and salary administration, training and career development, employee records, and benefit administration. In a small organization one person may be able to handle all the duties; in larger organizations, personnel workers are more specialized and may be limited to a single aspect of personnel work. Personnel offices are usually located to offer easy access to the public and designed to provide a pleasant atmosphere for visitors. They tend to be pleasant places to work with work hours structured to include a standard thirty-five to forty hours a week with exceptions, such as for those who may have to travel extensively to recruit.

TRAINING AND OTHER QUALIFICATIONS NEEDED

A college degree is required for most starting positions in this field. Required college majors may include personnel or industrial relations, although some employers may prefer a general business or liberal-arts education.

SOURCES OF ADDITIONAL INFORMATION

American Society for Personnel Administration, 606 North Washington Street, Alexandria, VA 22314.

American Society for Training and Development, 1630 Duke Street, Box 1443, Alexandria, VA 22313.

PHOTOGRAPHERS

NATURE OF THE WORK

Photographers use their cameras and film to portray people, places, and events much as a writer uses words. They specialize in scientific, medical, engineering, news, and other areas. Some develop and print their own photographs; others have this done elsewhere. In addition to knowing how to use their equipment, they must know how to compose their pictures with creativity and to recognize a potentially good photograph. Still photographers may specialize in portrait, fashion, or industrial work. Scientific and biological photographers provide illustrations and documentation for scientific publications and research reports. Photojournalists specialize in capturing newsworthy events for publications, such as newspapers, and for television news shows.

TRAINING AND OTHER QUALIFICATIONS NEEDED

There are no set entry requirements for education and training. Employers are looking for people with photographic skill and knowledge, but that can be obtained through practice and experience as well as through formal training, perhaps a combination of both. Training is available in art schools and two- and four-year colleges.

EARNINGS

Most experienced photographers earned between $24,600 and $33,800 in the latest survey.

SOURCE OF ADDITIONAL INFORMATION

Professional Photographers of America, Inc., 1090 Executive Way, Des Plaines, IL 60018.

PROTESTANT MINISTERS

NATURE OF THE WORK

Protestant ministers lead their congregations in worship services and administer the various rites of their churches. They prepare and deliver sermons and give religious instruction.· They perform marriages, conduct funerals, counsel, visit the sick and shut-ins, and serve church members in many other ways too. They provide the spiritual leadership for their congregations. Their working hours may be long and irregular because they are on call for any type of emergency that may occur and may work long hours on administrative, educational, or community activity matters.

TRAINING AND OTHER QUALIFICATIONS NEEDED

The primary prerequisite to this work is to be especially called. Other than that, churches and denominations have varying requirements for ordination. Some have no formal educational requirements; others require some amount of study in Bible colleges, seminaries, or regular colleges. Many denominations require a three-year course of professional study in an accredited school or seminary. Required or not, a good general education and the discipline of formal biblical studies and counseling courses will greatly increase the effectiveness of a ministry.

EARNINGS

Salaries of Protestant clergy vary greatly depending on age, experience, denomination, size and wealth of the congregation, and geographic location. Based on limited information, the estimated median annual income is about

$23,000. Ministers of large, wealthier churches will earn more; however, many ministers of small churches serve for little or nothing. Also, fringe benefits such as housing can add as much as 25 percent more.

SOURCES OF ADDITIONAL INFORMATION

Counsel should be sought from a minister of your own church. Information can also be obtained from the ordination body of the appropriate denomination. Each theological school can supply information about admission requirements.

PUBLIC-RELATIONS WORKERS

NATURE OF THE WORK

Public-relations workers help businesses, governments, universities, and other organizations build and maintain a positive public reputation. They apply their skills in many different areas, such as in press, community or consumer relations, political campaigning, interest-group representation, fund raising, or employee recruiting. In addition to telling the company's story, public-relations people also keep the company apprised of public attitudes and concerns. Public-relations (P.R.) personnel put together information that keeps the public aware of their organization's policies, activities, and accomplishments and keeps management aware of the public's attitudes. After preparing the information, they contact various media forms, such as newspapers and broadcast stations, to get the information disseminated.

TRAINING AND OTHER QUALIFICATIONS NEEDED

Although most beginners have a degree in journalism, communications, or public relations, some employers desire a degree related to the firm's business, such as science. A college degree is a definite plus in entering this field. Some form of experience with the news media is a good background for public relations. Many editors, reporters, and workers in closely related fields enter public relations.

EARNINGS

In the federal government, starting salaries for college graduates start at $19,500, and for those with graduate degrees about $23,800. In the private sector, the average is about $26,100. According to a survey, salaries for top public relations people averaged about $45,000—about $32,000 in non-profit organizations to $60,000 in industrial firms.

SOURCES OF ADDITIONAL INFORMATION

Career Information, Public Relations Society of America, Inc., 33 Irving Place, New York, NY 10003.

PR Reporter, Dudley House, P.O. Box 600, Exeter, NH 03833.

PURCHASING AGENTS/BUYERS

NATURE OF THE WORK

If an organization does not have the right materials, supplies, or equipment when needed, the entire production process or work flow is interrupted or halted. Purchasing agents, also called industrial buyers, obtain goods and services of the quality required at the lowest possible cost and see that adequate materials and supplies are always available. They buy supplies when the stock on hand reaches a predetermined point, when a department needs and requests it, or when market conditions are especially favorable. They usually work a standard thirty-five- to forty-hour week, although some overtime may be necessary, as well as travel to suppliers, seminars, or trade shows.

TRAINING AND OTHER QUALIFICATIONS NEEDED

There are no standard educational requirements for entry-level positions, although many large employers require a college degree in business administration or management. A few colleges offer a degree in purchasing. Some technologically oriented companies may require an engineering degree or a degree in one of the physical sciences. Courses in purchasing, accounting, economics, and statistics are helpful. An associate degree is sometimes satisfactory, and some companies promote clerical and technical people into purchasing jobs.

SOURCES OF ADDITIONAL INFORMATION

National Association of Purchasing Management, Inc., P.O. Box 22160, Tempe, AZ 85285.

National Institute of Governmental Purchasing, Inc., 115 Hillwood Avenue, Falls Church, VA 22046.

RADIO AND TELEVISION ANNOUNCERS AND NEWSCASTERS

NATURE OF THE WORK

In small radio stations, the duties of the announcer are quite varied and may include presenting music, news, weather, sports, commercials, interviewing guests, and other activities. It may also include operating equipment, selling commercial time, and writing copy for advertisers. In television stations and larger radio stations, duties are probably more geared toward a particular kind of programming. These specialized areas, such as sports and weather, require thorough familiarity with the subjects. Television news broadcasting requires specialized on-camera personnel, such as anchors, television news reporters, and analysts. Announcers often work in well-lighted, air-conditioned, and soundproofed studios; but when broadcasting from the location where the news is being made, the environment may even be hazardous, involving fires, floods, or other emergency situations. The fast pace and deadlines can be stressful, but most find the nature of the work and the ability to be creative most satisfying.

TRAINING AND OTHER QUALIFICATIONS NEEDED

Formal training for this can be obtained from a technical school, not just a college or university. Either will help; major importance, however, will be given by an employer to a taped audition, which will demonstrate an applicant's delivery, voice, and, for television, appearance and style. New-hires usually start out as production assistants, researchers, or reporters and are given a chance to move into announcing if they show an aptitude for broadcasting. Courses in English, public speaking, voice, drama, music, electronics, or sports can all add to your potential in this field.

EARNINGS

Median annual salaries of full-time radio announcers surveyed were approximately $20,000. Salaries ranged from below $10,400 to above $51,000. Salaries vary markedly, depending on the size of the station (radio or television), size of the market, listening or viewing area and population, and other factors. Annual salaries for TV announcers averaged from $19,000 to $204,000 at stations in large markets.

SOURCES OF ADDITIONAL INFORMATION

Broadcast Education Association, 1771 N Street N.W., Washington, DC 20036.

For information on FCC licensing procedures, write Federal Communications Commission, 1919 M Street N.W., Washington, DC 20552.

RECEPTIONISTS

NATURE OF THE WORK

Receptionists greet customers and other visitors, determine their needs, and refer callers to the person who can help them. Other duties vary with the function they are serving. Some, such as in doctors' offices, may have to obtain personal and financial information from visitors, then refer patients to the proper waiting rooms. Some arrange appointments; others may escort or arrange escorts. When not otherwise busy, they may type, file, and do other clerical duties. Often a receptionist will also be a switchboard operator, receiving and routing calls. Hours are usually regular; work locations usually pleasant, well-lighted, and quiet.

TRAINING AND OTHER QUALIFICATIONS NEEDED

A high school diploma is usually required. Personal characteristics are of the utmost importance, especially a neat appearance, a pleasant voice, and an even disposition. Previous training in clerical skills will be an asset in obtaining a job as a receptionist, in addition to aiding future promotion.

SOURCES OF ADDITIONAL INFORMATION

Many state employment agencies can provide additional information about job opportunities, salary, and other information in your area.

SECONDARY SCHOOL TEACHERS

NATURE OF THE WORK

The primary function of a secondary school teacher is to instruct students in a specific subject, such as English, foreign languages, mathematics, social studies, or science. Within a teacher's specialized subject area, he may teach a variety of courses. The teacher develops lesson plans, prepares and gives examinations, and arranges class projects and other activities. Teachers use a variety of instructional material, including films, slides, and computer terminals. In addition to regular classes, teachers perform other duties, such as supervising homerooms and study halls, advising student groups, and attending meetings and workshops.

TRAINING AND OTHER QUALIFICATIONS NEEDED

All states require that teachers be certified for public school, although not all require it for teaching in Christian or other private schools. Certification requirements vary, but all states require a bachelor's degree from an approved teacher-training program with a prescribed number of credits in the subject they plan to teach. Some states require a written examination; some have health, citizenship, or character requirements. About half the states require graduate degrees.

EARNINGS

According to the National Education Association, public secondary school teachers average $30,300 a year, with salaries highest in the Mid-Atlantic and in the far western states.

SOURCES OF ADDITIONAL INFORMATION

National Education Association, 1201 16th Street N.W., Washington, DC 20036.
National Council for Accreditation of Teacher Education, 2039 K Street N.W., Suite 500, Washington, DC 20006.

SECRETARIES AND STENOGRAPHERS

NATURE OF THE WORK

Secretaries and stenographers are at the center of communications within an organization. Secretaries perform a variety of administrative duties: scheduling, telephone answering, giving information, organizing and maintaining files, taking dictation, and typing. They route mail, compile reports, prepare correspondence, and have many other duties. Some managers delegate decision making to their executive secretaries, usually within narrowly defined parameters, where precedent often dictates the action taken. Stenographers typically take dictation and transcribe their notes on a typewriter, which can call for specialized knowledge, if working in a technical profession. For example, court reporters are a specialized type of stenographer, who use specialized equipment and technique.

TRAINING AND OTHER QUALIFICATIONS NEEDED

A high school diploma is usually required. Most employers prefer applicants who have had training at a business school or college. Courses vary from a few months to one or two years with a broad range of subjects covered. Your typing speed should be sixty-five words per minute or better. A knowledge of shorthand and a speed of at least ninety words per minute will help get a job, even though the skill is not required everywhere.

SOURCES OF ADDITIONAL INFORMATION

Professional Secretaries International, 301 East Armour Boulevard, Kansas City, MO 64111.

National Association of Legal Secretaries, 2250 East 73rd Street, Suite 550, Tulsa, OK 74136.

National Shorthand Reporters Association, 118 Park Street S.E., Vienna, VA 22180.

SYSTEMS ANALYSTS

NATURE OF THE WORK

Systems analysts plan efficient methods of processing data and handling the results. They help managers analyze problems by breaking the problems into component parts. They use various techniques, such as cost accounting, sampling, and mathematical model building to analyze a problem and devise a new system. Once accepted, they translate the logical requirements of the system into the capabilities of the computer equipment, or hardware. They also prepare applications for programmers to follow and work with them to debug, or eliminate errors from the system. Some improve existing systems; others do research and devise new systems.

TRAINING AND OTHER QUALIFICATIONS NEEDED

Educational requirements vary greatly. Some employers want degrees in computer science, information science, or data processing. Others prefer such fields as accounting, business management, or even the physical sciences, depending on the job. Since the systems analyst marries the computer with the manager's needs, an employer may emphasize either end of the equation for an educational background. Because of this, an aspiring systems analyst should have courses not only in data processing, information science, and computers but also in general business to provide as much balance as possible. Many enter this field from computer-programming experience because computer knowledge is essential.

SOURCES OF ADDITIONAL INFORMATION

Association for Systems Management, 24587 Bagley Road, Cleveland, OH 44138.

Information about the Certificate in Data Processing is available from The Institute for Certification of Computer Professionals, 2200 East Devon Avenue, Suite 268, Des Plaines, IL 60018.

TELEPHONE AND PBX INSTALLERS AND REPAIRERS

NATURE OF THE WORK

These are craft workers who install, service, and repair telephones and switchboard systems on customers' property. They are sometimes referred to as services and systems technicians. They install new systems and make changes to existing systems by adding, relocating, or removing equipment or facilities. There are various specialties in this field: telephone installers, PBX installers, telephone repairers, and PBX repairers. One person, however, may sometimes be responsible for two or more of these duties and sometimes all of them. These jobs were formerly associated primarily with the telephone utilities, but with the proliferation of private telephone companies, this is no longer the case. Many private businesses own their own telephone equipment and employ technicians to handle the repairs, installations, and relocations.

TRAINING AND OTHER QUALIFICATIONS NEEDED

A high school education is usually required. An applicant should be adept at using hand tools and be able to read blueprints and interpret work orders. A basic knowledge of electricity and electronics plus a practical problem-solving ability will be helpful.

EARNINGS

Pay scales vary greatly across the country. Generally, it takes four to five years to advance from the beginning to the top of the pay scale. The A.T.&T. and Bell system average union pay was $640 per week during the latest survey available.

SOURCES OF ADDITIONAL INFORMATION

United States Telephone Association, 900 19th Street N.W., Washington, DC 20006.

TELEPHONE OPERATORS

NATURE OF THE WORK

Telephone operators may be employed by one of the many telephone companies that provide commercial phone service. Or thay may be employed by a private business that receives so many calls that it has to operate its own private branch exchange (PBX), or switchboard. Businesses will typically do this so the public will only have to know one number and not have to call maybe dozens or hundreds of numbers to find.the person they want to speak with. The PBX enables all calls to come in on one number to a central location where they are answered by one or more operators who, in turn, route the calls to individual instruments in different offices. Some handle other duties; for instance, a police communications operator, who handles incoming emergency calls from citizens then transmits messages to and from units in the field. There are many other specialty telephone-operator jobs. Operators may be required to work odd-hour shifts, but otherwise the work can be pleasant and interesting.

TRAINING AND OTHER QUALIFICATIONS NEEDED

Aspirants to this kind of work should enjoy working with the public and be pleasant, courteous, and patient, not objecting to sitting in a chair for long periods of time. A clear, pleasing voice and good hearing are important, as well as good eye-hand coordination and manual dexterity. A high school diploma is sufficient, and most companies will train you if you have no previous experience.

EARNINGS

Operators surveyed averaged $15,500 annually in 1988. The union average was $24,000. Government operators averaged $15,700 that year, with $11,484 average for beginners.

SOURCE OF ADDITIONAL INFORMATION

United States Telephone Association, 900 19th Street N.W., Washington, DC 20006.

TELLERS

NATURE OF THE WORK

You usually think of banks as the only places that use tellers, but you may find this term used to apply to those in Christian organizations who receive and process the thousands of pieces of daily mail that contain contributions. In banks the teller deals directly with the public and processes deposits, withdrawals, and other transactions. Some specialize in certain types of transactions. In banks, of course, a personable nature is very important because of the constant face-to-face contact with the public. In all cases accuracy is probably the single most important factor, so tellers should be gifted at using numbers and have manual dexterity. The job is usually characterized by pleasant working conditions, repetitive work, sometimes constant public contact, and often standing for long periods of time.

TRAINING AND OTHER QUALIFICATIONS NEEDED

A high school diploma is usually required. Employers look for neatness, maturity, tact, and courtesy. Clerical skills, including the use of a calculator, are important. These skills can often be learned in high school.

EARNINGS

In 1988, full-time tellers averaged between $9,200 and $20,300.

SOURCES OF ADDITIONAL INFORMATION

American Bankers Association, Bank Personnel Division, 1120 Connecticut Avenue N.W., Washington, DC 20036.

VISUAL ARTISTS AND DESIGNERS

NATURE OF THE WORK

Some professional artists are painters who produce works of art intended to be displayed in homes and galleries. Most, however, are commercial and graphic artists and designers who illustrate and design the flood of magazine, newspaper, and television advertisements, as well as catalogs, brochures, instruction manuals, technical literature, book and record jackets, textiles, and many

211

other items requiring visual appeal. Illustrators paint or draw pictures. Among them are fashion illustrators, medical illustrators, cartoonists, and animators. Many designers merely create and supervise, deciding such things as art, photography, style, and layout. Designers include package designers, book designers, textile designers, and graphic designers. Many in these fields have full-time salaried jobs, though many are freelancers. Although freelancing offers a more flexible schedule, it can be as much or more demanding. Both are faced with frequent rush jobs and tight deadlines.

TRAINING AND OTHER QUALIFICATIONS NEEDED

Formal education is not a primary criterion in this field; demonstrated ability is. A potential employer will want to see an applicant's portfolio, that is, samples of your best work. Evidence of talent and flair in these portfolios is the most important factor influencing a hiring decision. While a good portfolio is all that is needed, some believe such a portfolio can only be put together after necessary training and education. Art training can be accomplished in a specialized technical school or in two- and four-year colleges.

EARNINGS

Entry-level paste-up or layout jobs may make as low as minimum wage; experienced art directors may make as much as $30,000 to $40,000. Some starting freelancers may charge less than minimum wage for their work; others make a comfortable living after gaining experience and a reputation. Federal government workers in art-related jobs averaged $22,338.

SOURCES OF ADDITIONAL INFORMATION

The Society of Illustrators, 128 East 63rd Street, New York, NY 10021.

American Institute of Graphic Artists, 1959 3rd Avenue, New York, NY 10021.

WRITERS AND EDITORS

NATURE OF THE WORK

Writers develop original fiction and nonfiction prose for books, magazines, trade journals, newspapers, technical studies and reports, company newsletters, radio and television broadcasts, and advertisements. Editors supervise writers and select and prepare material for publication or broadcasting. Writers start by selecting or being assigned a topic, then gathering information by research and interviews, organizing the material, and finally putting it in words that will most effectively convey the message to readers. Editors do some writing and almost always do much rewriting. Their main job is to plan the contents of the publication and to supervise its preparation.

TRAINING AND OTHER QUALIFICATIONS NEEDED

A college degree is usually, but not always required. There is no agreement on the best major course of study. Journalism would seem the most obvious one, but some employers prefer a general liberal-arts education or, if for technical writing, a more specialized degree. Communications is also a good background. Whatever the educational background, writers and editors need the ability to express themselves with the written word, clearly and logically. Any kind of writing experience is desirable.

EARNINGS

According to a survey, beginning salaries for writers and editorial assistants ranged from $18,000 to $26,600. More experienced writers and researchers ranged from $20,800 to $37,900; experienced editors from $22,200 to $39,800; supervisory editors up to $49,400.

SOURCES OF ADDITIONAL INFORMATION

The Newspaper Fund, Inc., P.O. Box 300, Princeton, NJ 08540.

American Society of Magazine Editors, 575 Lexington Avenue, New York, NY 10022.

Appendix E _____
SELECTED AVERAGE SALARIES IN THE UNITED STATES

The following information is a compilation of average monthly and annual salaries in the United States for selected occupations.

Job titles followed by Roman numerals represent different levels of experience, responsibility, and accompanying differences in salary. For example, an Accountant I is the lowest level; Accountant VI the highest.

The average figure shown is the arithmetic mean of the salaries of the employees surveyed.

Data Source: *White-Collar Pay: Private Service-Producing Industries, March 1989*. U.S. Department of Labor, Bureau of Labor Statistics, 1990. For subsequent years, slightly adjust for cost of living changes.

Average Salaries—United States

(Employment and average salaries in private service-producing industries for selected professional, administrative, technical, and clerical occupations, United States, except Alaska and Hawaii, March 1989)

Occupation and Level	Average Monthly Salary	Average Annual Salary
ACCOUNTANTS		
I	$1,839	$22,073
II	2,169	26,031
III	2,784	33,404
IV	3,609	43,304
V	4,552	54,627
VI	5,688	68,252
CHIEF ACCOUNTANTS		
II	4,600	55,196
III	6,013	72,156
IV	7,777	93,321
AUDITORS		
I	1,972	23,664
II	2,377	28,519
III	2,922	35,059
IV	3,615	43,384
PUBLIC ACCOUNTANTS		
I	2,111	25,335
II	2,292	27,505
III	2,616	31,390
IV	3,378	40,532
PERSONNEL SPECIALISTS		
I	1,852	22,229
II	2,116	25,395
III	2,700	32,395
IV	3,518	42,214
V	4,485	53,816
PERSONNEL SUPERVI-SORS/MANAGERS		
I	3,654	43,844
II	4,564	54,771
III	6,053	72,632
IV	7,671	92,049

Occupation and Level	Average Monthly Salary	Average Annual Salary
DIRECTORS OF PERSONNEL		
I	$3,436	$41,229
II	4,409	52,906
III	5,951	71,414
IV	7,918	95,012
ATTORNEYS		
I	3,030	36,365
II	3,603	43,239
III	4,620	55,440
IV	6,212	74,547
V	7,634	91,607
VI	9,883	118,601
BUYERS		
I	1,918	23,013
II	2,356	28,266
III	3,154	37,849
IV	3,838	46,058
COMPUTER PROGRAMMERS		
I	1,909	22,903
II	2,242	26,901
III	2,681	32,172
IV	3,266	39,196
V	3,867	46,400
SYSTEMS ANALYSTS		
I	2,658	31,893
II	3,188	38,256
III	3,804	45,650
IV	4,485	53,823
V	5,457	65,488
SYSTEMS ANALYSTS MANAGERS		
I	4,139	49,665
II	4,717	56,605
III	5,699	68,393
CHEMISTS		
III	3,039	36,469
IV	3,627	43,526
V	4,852	58,228

217

Occupation and Level	Average Monthly Salary	Average Annual Salary
ENGINEERS		
I	$2,445	$29,340
II	2,834	34,005
III	3,342	40,098
IV	4,000	48,003
V	4,749	56,989
VI	5,510	66,118
VII	6,273	75,280
VIII	6,937	83,248
REGISTERED NURSES		
I	2,050	24,605
II	2,369	28,434
II Specialists	2,675	32,105
III	3,388	40,651
IV	3,472	41,662
LICENSED PRACTICAL NURSES		
I	1,336	16,027
II	1,540	18,481
III	1,896	22,755
NURSING ASSISTANTS		
I	804	9,647
II	952	11,420
III	1,213	14,562
IV	1,507	18,088
MEDICAL MACHINE TECHNI-CIANS		
I	1,381	16,568
II	1,786	21,432
III	2,149	25,790
IV	2,651	31,817
ENGINEERING TECHNICIANS		
I	1,538	18,462
II	1,862	22,347
III	2,315	27,781
IV	2,773	33,274
V	3,049	36,594

Occupation and Level	Average Monthly Salary	Average Annual Salary
DRAFTERS		
II	$1,658	$19,896
III	1,893	22,717
IV	2;397	28,766
V	2,988	35,853
COMPUTER OPERATORS		
I	1,234	14,807
II	1,570	18,837
III	1,948	23,377
IV	2,274	27,284
V	2,634	31,612
PHOTOGRAPHERS		
II	1,857	22,289
III	2,272	27,268
IV	2,821	33,857
PERSONNEL CLERKS/ASSISTANTS		
I	1,196	14,357
II	1,459	17,503
III	1,731	20,769
IV	2,143	25,719
PURCHASING CLERKS/ASSISTANTS		
I	1,272	15,263
II	1,522	18,265
III	1,969	23,625
GENERAL CLERKS		
I	902	10,823
II	1,130	13,555
III	1,440	17,283
IV	1,769	21,223

Appendix F

POTENTIAL CHRISTIAN EMPLOYERS

COMPREHENSIVE LISTING

The following is a list of over two thousand ministries, companies, associations, and fellowships, along with addresses and telephone numbers. Most of these are a potential source of employment for the Christian job seeker. A few on the list may not have a paid staff, such as the associations, but they are included to give the reader as much comprehensive information as possible. Such organizations may be able to give helpful referral information.

For most of the information, we are indebted to the National Association of Evangelicals and their directory, the *National Evangel*. Most of the organizations listed are members of or are somehow affiliated with the NAE.

For information on membership or other questions, contact the National Association of Evangelicals, P.O. Box 28, Wheaton, IL 60189.

ADVERTISING AND GRAPHIC ARTS SERVICE ORGANIZATIONS

Aslan Group Ltd., The, 3595 Webb Bridge Rd., Alpharetta, GA 30201 404-442-1500

Austin/Lyman Advertising, 10 S. 5th St., Apt. Ste. No. 330, Minneapolis, MN 55402-2496 612-332-1557

Bartley Associates, Inc., 482 Congress St., Portland, ME 04101 207-773-0039

Ben Wood & Associates, Inc., 400 W. Roosevelt Rd., Ste. 2 N.W., Wheaton, IL 60187 312-665-6633

Bjorkman Designs, Steve, 1711 Langley, Irvine, CA 92714 714-261-1411

B/M/C Advertising, Inc., 11331 E. 58th St., Tulsa, OK 74146 918-252-9292

Bozell, Jacobs, et al, 100 N. Sixth St., Minneapolis, MN 55403

Brewer Jones & Feldman, 144 Merchant/Tri County, Cincinnati, OH 45246

Carol DeChant & Associates, (author tours), Public Relations, 2930 N. Commonwealth, Chicago, IL 60657

Company Carr Advertising, 5529 Harroun Rd., Sylvania, OH 43560

Concept Associates, Inc., 1230 N. Mesa Dr., Ste. 7-272, Mesa, AZ 85201 602-835-8845

Creative Christian Concepts, 2801 S.W. College Rd., Ste. 22, Ocala, FL 32674 904-237-4320

C Reimer Advertising Ltd., 2265 Pembina Hwy., Ste. 104, Winnipeg, Manitoba R3T 5J3, Canada 204-269-8093

Cummings Media Inc., 4742 N. 24th St., Ste. 350, Phoenix, AZ 85016 602-468-7800

Dan Roberts Public Relations, (marketing & promotion consulting), P.O. Box 727, Moreno Valley, CA 92337 714-653-3328

Del Rey Communications, P.O. Box 50111, Chicago, IL 60650 312-655-0020

Development Marketing Services, 17772 Irvine Blvd., Ste. 101, Tustin, CA 92680 714-832-1034

Domain Communications, 289 Main Pl., Carol Stream, IL 60188; P.O. Box 337, Wheaton, IL 60189 312-668-5300

Doug Ross Communications, 950 W. Southern Ave., Ste. 104, Tempe, AZ 85282 602-966-1744

Earle Palmer Brown & Spiro, 100 S. Broad St., Philadelphia, PA 19110 215-923-5400; cable address SPIRO

Ernest Philip Agency, 3838 Medical Dr., Ste. 101, San Antonio, TX 78229 512-558-4245

Foltz/Wessinger, Inc., P.O. Box 1297, Lancaster, PA 17603

Franklin Spier Advertising, 650 First Ave., New York, NY 10016

George Moll Advertising, 1829 Acorn Ln., Abingdon, PA 19001

Gottry Advertising & Marketing, 5001 W. 80th St., Ste. 655, Minneapolis, MN 55437

Harrison Associates, 15 Oakland Ave., Harrison, NY 10528 914-835-0900

Horizon Advertising, 915 N.E. Third Ave., Ft. Lauderdale, FL 33304 305-763-5651

Hugh Wallace Inc., 11332 Camarillo St., N. Hollywood, CA 91602 818-980-3212

Huntsinger, Jeffer, et al, 809 Brook Hill Cir., Richmond, VA 23227

Iversen-Norman Associates, 5 S. Buckout St., Irvington, NY 10533

J & R Kern Advertising, 303 Green St. N.E., Ste. 1A, Gainesville, GA 30501 404-536-1992

J. May Marketing/Media, 209 N. Hale St., Ste. 3, Wheaton, IL 60187 312-690-2525

JMK Design, 418 McKay Tower, Grand Rapids, MI 49503

Jordan Advertising Inc., 1100 Wheaton Oaks Ct., Wheaton, IL 60187 312-665-4965

J Richard Lee Inc., 700 1st. St., Oceanside, CA 95024 619-722-8232

K's ADV-Broadcasting, The, 109 N. Goliad, Rockwall, TX 75087 214-722-5040

Keener Marketing Inc., 124 E. Main, Dayton, TN 37321 615-775-3300

Kent Puckett Associates, 2300 Parklake Dr., Ste. 200, Atlanta, GA 30345 404-491-7774

Kernwood Agency, P.O. Box 7826, Charlottesville, VA 22906 804-973-5941

Killion McCabe & Associates Inc., 900 Coit Central Tower, 12001 N. Central Expwy., Dallas, TX 75243-3715 215-239-6000

Lloyd Daniel Corporation, The, P.O. Box 1196, Deerfield Beach, FL 33443 305-428-8986

Maddox Agency, 315 King George Ave., S.W., Roanoke, VA 24016

Maracom, 1000 Memorial Pkwy., P.O. Box 737, Willmar, MN 56201 612-235-3300

Maracom, 18 Thompson Rd., E. Windsor, CT 06088

Media Management, Stephen M. Wike, P.O. Box 21433, Roanoke, VA 24018 703-989-1330

Michael R. Ellison, Inc., P.O. Box 15000, Phoenix, AZ 85060 602-952-1400

Mid Missouri Christian Ministries, P.O. Box 650, Hwy. 32 E., Salem, MO 65560 314-729-2404

Mulvey Advertising, Inc., P.O. Box 489, Greenville, PA 16125 412-588-9810

Pan American Broadcasting Co., 10201 Torre Ave., Ste. 320, Cupertino, CA 95014 408-996-2033

Paragon Advertising Agency, Inc., 7075 Industrial Rd., P.O. Box 335, Florence, KY 41042 606-727-4000

Paul J. Hughes Advertising, Court Square/Penthouse, 269 W. Main St., Lexington, KY 40507 606-276-2511

PDI Advertising, 1223 Potomac St., N.W., Washington, D.C. 20007 202-337-0800

Quadrus Media Ministry, 128 Kishwaukee St., Ste. 300, Rockford, IL 61104 815-987-3970

Rainbow Graphics, 901 Eastern N.E., Grand Rapids, MI 49503 616-459-6273

Russ Reid Company, 2 N. Lake Ave., #600, Pasadena, CA 91101

Sam K Pate Associates, Inc., P.O. Box 4315, 141 Oakdale, Lynchburg, VA 24502 804-237-2903

Schultz & Sibley, 219 Ford St., West Conshohocken, PA 19428 215-825-7427

Screen Communications, 755 Winslow Way E., Bainbridge Island, WA 98110 206-842-9000

Soma Communications Inc., 2227 Meadow Dr., Carrollton, TX 75007 800-327-3383; 214-307-7000

Stephen & Brady, 1850 Hoffman St., Madison, WI 53704

Strang Communications, 190 N. Westmonte Dr., Altamonte Springs, FL 32714 407-869-5005

Sussman & Sugar, Inc., 24 W. 40th St., New York, NY 10019

Van Brunt & Company, 300 E. 42nd St., New York, NY 10017 212-949-1309

Variedades Cristianos Internacional, P.O. Box 1331, San Juan, PR 00902 809-797-4778; 809-797-0825

Vision Communications, 7643 Brookhaven Rd., Philadelphia, PA 19151 215-879-1065

Walter Bennett Company, 1634 Spruce St., Philadelphia, PA 19103 215-545-2003

Wilson Advertising Associates Inc., 505 N. Brand Blvd., Ste. 700, Glendale, CA 91209; P.O. Box 1947, Glendale, CA 91203 818-246-2200

WJH Communications, 421-23, S. Oak Park Ave., #C-1, Oak Park, IL 60302 312-383-2998

Wm. R. Biggs/Gilmore Associates Inc., 660 Cascade W. Pkwy., Grand Rapids, MI 49546

ARTS IN MINISTRY AGENCIES

Artists in Christian Testimony, (ACT-artistic communication into mission strategy), (Service and Mobilization), P.O. Box 1002, 9521 Business Center Dr., Bldg. 9, Ste. A, Cucamonga, CA 91730 714-987-3274

Fellowship of Artists for Cultural Evangelism, 1605 E. Elizabeth St., Pasadena, CA 91104 213-794-7970

Violetiles (hand-decorated ceramic tiles with scriptures), 279 Vischer Ferry Rd., Clifton Park, NY 12065 518-371-5301

Consulting/Legal Assistance Organizations

CHURCH GROWTH ORGANIZATIONS

Church Growth Center, (evangelism, discipleship), Corunna, IN 46730 219-281-2452; 800-626-8515

Church Growth Services, P.O. Box 2409, South Bend, IN 46680 219-291-4776

Churches Alive!, P.O. Box 3800, San Bernardino, CA 92413 714-886-5361

Churches Vitalized, Inc., 480 Brightspur Ln., Ballwin, MO 63011 314-394-2832

Institute for American Church Growth, 709 E. Colorado Blvd., Ste. 150, Pasadena, CA 91101 818-449-4400; 800-423-4844

FINANCIAL CONSULTING ORGANIZATIONS

Evangelical Council for Financial Accountability, P.O. Box 17456, Washington, D.C. 20041 703-435-8888; 800-3BE-WISE

LEGAL SERVICES ORGANIZATIONS

Christian Legal Society, P.O. Box 1492, Merrifield, VA 22116 703-642-1070

John M. Perkins Foundation for Reconciliation & Development, 1581 Navarro Ave., Pasadena, CA 91103 818-791-7439

Lawyers Christian Fellowship, 3931 E. Main St., Columbus, OH 43213 614-231-6614

Mennonite Conciliation Service 21 S. 12th St., Akron, PA 17501 717-859-1151

National Legal Foundation, The, P.O. Box 64845, Virginia Beach, VA 23464 804-424-4242

The Association of Christian Conciliation Services (Christian Legal Society), Samuel Ericsson, dir., P.O. Box 1492, Merrifield, VA 22116 703-642-1070

Christian Legal Society (CLS) is a national fellowship of lawyers, judges and law students committed to integrating their Christian faith with professional responsibilities. CLS seeks to fulfill this mission through various ministries, including the Center for Law and Religious Freedom which publishes the *Religious Freedom Reporter,* and its public ministries staff, who equip various local Christian conciliation chapters.
Working the context of the local churches, the Association of Christian Conciliation Services (ACCS) and local Christian Conciliation Services (CCS) conduct alternate dispute resolution training and help Christians to resolve legal conflicts by applying biblical principles.

Alabama

CCS of Alabama, Daniel Benton, dir., P.O. Box 471, Fairhope, AL 36532 205-928-0282

Arizona

CCS of Southern Arizona, Gail Jansen, chrm., 6842 E.Tanque Verde, Ste. E., Tucson, AZ 85715 602-886-2112

California

Bay Area CCS, Timothy J. Arensmeier, dir., P.O. Box 617, Novato, CA 94948 415-382-9162
CCS of Los Angeles, Peter Robinson, dir., 1800 N. Highland Ave., Ste. 502, Hollywood, CA 90028 213-467-3331

CCS of Orange County, Kimberly Parker, dir., 3855 E. LaPalma, Ste. 112, Anaheim, CA 92807 714-630-2622
CCS of San Diego, Robert Goff, dir., 3430 Camino del Rio, N., Ste. 300, San Diego, CA 92108-1796 619-563-9965

Colorado

Bear Valley Baptist Peacemakers, c/o Anthony Sturniolo, 2600 S. Sheridan Blvd., Denver, CO 80227 303-861-1444
CCS of Colorado Springs, (Mr.) Terry Jackson, dir., P.O. Box 25658, Colorado Springs, CO 80935-5658 303-597-4677; 303-635-1190
CCS of Denver, Richard Wise, dir., 1980 S. Wolff, Denver, CO 80219 303-936-8919

District of Columbia

CCS of Metropolitan Washington, F. Mather Archer, dir., P.O. Box 396, Fairfax, VA 22030 703-591-1142

Florida

CCS of Brevard, Francis M. Bradley, dir., 427 Timberlake Dr., Melbourne, FL 32940 305-242-1421
CCS of Central Florida, Kenneth Enslow, pres., P.O. Box 1649, Orlando, FL 32802-0767 305-658-3005

Georgia

CCS of Atlanta, David Montgomery, dir., 120 Allen Rd., Ste. B, Atlanta, GA 30328 404-851-9466

Guam

CCS of Guam, (Mr.) Pat Wolff, dir., P.O. Box CE, Agana, GM 96910 671-646-1527

Illinois

CCS of Northern Illinois, John Steven Cole, dir., 100 S. York St., #214, Elmhurst, IL 60126 312-834-4740

Kansas

Heart of America CCS, Kenneth Peery, dir., 6750 W. 75th St., 1-B, Overland Park, KS 66204 913-362-2102

Kentucky

CCS of Louisville, Frank James, dir., 1013 S. 5th St., Louisville, KY 40203 502-585-4673

Michigan

CCS of Central Michigan, Anne Bachle, dir., 1441-1/2 E. Michigan Ave., Lansing, MI 48912 517-485-2270

CCS of Southeastern Michigan, Judy Darlington, dir., 27350 W. Chicago, Redford, MI 48239 313-937-3939

Minnesota

CCS of Minnesota, Nellie Waldin-Frisch, dir., 5701 Normandale Rd., #326, Minneapolis, MN 55424 612-922-2048

Mississippi

CCS of Central Mississippi, Frances Harrison, dir., P.O. Box 2164, Jackson, MS 39205 601-352-7300

Missouri

Heart of America CCS, Kenneth Peery, dir., 6750 W. 75th St., 1-B, Overland Park, KS 66204 913-362-2102

Montana

CCS of Montana, C. Ken Sande, dir., 929 Alderson Ave., Billings, MT 59101 406-256-1583

Nevada

CCS of Nevada, Brian Hall, dir., P.O. Box 2995, Reno, NV 89505 702-851-2279

New York

CCS of Western New York, W. Dennis Huber, dir., P.O. Box 183, Niagara Square Station, Buffalo, NY 14202-0183 716-683-5544

North Carolina

Triangle CCS, William Montgomery, dir., P.O. Box 40783, Raleigh, NC 27629-0783 919-876-6806

North Dakota

CCS of North Dakota, Michael Dwyer, dir., 1501 N. 12th St., Bismarck, ND 58502 701-255-6601

Ohio

CCS of Akron, Frank Walker, dir., 680 E. Market St., Ste. 304, Akron, OH 44304 216-253-9332

CCS of Cincinnati, Robert Burns, dir., P.O. Box 19167, Cincinnati, OH 45219 513-861-HOPE

Reconciliation Ministries, Inc., Bryan Sanders, dir., c/o Logos Development Corp., 121 Keep Ct., Elyria, OH 44035 216-324-3550; 216-236-8833

Oklahoma

CCS of Oklahoma City, Tom Parrott, dir., 8800 Northridge Terr., Oklahoma City, OK 73132 405-720-9207

Oklahoma CCS, Inc., James Head, dir., 228 W. 17th Pl., Tulsa, OK 74119 918-584-4187

Oregon

CCS of Portland/Vancouver, David Blair, coord. dir., P.O. Box 9070, Portland, OR 97207 503-667-1776

Pennsylvania

CCS of Western Pennsylvania, Rick Givan, dir., P.O. Box 1805, Butler, PA 16003 412-285-5102

CCS of Pittsburgh, Judith Anderson, dir., 719 E. End Ave., Pittsburgh, PA 15221 412-371-6562

South Carolina

CCS of Spartanburg, Edward Bailey, dir., 180 Library St., Spartanburg, SC 29301 803-582-3740

Tennessee

CCS of East Tennessee, G. Turner Howard, pres., 7323 Bennington Dr., N.W., Knoxville, TN 37909 615-694-8906

CCS of Middle Tennessee, David Zinn, pres., 2114 Parkway Towers, Nashville, TN 37219 615-244-6632

Texas

CCS of Dallas-Ft. Worth, Steve Carlock, dir., 1209 N. Haskell Ave., Ste. A, Dallas, TX 75204 214-824-0521

CCS of Greater Houston, Walt Carpenter, dir., One Park Pl., Ste. 200, Houston, TX 77084 713-578-8787

CCS of San Antonio, Thomas Sisson, dir., 6243 Inner State Hwy., IH-10 West, San Antonio, TX 78201 512-735-2200

Virginia

CCS of Metropolitan Washington, F. Mather Archer, dir., P.O. Box 396, Fairfax, VA 22030 703-591-1142

Commonwealth CCS, (Ms.) Kit Webb, dir., P.O. Box 4249, Virginia Beach, VA 23454 804-397-0905

Washington

CCS of Puget Sound, Chip Zimmer, dir., 424 N. 130th St., Seattle, WA 98133 206-367-2245

CCS of Inland Empire-Spokane, Richard Carpenter, dir., 15123 Little Spokane Dr., Spokane, WA 99208 509-466-3425

Canada

CCS of British Columbia, Flyn Ritchie, dir., 84-8790 Forest Grove Dr., Burnaby, British Columbia V5A 4C9, Canada 604-589-1108

CCS of Edmonton, Robert Evans, pres., 5241 Calgary Trail, S., Ste. 406, Edmonton, Alberta T6H 5G8, Canada 403-438-4493

CCS of Toronto, Anthony Baker, coord., P.O. Box 160, Etobicoke, Ontario M9C 1X8, Canada 416-266-1773

MANAGEMENT/PERSONNEL/ PUBLIC RELATIONS CONSULTING ORGANIZATIONS

Christian Booksellers Association (CBA), (Trade Assoc. for Christian Booksellers), P.O. Box 200, Colorado Springs, CO 80901 719-576-7880

227

Christian Ministries Management Association, P.O. Box 4638, Diamond Bar, CA 91765 714-861-8861

Christian Public Relations Fellowship, c/o Juleen Turnage, secretary of information, General Council of the Assemblies of God, 1445 Boonville Ave., Springfield, MO 65802 417-862-2781

Dan Porter, (management consultant, audio consultant), P.O. Box 727, Moreno Valley, CA 92337 714-653-3328

Media Management, 4736 Starkey Rd., Roanoke, VA 24014 703-989-1330

POLITICAL AND ADVOCACY ORGANIZATIONS

American Family Association, (decency awareness), Donald E. Wildmon, exec. dir., 107 Parkgate, P.O. Drawer 2440, Tupelo, MS 38803 601-844-5036

Bread for the World, (Christian citizens' movement), 802 Rhode Island Ave. N.E., Washington, D.C. 20018 202-269-0200; 800-82-BREAD

Christian Leaders for Responsible Television, (CLeaR-TV), P.O. Drawer 2440, Tupelo, MS 38803 601-844-5036

Christian Mandate for America, P.O. Box 2500, Culpeper, VA 22701 703-825-4040

Christians in Government, P.O. Box 71654, Los Angeles, CA 90071 213-250-2824

Christians for Urban Justice, One Aspinwall Rd., Dorchester, MA 02124 617-825-6080

Citizens for Decency Through Law, Inc., William D. Swindall, national dir., 2845 E. Camelback Rd., Ste. 740, Phoenix, AZ 85016 602-381-1322

Concerned Women for America, (decency awareness), 122 C St., N.W., Ste. 800, Washington, D.C. 20001

Evangelicals for Social Action, 712 G St. S.E., Washington, D.C. 20003 202-543-5330

Focus on the Family, Pomona, CA 91799 714-620-8500

Morality in Media, (decency awareness), Morton H. Hill, pres., 475 Riverside Dr., New York, NY 10115

National Black Evangelical Association, 5736 N. Albina St., Portland, OR 97217 503-289-0143

National Christian Association, (decency awareness), Brad Curl, dir., P.O. Box 40945, Washington, D.C. 20016

National Consultation on Pornography, Inc., (decency awareness), Jerry R. Kirk, pres., 5742 Hamilton Ave., Cincinnati, OH 45224

Religious Alliance Against Pornography, (RAAP), Jerry R. Kirk, chairman, 800 Compton Rd., Ste. 9224, Cincinnati, OH 45231 513-521-6227

Counseling/Guidance Organizations

ADOPTION/ CRISIS PREGNANCY COUNSELING AGENCIES

Bethany Christian Services (adoption; pregnancy counseling services), 901 Eastern Ave. N.E., Grand Rapids, MI 49503-1295 616-459-6273, corporate office; crisis prgnancy hotline, #1-800-BETHANY

Crisis Pregnancy Center, Inc., 1124 N. 3rd Ave., Tucson, AZ 85705-7474 602-622-5774

Deaconess Home, (The Home of Redeeming Love), (Free Meth. Ch. of N. Am.), (care for unwed mothers & a certified adoption agency), 5401 N. Portland Ave., Oklahoma City, OK 73112 405-942-5001

Evangelical Adoption and Family Service, Inc., (NAE service agency), 119 Church Street, North Syracuse, NY 13212 315-458-1415

Evangelical Child and Family Agency, (NAE affiliate), Doris Wheeler, executive director, 1530 N. Main St., Wheaton, IL 60187 312-653-6400

Give Us This Day, Inc., (counseling/referral/adoption services), 2207B Portland Rd., P.O. Box 796, Newberg, OR 97132 503-538-2111; 503-628-2041

Hotline Help Center, (crisis-intervention, prevention & treatment), P.O. Box 999, Anaheim, CA 92805 714-778-1000

Life Line Homes, Inc., (social service agency of Free Meth. Ch. N. Am.), (endowment for youth ministries provides grants for worthy projects), P.O. Box 12366, Kansas City, KS 66112 913-262-3050

New Life Homes & Family Service, (Christian social service agency), c/o Greater Minneapolis Association of Evangelicals, 3361 Republic Ave., Ste. 201, Minneapolis, MN 55426 612-920-8117

Open ARMS, (Abortion related ministries), National Headquarters: P.O. Box 7188, Federal Way, WA 98003 206-839-8919

PLAN (Plan Loving Adoptions Now), (adoptions), P.O. Box 667, McMinnville, OR 97128 503-472-8452

Regular Baptist Child Placement Agency, Box 16353, Seattle, WA 98116

Shepherd Care Ministries, Inc., (counseling & training program-crisis pregnancy-adoption agency), 5935 Taft St., Ste. B., Hollywood, FL 33021 305-981-2060; 305-621-1991

Wales Goebel Ministry, (Lifeline Adoption ·Agency), 2908 Pump House Rd., Birmingham, AL 35243 205-967-4888

ALCOHOL/DRUG COUNSELING AGENCIES

Calvary Rehabilitation Center, (alcohol & drug counseling), 329 N. Third Ave., Phoenix, AZ 85003 602-254-7092

Hotline Help Center, (crisis-intervention, prevention & treatment), P.O. Box 999, Anaheim, CA 92805 714-778-1000

New Life for Girls (women w/drug & alcohol related problems), R.D. 3, Box D700, Dover, PA 17315 717-266-5414

Overcomers Outreach, Inc. (ministry to Christian alcoholics) 17027 E. Janison Dr. Whittier, CA 90603 213-697-3994

CAREER GUIDANCE SERVICE ORGANIZATIONS

IDAK Group, Inc., 7931 N.E. Halsey, Portland, OR 97213 503-252-3494

IDAK Interface Group, (5 offices Los Angeles/Orange Counties), 10900 Los Alamitos Blvd., Los Alamitos, CA 90720 213-431-4099

IDAK Nashville Group, 100 Winners Circle, Brentwood, TN 37027 615-373-4111

IDAK Sorensen Group, 7600 France Avenue South, Edina, MN 55435 612-831-3516

Intercristo, (div. of Crista Ministries, Inc.), (provides career planning, placement & decision making services), 19303 Fremont Ave. N., Seattle, WA 98113 206-546-7330; 800-426-1342

CHAPLAINCY ORGANIZATIONS

Correctional Institutions Chaplaincy, 195 N. Main, Milpitas, CA 95035 408-263-6900

Hope Hospital Chaplains, 1800 W. Charleston Blvd., Las Vegas, NV 89102 702-383-2434

Hospital Chaplains' Ministry of America, Inc., 710 N. Euclid St., P.O. Box 4308, Anaheim, CA 92803-4308 714-635-4262

Officer Alive/Law Enforcement Ministries, Inc., P.O. Box 1235, Hillsboro, OR 97123 503-648-5373

Police Chaplain Corps, c/o Greater Minneapolis Association of Evangelicals, 3361 Republic Ave., Minneapolis, MN 55426 612-920-8147

Waikiki Beach Chaplaincy, P.O. Box 15488, Honolulu, HI 96815 808-923-3137

COUNSELING AND COUNSELING ASSOCIATIONS

The American Association of Christian Counselors (AACC), P.O. Box 55712, Jackson, MS 39216 601-981-2180

The American Association of Christian Counselors (AACC) promotes excellence in Christian counseling by providing members with information, educational resources and affiliation with other Christian counselors. One of many tools prepared by the AACC is the *Christian Journal of Psychology and Counseling*, a quarterly periodical presenting the ideas, research and developments of practical interest by leading Christian professionals. Also published is a registry of AACC members.

Center for Pastoral Renewal, The, P.O. Box 8617, Ann Arbor, MI 48107 313-761-8505

Family Life Ministries, Mt. Paran Church of God, 2055 Mt. Paran Rd., Atlanta, GA 30327 404-261-0720

Lombard Mennonite Peace Center, 528 E. Madison, Lombard, IL 60148 312-627-5310

Narramore Christian Foundation, Box 5000, 1409 N. Walnut Grove Ave., Rosemead, CA 91770 818-288-7000

National Association of Nouthetic Counselors, (Granada Pastoral Counseling Center), c/o Tartan farm, 1291 Clotfelter Rd., Bogart, GA 30622 404-769-5794

Network of Christian Counseling Centers, Inc., The, P.O. Box 1138, St. Petersburg, FL 33731 813-823-2436

New Hope and Freedom Counseling Ministries, Inc., (United Association of Christian Counselors, Intl.), (individual, couples, sex & family therapy), 1303 N. Franklin St., Wilmington, DE 19806 302-654-6441

New Hope and Freedom Counseling Ministries, Inc., (United Association of Christian Counselors, Intl.), (individual, couples, sex & family therapy), 3837 Walnut St., Harrisburg, PA 17109 717-545-4103

Paradise Valley Counseling Inc., John Booth, dir., 10210 N. 32nd St., Ste. 211, Phoenix, AZ 85028 602-867-9777

United Association of Christian Counselors, International (UACCI), 3837 Walnut St., Harrisburg, PA 17109 717-652-7688

The United Association of Christian Counselors, International (UACCI) is a nonprofit association of Christians committed to discovering and sharing God's answers to man's personal and interpersonal problems in a clearly professional way.

The association exists to encourage and promote Christian counseling through an organization that can minister to professionals and to the general Christian community.

Christian Association for Psychological Studies, Inc. (CAPS), P.O. Box 628, Blue Jay, CA 92317 714-337-5117

CAPS International is a professional association of psychologists, psychiatrists, counselors, social workers, sociologists, pastors, paraprofessionals, psychiatric nurses, students and other persons in related fields in the helping professions.

The association exists to promote four objectives: development and communication of thought regarding theoretical and applied relationships between Christians in psychologically related fields and professions; professional and educational services in relation to the general Christian community; and witness and expression of views and values to the secular community regarding Christianity and psychologically related issues.

Regional Executive Secretaries

East

Samuel Barkat, Ph.D., 1812 Blossom Court, Yorktown Heights, NY 10598 914-941-7200, ext. 214

Midwest

Marcia Zwier, Ph.D., 16 Portsmouth, N.E., Grand Rapids, MI 49503 616-459-1933

Rocky Mountains-Plains

James R. Beck, Ph.D., Denver Seminary, P.O. Box 10,000, Denver, CO 80210 303-781-3495

Southeast

James M. Siwy, Ph.D., Atlanta Counseling Center, 6111 Peachtree-Dunwoody, Bldg. C, Atlanta, GA 30328 404-396-0232

Southwest

John F. Shackelford, Psy.D., 105 Thompson Dr., Richardson, TX 75080 214-238-9245

Western

Leonard J. Cerny, II, Ph.D., 746 E. Chapman Ave., Orange, CA 92666 714-532-6761

FINANCIAL PLANNING/ADVISEMENT ORGANIZATIONS

Evangelical Council for Financial Accountability, P.O. Box 17456, Washington, D.C. 20041 703-435-8888; 800-3BE-WISE

231

Education/Christian Education

American Association of Bible Colleges (AABC), 130-F North College, P.O. Box 1523, Fayetteville, AR 72702 501-521-8164

The AABC is the recognized institutional accrediting agency in the field of undergraduate and church-vocational education. You may write to them for a complete listing of Bible colleges in the United States and Canada.

Christian College Coalition, 329 Eighth St. N.E., Washington, D.C. 20002 202-293-6177

The Christian College Coalition is an association of over 75 Christ-centered liberal arts colleges. Members of the Christian College Coalition are four-year accredited schools committed to (1) integrating the Christian faith with the academic disciplines and daily life of students, faculty, and administrators, and (2) maintaining a faculty and administration of professional excellence and personal commitment to Christ. You may write for a complete listing of colleges in the coalition.

Christian College Consortium, 6 Pine Tree Drive, Suite 180, St. Paul, MN 55112 612-638-6155

Organized in 1971, the Christian College Consortium consists of 13 colleges which are united by regional accreditation, a concentration upon liberal arts studies, educational strengths that can be shared and a common affirmation of faith. The Consortium colleges maintain active membership in the Christian College Coalition. You may write them for a complete listing of colleges in the consortium.

CHRISTIAN DAY SCHOOL ASSOCIATIONS

American Association of Christian Schools, (National Organization of Fundamentalist Christian Schools K–12), P.O. Box 1088, Fairfax, VA 22030 703-273-6114

Association of Christian Schools International (ACSI), P.O. Box 4097, Whittier, CA 90607, 731 N. Beach Blvd., La Habra, CA 90631 213-694-4791

Association of Christian Schools International (ACSI) is a service organization serving Christian schools across the United States and around the world. A professional organization, ACSI is designed to improve the quality of Christian school education.

ACSI administrative personnel conduct local teacher conventions and administrator conferences in each ACSI region along with numerous student activities. All are designed to upgrade the ministry of each Christian school.

United States

Consultant for Academic Affairs, Dr. Anthony C. Fortosis, dir., 1001 E. Beltline, N.E., Grand Rapids, MI 49505 616-949-5300

Early Education, Eunice Dirks, dir., P.O. Box 4097, Whittier, CA 90607 213-694-4791

Mid-America Region, Jim Burdick, dir., 4041 Batton St., Ste. 100,

North Canton, OH 44720 216-499-0051

Missions, Dr. Philip M. Renicks, dir., P.O. Box 960, Northport, AL 35476 205-333-9572

North California, North Nevada-Hawaii Region, Dr. Richard Wiebe, dir., 770 E. Shaw, Ste. 127, Fresno, CA 93710 209-224-6993

Northeast Region, Jay B. Katz, dir., 517 Carlisle Ave., York, PA 17404 717-848-6006; 717-854-4904

Northwest Region, Dr. Eugene Fadel, dir., 1417 N.E. 76th St., Ste. 16, Vancouver, WA 98665 206-694-1037

Operations, Gus Enderlin, dir., P.O. Box 4097, Whittier, CA 90607 213-694-4791

South California, South Nevada Region, Dr. Jerry Haddock, dir., P.O. Box 4097, Whittier, CA 90607 213-694-4791

Southcentral Region, John Schimmer, dir., 4300 Alpha Rd., Ste. 205, Dallas, TX 75244 214-991-2822

Southeast Region, Ollie E. Gibbs, dir., 636 Exchange Pl., Ste. 101, Lilburn, GA 30247; P.O. Box 57-30226, Lilburn, GA 30226 404-923-5650

Southwest Region, Doug Horney, dir., Grace Christian School, 2940 W. Bethany Hm. Rd., Phoenix, AZ 85017 602-242-2010

Canada

Eastern Canada Region, David Harris, dir., Heritage Christian School, 80 Springside Dr., Hamilton, Ontario L9B 1M7, Canada 416-575-9090

Western Canada Region, Ken Penner, dir., Box 988, Three Hills, Alberta T0M 2A0, Canada 403-443-7337

Christian Schools International (CSI), 3350 East Paris Ave. S.E., P.O. Box 8709, Grand Rapids, MI 49518-8709 616-957-1070; 800-635-8288

Christian Schools International (CSI) is organized to unite, strengthen, and serve Christian schools in the United States, Canada and throughout the world. It joins individual schools in common purposes, helping those schools do things which each school would find difficult or impossible to do alone.

CSI's goal is to serve its constituency while promoting Christian education internationally. The organization is divided into 13 geographic districts. CSI publishes the *Christian Educators Journal*.

United States
District 1

(Maine, Maryland, Massachusetts, New Jersey, New York, Pennsylvania, Vermont), George Lawrence, asst. treas., Phil-Mont Christian Academy, 35 Hillcrest Ave., Erdenheim, PA 19118

District 2

(Michigan), Gordon VanHarn, vice pres., Calvin College, 3201 Burton S.E., Grand Rapids, MI 49546

District 3

(Illinois, Indiana, Missouri, Ohio), Arnold Hoving, treas., 11221 Timberview Ln., La Grange, IL 60525

District 4

(Eastern Wisconsin), Neal Buteyn, 717 Bluff Ave., Sheboygan, WI 53081

District 5

(Colorado, Eastern Iowa, Texas), William Dieleman, 518 Woodlawn Dr., Pella, IA 50219

District 6

(Western Iowa, Minnesota, Nebraska, South Dakota, Western Wisconsin), Dr. Martin Dekkenga, 105 2nd Ave., Sioux Center, IA 51250

District 7

(Alaska, Washington), Jay Anema, 1906 N.E. 100th St., Seattle, WA 98125

District 8

(Arizona, California, New Mexico), James A. Zoetewey, 17038 California St., Bellflower, CA 90706

District 9

(Florida), James Hofman, pres., Bradenton Christian School, 3304 43rd St., West Bradenton, FL 33529

District 13

(Alabama, Georgia, Louisiana, Mississippi, North Carolina, Tennessee), Donald Holwerda, Chattanooga Christian School, 3354 Broad St., Chattanooga, TN 37407

Canada

C.S.I. Schools of Canada, 777 Hwy. 53 E., Box 7220, Ancaster, Ontario L9G 3L4, Canada

District 10

(New Brunswick, Nova Scotia, Ontario), Jack Zondag, 5 Beverlyglen, R. #1, Lynden, Ontario L0R 1T0, Canada

District 11

(Alberta, Manitoba, Montana, Saskatchewan), Alyce Oosterhuis, sec., The King's College, 10766 97th St.,

Edmonton, Alberta T5H 2M1, Canada

District 12

(British Columbia), Al DeJong, asst. sec., 20915 132nd Ave., Maple Ridge, British Columbia V2X 7E7, Canada

Southern Association of Christian Schools, c/o Rev. Rich Cannon, French Camp Academy, French Camp, MS 39745 601-547-6113

CHRISTIAN EDUCATION SUNDAY SCHOOL ORGANIZATIONS

Alaska

Alaska Christian Education Convention Association, 2440 E. Tudor Rd., Box 150, Anchorage, AK 99507 907-349-3764; Or: Eileen Starr, 1741 Lake Otis Pkwy., Anchorage, AK 99508 907-272-8760

Arizona

Greater Arizona Christian Education Association (G.R.A.C.E.), Tim Reed, 1440 W. Prince Rd., Tucson, AZ 85705 602-887-6447

California

Bay Area Sunday School Association (BASS), Wally Glucklich, chrm., Box 2829, Castro Valley, CA 94546 415-483-6266

B.R.A.S.S. Conventions (San Bernardino Riverside Area Sunday School Association), Frances Andersen, exec. dir., 1787 Prince Albert Dr.,

Riverside, CA 92507 714-683-1009 evenings

Central Valley Christian Education Convention, Ramona, P.O. Box 4286, Visalia, CA 93278 209-732-4787

Church Leadership & Sunday School Convention of Sacramento (CLASS), 4400 58th St., Sacramento, CA 95820 916-344-7966

Greater Los Angeles Sunday School Association (GLASS), Wes Rylander, admin., P.O. Box 296, Rosemead, CA 91770-0296 818-288-8720

Greater Redding Area Christian Education (G.R.A.C.E.), P.O. Box 720321, Redding, CA 96099 916-244-9530

Greater San Jose Sunday School Association, Walt Huckaby, chrm., 16330 Los Gatos Blvd., Los Gatos, CA 95030 408-356-5126

Kern County Sunday School Association, c/o Dr. Dean Haddock, 4800 Easton Dr., Ste. 109, Bakersfield, CA 93309 805-326-8167

San Diego Sunday School Association (SANDSS), Paul Whitmoyer, pres., P.O. Box 1776, Spring Valley, CA 92077 619-670-6657

Youth Specialties Ministries, 1224 Greenfield Dr., El Cajon, CA 92021 619-440-2334

Colorado

Mountain Area Sunday School Association (MASS), Dennis Williams, P.O. Box 5881, Denver, CO 80217 303-696-6277; 303-795-5804

District of Columbia

(See Maryland)

Illinois

Central Illinois Sunday School Convention, Gary Losey, exec. dir.,

4100 War Memorial Dr., Peoria, IL 61614 309-688-0625

Greater Chicago Sunday School Association, Cliff Raad, 202 Chicago Ave., Oak Park, IL 60302 312-383-7550

Greater Rockford Area Sunday School Association, Mr. Russ Anderson, chrm., P.O. Box 4005, Rockford, IL 61110 815-987-8900

National Christian Education Association (NCEA), (NAE commission), 450 Gundersen Dr., Carol Stream, IL 60188 312-665-0500

Tri-State Sunday School Conference (Mo., Iowa, Ill.), Ronn Read, Lighthouse Ministries, 1400 Highland Lane, Quincy, IL 62301 217-222-1444

Indiana

Three Rivers Sunday School Association, Douglas Barcalow, chrm., Ft. Wayne Bible College, 1025 Rudisell Blvd., Ft. Wayne, IN 46807 219-456-2111

Iowa

Iowa State Sunday School Association, Steve Siemens, pres., Iowa Christian College & Equip. Cntr., 2847 Indianola Ave., Des Moines, IA 50315 515-244-6578; 515-265-7169

Kansas

Christian Education Conference, c/o Bible Supply & Gift Co., Mark Holmgren, 1020 Kansas Ave., Topeka, KS 66612 913-233-4219

Kansas Leadership & Sunday School Association, P.O. Box 9184, Wichita, KS 67277-0184 316-943-1800

Mid-America Church Leadership Conference, c/o Manhattan Christian College, Gary Edwards, 1415 An-

235

derson Ave., Manhattan, KS 66502
913-539-3571

Kentucky

Good News, 308 E. Main St., Wilmore, KY 40390 606-858-4661

Maine

Maine Association of Christian Educators, (formerly Maine Sunday School Association), Rev. H. Kenneth Dutille, Jr., Christian Civic League of Maine, P.O. Box 5459, Augusta, ME 04330 207-622-7634

Maryland

Baltimore Area Sunday School Association, Amos Gregory, chrm., P.O. Box 24008, Baltimore, MD 21227 301-789-1438

Greater Washington Christian Education Association, 2130 E. Randolph Rd., Silver Spring, MD 20904 301-431-4141 (ask for Norma Down, prog. coord.)

Massachusetts

Evangelistic Association of New England, 88 Tremont St., Ste. 600, Boston, MA 02108 617-523-3579

New England Association of Christian Education, 88 Tremont St., Boston, MA 02108 617-523-3579

Michigan

International Christian Education Association, 24200 Woodward Ave., Pleasant Ridge, MI 48069 313-399-6500

Midwest Christian Sunday School Association, Marvin Bolt, Exec. Sec., Wyoming, MI 49509 616-243-1016

Minnesota

Minnesota Sunday School Association, Timothy Johnson, 3745 - 26th Ave. S., Minneapolis, MN 55406 612-729-4384

Nebraska

Central Nebraska Sunday School Association, c/o Mr. John Springer, chrm., Rt. 2, Aurora, NE 68818 402-694-3918

New Jersey

Northern New Jersey Sunday School Convention, Ken Sewall, chrm., 44 Lakewood Terr., Bloomfield, NJ 07003 201-743-0650

New York

Greater New York Sunday School Association, Paul Lenz, P.O. Box 603, Lynbrook, NY 11563 516-221-0231

New York State Sunday School Association, Dr. Charles Massey, P.O. Box 587, Kenmore, NY 14217 716-631-3221

North Carolina

Mid-Atlantic Sunday School Association (N.C. & S.C., Va., Tenn. & Ga.), Elizabeth Burchett, sec., P.O. Box 29045, Charlotte, NC 28229 704-375-8935; David Peterson, chrm., 1614 Red Forest Rd., Greensboro, NC 27410 919-288-8965

North Dakota

North Dakota State Sunday School Association, c/o Carol Potratz, Bismarck Baptist Church, 2211 La Forest, Bismarck, ND 58501 701-223-4445

Ohio

Central Ohio Christian Education Conference, Heritage Christian Books & Supply, 173 Cline Ave., Mansfield, OH 44907 419-526-3166

North American Christian Convention, Box 39456, Cincinnati, OH 45239 513-385-2470; (Note: sponsored by Christian Chs. & Chs. of Christ)

Ohio Christian Education Association, c/o Church of the Saviour, 120 Cleveland S.W., Canton, OH 44702 (Bruno Gladkoski, pres., A/G District office, Columbus, OH 614-890-2290)

Oklahoma

National Association of Directors of Christian Education (NADCE), 8405 N. Rockwell, 5 Plaza Square, Ste. 222, Oklahoma City, OK 73132; Michael Lawson (Dallas Sem. Prof.) 214-824-3094

Northeast Oklahoma Christian Education Association, Bud Proffitt, pres., 14127 E. 12th, Tulsa, OK 75108 918-250-0404; 918-252-3166

Oklahoma Christian Education Association (OCEA), Box 457, Bethany, OK 73008; contact person: Robin Jones-KQCV Radio, 1919 N. Broadway, Oklahoma City, OK 73103 405-521-1412

Oregon

Greater Salem Association of Christian Educators, 555 Gaines N.E., P.O. Box 7354, Salem, OR 97301 503-581-2129

Pennsylvania

Central Pennsylvania Christian Education Conference, Bruce McCracken, 901 Eden Rd., Lancaster, PA 17601 717-569-7071

Delaware Valley Christian Education Convention, c/o Philadelphia College of Bible, Langhorne Manor, Langhorne, PA 19047 215-752-5800 ext. 277

Greater Philadelphia Area Sunday School Association (PASSA), Rev. Earl W. Parrott, pres., P.O. Box 28882, Philadelphia, PA 19151 215-748-8568 (church member)

Greater Pittsburgh Christian Education Conference, (inactive at present time; for info: call Mike Hupp 412-795-1718; 412-795-2072)

Pennsylvania State Sunday School Association, 5915 Fox St., Harrisburg, PA 17112 717-652-1930

South Dakota

South Dakota Sunday School Association, Darrell Modica, contact person, Crossroads Book & Music Store, 3817 S. Western, Sioux Falls, SD 57105 605-338-5951

Texas

Texas State Sunday School Convention, P.O. Box 153767, Irving, TX 75015 817-481-4949

Utah

Intermountain Christian Education Association, Dr. Bob Donahue, chrm., P.O. Box 7714, Salt Lake City, UT 84107 801-328-0768; or Pastor Jerry Wolf 801-486-0522

Washington

Christian Growth Conference, Greater Yakima Association of Evangelicals, P.O. Box 989, Yakima, WA 98907

Greater Tacoma Christian Education Conference, Rev. Ray Dimino, chrm., 206-352-9044; information: Carol, P.O. Box 110548, Tacoma, WA 98411-0548 206-564-6118

Spokane Christian Workers Conference, Daryl Bursch, chrm., N. 2828 Laura Rd., Spokane, WA 99212 509-926-1982; 509-534-8575

Wisconsin

Wisconsin Sunday School Association, Rev. David Eisley, sec., P.O. Box 673, Oshkosh, WI 54902-0673 414-231-8231

EDUCATIONAL SUPPORT ORGANIZATIONS

Accelerated Christian Education, Inc., P.O. Box 1438, Lewisville, TX 75067 214-462-1776

Advanced Training Institute of America, (a ministry of the Institute in Basic Youth Conflicts), Box One, Oak Brook, IL 60522-3001 312-323-9800

Alpha Omega Publications, P.O. Box 3153, Tempe, AZ 85281 602-438-1092

Bread for the World Institute on Hunger and Development, 802 Rhode Island Ave. N.E., Washington, D.C. 20018 202-269-0200; 800-82-BREAD

Christian Educators Association International, 1615 Howard, Pasadena, CA 91104; P.O. Box 50025, Pasadena, CA 91105 818-798-1124

Christian Home Educators Fellowship, P.O. Box 471363, Tulsa, OK 74147

Evangelical Teacher Training Association (ETTA), P.O. Box 327, Wheaton, IL 60189 312-668-6400

Leadership Dynamics, Intl., (church training curriculum), 6666 Powers Ferry Rd., Ste. 120, Atlanta, GA 30339 404-980-0626; 800-843-1262

National Association of Christian Educators, Box 3200, Costa Mesa, CA 92628 714-546-5931

National Association of Directors of Christian Education, 8405 N. Rockwell, 5 Plaza Square, Ste. 222, Oklahoma City, OK 73132

National Christian Education Association (NCEA), (NAE commission), Paul Hirschy, chairman, 302 Lake St., Huntington, IN 46750 219-356-2312

New Horizons Youth Ministries, (Schools-Special), 100 S. 350 E., Marion, IN 46953 317-668-4009; 800-333-4009

Professional Resource Outreach to Youth, (P.R.O. Youth), 1508 N.E. 98th Ave., Vancouver, WA 98664 206-892-5343

Seattle Area Literacy Tutors, 1013 8th Ave., Seattle, WA 98104 206-621-7323

The Teaching Home, P.O. Box 20219, Portland, OR 97220-0219 503-253-9633

Wisdom Publications, (home schooling materials), P.O. Box 3154, LaVale, MD 21502 301-759-3218

SPECIAL EDUCATION INSTITUTES

Children's Bible Fellowship of N.Y. Hope Town Resident Christian School, Rev. Winfield R. Ruelke, D. D., pres., P.O. Box 670, Carmel, NY 10512 914-225-2005

Elim Christian School Special Education, 13020 S. Central, Palos Heights, IL 60463 312-389-0555

Hope Town Resident Christian School, (see Children's Bible Fellowship of N.Y.)

TRAINING AND SEMINAR MINISTRIES

Leadership Dynamics, Intl., (church training curriculum), 6666 Powers Ferry Rd., Ste. 120, Atlanta, GA 30339 404-980-0626; 800-843-1262

National Training Institute, 1000 S. Interregional Hwy., Round Rock TX 78664 800-531-6789

Susan-Gift Porter, (Christian family concert artist—family crusades, concerts, camps, children's evangelism), P.O. Box 727, Moreno Valley, CA 92337 714-653-3328

U.S. Center for World Mission, 1605 Elizabeth St., Pasadena, CA 91104 818-797-1111

Health Care Services

HEALTH CARE SUPPORT ORGANIZATIONS

Christian Medical & Dental Society, P.O. Box 177, Summer, IA 50674 319-578-5137

Christian Medical & Dental Society, 1616 Gateway Blvd., P.O. Box 689, Richardson, TX 75083 214-783-8384

Disability Communication Consultants, 540 Tubman Court, San Jose, CA 95125

Handi Vangelism, (BCM Intl., bereaved parents ministries), 237 Fairfield Ave., Upper Darby, PA 19082 215-352-7177

Hospital Christian Fellowship, Inc., (Evangelistic health care organiz.), P.O. Box 4004, San Clemente, CA 92672 714-496-7655

LNE' Ministries, (mentally retarded or physically disabled people and seriously or terminally ill children), St. Andrews Presbyterian Church, P.O. Box 125, Strathmore, CA 93267 209-568-2238

Love & Action, (a Christian ministry of compassion to people with AIDS), Jeffrey A. Collins, exec. dir., 3 Church Circle, #108, Annapolis, MD 21401 301-268-3442

Nurses' Christian Fellowship, P.O. Box 7895, Madison, WI 53707 608-274-9001

Nursing Home Ministries, Inc., P.O. Box 02519, Portland, OR 97202 503-238-0647

MENTAL HEALTH CARE CENTERS

Shepherds Baptist Ministries, (agency for mentally retarded/General Assoc. of Regular Baptists), P.O. Box 400, 1805 - 15th Ave., Union Grove, WI 53182 414-878-2451

MEDICAL AND DENTAL CLINICS

Worldwide Dental Health Service, (Missionary Dentists), P.O. Box 7002, Seattle, WA 98133 206-546-1200; 206-771-3241

239

NURSING HOME AND RETIREMENT CARE CENTERS

Alliance Home, The, (C&MA), Jack R. Seward, exec. admin., 770 S. Hanover St., Carlisle, PA 17013 717-249-1363

Alliance Retirement Center of Deland, Inc., The, (C&MA), Don E. Anderson, exec. dir., 600 S. Florida Ave., Deland, FL 32720 904-734-3481

Brethren Care, Inc., (The Breth. Ch., Ashland, OH), Darrel Barnes, admin., 2000 Center St., Ashland, OH 44805 419-289-1585

Brethren Care of South Bend, Ind., Inc., St. Paul's Retirement Community, Inwood Rd., South Bend, IN 46614 219-291-8205

Brethren's Home of Indiana, Inc., The, (The Breth Ch., Ashland OH), Gene A. Geaslen, admin., Rt. 2, P.O. Box 97, Flora, IN 46929 219-967-4571

Buhler Sunshine Home, (Menn. Breth. Chs.), 412 W. C St., Buhler, KS 67522 316-543-2251

Carmen Home, (Intl. Pent. Hol. Ch.), P.O. Box 10, Carmen, OK 73726 405-987-2577

Casa De Verdugo (Verdugo Home, Inc.,), (Bapt. Gen. Conf.), Elaine Johnson, admin., 155 - 175 N. Girard St., Hemet, CA 92344 714-658-2274

Christian Homes, Inc., (Evang. Free Ch. of Am.), Holdrege, NE 68949 308-995-4493

Clawson Manor, New Life, Inc., (Free Meth. Ch. of N. Am.), Leon T. Boree, admin., 255 W. 14th Mile Rd., Clawson, MI 48017 313-435-5650

Colonial Oaks Retirement Center, (The Wesleyan Ch.), 4275 Colonial Oaks Dr., Marion, IN 46953 317-674-9791

Corn Heritage Village, (Menn. Breth. Chs.), Corn, OK 73024 405-343-2295

Dallas Nursing Home, (Menn. Breth. Chs.), 348 W. Ellendale, Dallas, OR 97338 503-623-5581

Dayview Care Center, (Missionary Ch.), 1885 Dayton-Lakeview Rd., New Carlisle, OH 45344 513-845-8219

Elim Home, (Evang. Free Ch. of Am.), 730 - 2nd St. S.E., Milaca, MN 56353 612-983-2185

Elim Home, (Evang. Free Ch. of Am.), 101 S. 7th Ave., Princeton, MN 55371 612-389-1171

Elim Home, (Evang. Free Ch. of Am., North Central District), 409 Jefferson Ave., S.W., Watertown, MN 55388 612-955-2691

Elim Home, (Evang. Free Ch. of Am.), 3534 S. University Dr., Fargo, ND 58103 701-237-4392

Elim Park Baptist Home, Inc., (Bapt. Gen. Conf.), David MacNeill, pres., 140 Cook Hill Rd., Cheshire, CT 06410 203-272-3547

Evangelical Congregational Church Retirement Village, (Evang. Cong. Ch.), S. Railroad St., Myerstown, PA 17067 717-866-6541

Evangelical Free Church Home, (Evang. Free Ch. of Am.), 112 W. 4th St., Boone, IA 50036 515-432-1393

Fairhaven Christian Home, Inc., (Evang. Free Ch. of Am.), 3470 N. Alpine Rd., Rockford, IL 61111 815-877-1441

Fairhaven Retirement Center, (World Gospel Mission), 4360 63rd St., Sacramento, CA 95820-4252 916-452-2100

Fairview Baptist Home, (Bapt. Gen. Conf.), Wesley Ringdahl, admin., 7 S. 241 Fairview Ave., Downers Grove, IL 60516 312-852-4350

Fairview Fellowship Home, (Menn. Breth. Chs.), 605 E. State St., Fairview, OK 73737 405-227-3784

Fred Lind Manor, (formerly Baptist Rest Home), (Bapt. Gen. Conf.), Marion Hogg, admin., 1802 - 17th Ave., Seattle, WA 98122 206-324-1632

Friends Village, (Evangelical Friends Alliance), 628 S. Hiram, Wichita, KS 67213 316-267-8811

Friendsview Manor, (Evangelical Friends Alliance), 1301 E. Fulton St., Newberg, OR 97132 503-538-8383

Garden Valley Retirement Village Inc., (Menn. Breth. Chs.), 1505 E. Spruce, Garden City, KS 67846 316-276-7879

Golden Years Home, (Intl. Pent. Hol. Ch.), P.O. Box 39, Falcon, NC 28342 919-892-6048

Grandview Christian Home, (Bapt. Gen. Conf.), Greg Carlson, admin., 800 Second Ave. N.W., Cambridge, MN 55008 612-689-1474; 612-339-0018 (Minneapolis)

Heritage Village, (The Gerry Homes, Free Meth. Ch. of N. Am.), Gerry, NY 14740 716-985-4612

Hilty Memorial Home, (Missionary Ch.), P.O. Box 265, Pandora, OH 45877 419-384-3218

Hubbard Hill Estates Retirement Community, (Missionary Ch.), 28070 C.R. 24 W., Elkhart, IN 46517 219-295-6260

Inland Christian Home, (Chr. Ref. Ch.), 1950 S. Mountain Ave., Ontario, CA 91761 714-983-0084

Kern Crest Manor, (Menn. Breth. Chs.), 250 E. Tulare St., Shafter, CA 93263 805-746-6521

Lincoln Glen Manor and Intermediate Care, (Menn. Breth. Chs.), 2671 Plummer Ave., San Jose, CA 95125 408-265-3222

Locust Grove Rest Home, Rt. 3, P.O. Box 136, Harpers Ferry, WV 25425 304-535-6355

Maranatha Village, (A/G), Raymond J. Junker, admin., 233 E. Norton Rd., Springfield, MO 65803 417-833-0016

Mennonite Brethren Homes, Inc., 856 S. Reed Ave., Reedley, CA 93654 209-638-3615

Messiah Village, (Breth. in Christ Ch.), 100 Mt. Allen Dr., Mechanicsburg, PA 17055 717-697-4666

Michigan Christian Home Assoc., (Bapt.), 1845 Boston S.E., Grand Rapids, MI 49506 616-245-9179

New Carlisle Adult Care Home, (Missionary Ch.), 1884 Addison-New Carlisle Rd., New Carlisle, OH 45344 513-845-2150

Oregon Baptist Retirement Home, (Bapt. Gen. Conf.), Rosalie Miller, admin., 2545 N.E. Flanders St., Portland, OR 97232 503-232-5055

Parkside Homes, Inc., 200 Willow Rd., Hillsboro, KS 67063 316-947-2301

Piney Mountain Home, (Ch. of the United Breth. in Christ), Charles L. Kind, admin., 6375 Chambersburg Rd., Fayetteville, PA 17222 717-352-2721; 717-352-7861

Pleasant View Home, 108 N. Walnut, Inman, KS 67546 316-585-6411

Quaker Gardens, (California Friends Homes), 12151 Dale St., Stanton, CA 90680 714-530-9100

Reformed Presbyterian Home for the Aged, (Ref. Pres. Ch. of N. Am.), 2344 Perrysville Ave., Pittsburgh, PA 15214 412-321-4139

Rest Haven Christian Services, (Chr. Ref. Ch.), (Nursing Care & Ret. Living), 13259 S. Central Ave., Palos Heights, IL 60463 312-597-1000

Salem Home, 701 S. Main, Hillsboro, KS 67063 316-947-2272

Shell Point Village, (C&MA), Peter Dys, exec. dir., Shell Point Blvd., Fort Myers, FL 33908 813-466-1111

Sunset Manor, Inc., (Free Meth. Ch. of N. Am.), (Woodstock Homes), 920 N. Seminary Ave., P.O. Box 508, Woodstock, IL 60098 815-338-1749

Town and Country Manor, (C&MA), Dirk E. DeWolfe, exec. dir., 555 E. Memory Ln., Santa Ana, CA 92706 714-547-7581

Upland Manor, (Breth. in Christ Ch.), 1125 W. Arrow Hwy., Upland, CA 91786 714-985-1215

Village Retirement Center, The, (Menn. Breth. Chs.), 310 W. Ellendale Ave., Dallas, OR 97338 503-623-9211

Warm Beach Senior Community, (Free Meth. Ch. of N. Am.), 20420 Marine Dr. N.W., Stanwood, WA 98292 206-652-7585

Weidler Retirement Center, (indep. living div. of Oregon Baptist Retirement Home), Ted Wolcheck, admin., 1825 N.E. 108th, Portland, OR 97220 503-255-7160

Wesley Manor, (Free Meth. Ch. of N. Am.), 815 Kennedy St., 113A, New Westminster, British Columbia V3M 1R8 Canada 604-521-3172

Wesleyan Arms Retirement Center, (Wesleyan Ch.), 1901 N. Centennial St., High Point, NC 27260 919-884-2222

Wesleyan Village, (Wesleyan Ch.), (Wesleyan Bible Conference Assoc.), 8225 Wesley Dr., Brooksville, FL 34601 904-799-1644

Woodstock Christian Care, Inc., (Free Meth. Ch. of N. Am.), P.O. Box 508, Woodstock, IL 60098 815-338-1090

Media: Audio/Visual Production Organizations

AUDIO CASSETTE/RECORD PRODUCTION AND DISTRIBUTION ORGANIZATIONS

Accent Records, 71906 Hwy. 111, Rancho Mirage, CA 92270 714-346-0075

Airborn Communications, (Intl. Recording, Video, TV), P.O. Box 3064, Flint, MI 48502 313-736-5191

Angelsong Records, P.O. Box 2673, Beverly Hills, CA 90213 818-761-4481

Ark Records, P.O. Box 230073, Tigard, OR 97223 503-620-5680

BeeGee Records, Inc., 458 Fair Oaks, Pasadena, CA 91105 818-405-0356

Bible Alliance, (Talking Book Program, the Bible on audio cassettes for blind, visually impaired and print handicapped), P.O. Box 621, Bradenton, FL 34206 813-748-3031

Birdwing Records, (Sparrow), 9255 Deering Ave., Chatsworth, CA 91304 818-709-6900

Birthright Records, 458 Fair Oaks, Pasadena, CA 91105 818-405-0356

Bread N' Honey, P.O. Box 3391, Ventura, CA 93006 805-644-1821

Brentwood Music, Inc., P.O. Box 1028, Brentwood, TN 37027 615-373-3950; 800-333-9000

Calvary Music Group, The, 142 8th Ave. N., Nashville, TN 37203 615-244-8800

Canaan Records, (a div. of Word, Inc.), 5221 N. O'Connor Blvd., Ste. 1000, Irving, TX 75039 214-556-1900

Cloudburst Records, P.O. Box 31, Edmonton, KY 42129 502-432-3183

Colonial Regency Records, 2199 Nolensville Rd., Nashville, TN 37072 615-259-2247

Comstock Records, Box 3247, Shawnee, KS 66203 913-631-6060

Creative Sound Productions, 6290 Sunset Blvd., Ste. 1026, Hollywood, CA 90028 213-871-1010

Creed Records, (Nashboro), P.O. Box 5366, Nashville, TN 37206 615-227-5081

Crossroads Christian Communications, 100 Huntley St., Toronto, Ontario, Canada M4Y 2L1 416-961-8001

Crossroads Productions, 10451 Huron St., Denver, CO 80234 303-452-1018

DaySpring Records, (a div. of Word, Inc.), 5221 N. O'Connor Blvd., Ste. 1000, Irving, TX 75039 214-556-1900

Deka Records, P.O. Box 5712, High Point, NC 27262 919-431-5521

Destiny Records, P.O. Box 545, Corona del Mar, CA 92652

Epoch Universal Publication, 10802 N. 23rd Ave., Phoenix, AZ 85029

Family Life Institute, (Bible stories for kids & the family), P.O. Box 244, Nordland, WA 98358 206-385-0234

Globe Mission, Inc., (Perlita Lim Concert Ministry), P.O. Box 1212, Glendora, CA 91740 818-963-8833

Gold Tag Productions, P.O. Box 774, Rialto, CA 92376 714-820-1841

Good News Records, 8319 Lankershim Blvd. N., Hollywood, CA 91605 213-767-4522

Gotown Records, Ltd., 706 W. Mechanic St., Leesville, LA 71446-3446 318-238-0028

Greentree Records, (Benson), 365 Great Circle Rd., Nashville, TN 37228 615-259-9111

HSE Records, 1709 Church St., Nashville, TN 37203 615-320-1561

Happy Day Music Co., (BMI), P.O. Box 602, Kennett, MO 63857 314-888-2995

Hartford Music Co., Powell, MD 65730 417-435-2225

Heartwarming Records, (Benson), 365 Great Circle Rd., Nashville, TN 37228 615-259-9111

Herald Records, Box 218, Wellman Heights, Johnsonville, SC 29555 803-386-2600

Holy Spirit Records, 27335 Penn, Inkster, MI 48141 313-274-5905

Home Sweet Home Records, P.O. Box 7409, Dallas, TX 75209 214-353-0472

Hosanna Music Productions, 71 N. Laurel, Ventura, CA 93001 805-648-1076

Impact Records, (Benson), 365 Great Circle Rd., Nashville, TN 37228 615-259-9111

Jewel-Paula-Ronn Records, 1125, Shreveport, LA 71163 318-865-5318

Jim Records, P.O. Box 2550, Baton Rouge, LA 70821

Joe Keene Music Co., (BMI), P.O. Box 602, Kennett, MO 63857 314-888-2995

John Hall Ministries, P.O. Box 18344, 5009 Davis Blvd., Fort Worth, TX 76118 817-281-6605

KSS Records, P.O. Box 602, Kennett, MO 63857 314-888-2995

Kenwood Records, P.O. Box 5366, Nashville, TN 37206 615-227-5081

Klesis Records, P.O. Box 218, Wellman Heights, Johnsonville, SC 29555 803-386-2600

L.P.S. Records, Inc., (Fourth Corner Music/SESAC, Heartstone Music/BMI), 2140 St. Clair St., Bellingham, WA 98226 206-733-3807

Lamb & Lion Records, 15477 Ventura Blvd., Ste. 201, Sherman Oaks, CA 91403 818-788-2701

Lexicon Music/Light Records, P.O. Box 2222, Newbury Park, CA 91320 805-499-9894

Lodema Records, 5806 Arroyo Dr., Farmington, NM 78401 505-325-1684

Lorenz Creative Services, 40 Music Square E., Box 23088, Nashville, TN 37203 614-224-5588

Lutheran Braille Evangelism Association, 1740 Eugene St., White Bear Lake, MN 55110 612-426-0469

MCW Records, P.O. Box 50208, Nashville, TN 37205

Maiden Music, P.O. Box 777, Treviliams, VA 23170 703-967-0077

Mainroads Productions, Inc., 100 Huntley St., Toronto, Ontario, Canada M4Y 2L1 416-961-8001

Majega Records, 240 E. Radcliffe Dr., Claremont, CA 91711 714-624-0677

Manna Music & Manna Records, (ASCAP), 2111 Kenmere Ave., Burbank, CA 91504 818-843-8100

Maranatha! Music, P.O. Box 31050, Laguna Hills, CA 92654-1050 714-586-5778; 800-245-7664

Mark Five Records, P.O. Box 218, Wellman Heights, Johnsonville, SC 29555 803-386-2600

Master Disc Records, 711 E. Walnut St., #208, Pasadena, CA 91101 818-796-1600

Master's Collection, The, P.O. Box 362, Sta. A, Rexdale, Ontario, Canada M9W 5L3 416-681-2760; 800-263-9116 (Canada only)

MPM Productions, (record production), P.O. Box 727, Moreno Valley, CA 92337 714-653-3328

Music Emporium Record Co., 3100 23rd Ave., Meridian, MS 39301 601-483-5991

Myrrh Records, (a div. of Word, Inc.), 5221 N. O'Connor Blvd., Ste. 1000, Irving, TX 75039 214-556-1900

New Dawn Records, 1415 Lake Dr. S.E., Grand Rapids, MI 49506 616-459-6900

New Day Records, 2832 Spring Grove Ave., Cincinnati, OH 45225 513-681-8400

New Life Records, E. 122 Montgomery, P.O. Box 5378, Spokane, WA 99205 509-328-4207, 800-541-1565

New Pax Records (Benson), 365 Great Circle Rd., Nashville, TN 37228 615-259-9111

Neworld Media Records, South Blue Hill, ME 04615 207-374-5539

Nita Herndon Enterprises, 1920 N. Beverly St., Porterville, CA 93257 209-781-4093

North American Liturgy Resources, 10802 N. 23rd Ave., Phoenix, AZ 85029 602-864-1980; 800-528-6043

Old Towne Records, P.O. Box 2, Arcola, VA 22010 703-327-6367

Paragon Records (Benson), 365 Great Circle Rd., Nashville, TN 37228 615-259-9111

Paul Johnson Music Productions, Inc., P.O. Box 552, Woodland Hills, CA 91365 818-703-6707

Phydeaux Records, 1482 DeTracy St., San Jose, CA 95128 408-378-5279

Pressing Plant, 2727 Irving Blvd., Dallas, TX 75207 214-630-6401

QCA Records & Custom Pressing, 2832 Spring Grove Ave., Cincinnati, OH 45225 513-681-8400

Rite Record Productions, Inc., 9745 Mangham Dr., Cincinnati, OH 45215 513-733-5533

Roadshow Records, 870 Seventh Ave., New York, NY 10019 212-765-8840

Sand Island Records, Honolulu, HI (Mainland—P.O. Box 688, Eugene, OR 97440) 503-686-0779

Scratched Records, 4511 Roundup Trail, Austin, TX 78745

Season Records, 97 S. Hamilton Ave., Lindenhurst, NY 11757 516-884-5628

Seed Records, P.O. Box 2112, Shawnee Mission, KS 66201

Serenity Records, 10924 Beverly Hills Dr., Little Rock, AR 72211 501-225-3036

Shalom Records, 60446, Oklahoma City, OK 73106 405-521-0777

Singspiration Records, 1415 Lake Dr. S.E., Grand Rapids, MI 49506 616-698-6900

Snow Records and Productions, E1103 29th St., Spokane, WA 99203 508-624-9359

Sold Out to Jesus, P.O. Box 786, Micaville, NC 28755 704-682-3528

Solid Rock Records, 22020 Buenaventure, Woodland Hills, CA 91364 213-883-0640

Sonrise Records, Inc., 6290 Sunset Blvd., Ste. 1026, Hollywood CA 90028 213-871-1010

Sparrow Corporation, 9255 Deering Ave., Chatsworth, CA 91311 818-709-6900; 800-347-4777

Spearmans, The, (gospel singers), Dyer Rt., Cowen, WV 26206 304-226-3424

Stamps-Baxter Music Company (Benson), 365 Great Circle Dr., Nashville, TN 37228 615-244-1274

Star Song Records, 12929 Gulf Frwy., Ste. 201, Houston, TX 77034 713-484-5505

Sugar Records, P.O. Box 1181, Florissant, MO 63031 314-837-4095

Supreme Record Co., P.O. Box 150394, Nashville, TN 37215 615-298-3824

Susquehanna Sound Productions, 48 A St., Northumberland, PA 17857 717-473-9733

Sweetsong Records, P.O. Box 2041, Parkersburg, WV 26102 304-489-2911

Third Firkin Music Co., P.O. Box 884062, Walled Lake, MI 48088 313-624-2502

Tri-Power Records, P.O. Box 1101, Gresham, OR 97030

Vertie Records, Inc., P.O. Box 22398, Nashville, TN 37202 615-242-8102

Warrior Records, P.O. Box 43, Billings, MT 59103 406-252-4386

Word Record & Music Group (Canaan/Dayspring/Myrrh/Word), (a div. of Word, Inc.), 5221 N. O'Connor Blvd., Ste. 1000, Irving, TX 75039 214-556-1900

FILM, TV, AND VIDEO PRODUCTION AND DISTRIBUTION ORGANIZATIONS

Allied Film Laboratory, Inc., 737 Woodward Ave., Detroit, MI 48202 313-871-2222

Arrow Productions, P.O. Box 322, Waco, TX 76703 817-666-4545

Baptist Spanish Publishing House, P.O. Box 4255, El Paso, TX 79914 915-566-9656

Bauman Bible Telecasts, 4620 Lee Hwy., Arlington, VA 22207 703-243-1300

Bible Study Hour, 1716 Spruce St., Philadelphia, PA 19103 215-546-3696

Bill Rice Ranch Films, Rt. 2, Franklin Rd., Murfreesboro, TN 37129 615-893-2767

Christian Communication, 709 E. Colorado Blvd., Ste. 150, Pasadena, CA 91101 818-449-4400

Christian Communications Technology, 4708 Amberjack Dr., Virginia Beach, VA 23464 804-490-2869

Christian Leadership Training, 21300 Mack Ave., Grosse Pointe Woods, MI 48236 313-343-8856

CLP Video, 10946 Woodside Ave. N., Santee, CA 92071 619-448-1121

Cornerstone Pictures, 6331 Glade Ave., Ste. H204, Woodland Hills, CA 91367 213-716-7722

Covenant Video, (Evang. Covenant Ch.), 3200 W. Foster, Chicago, IL 60625 312-478-4676; 800-621-1290

245

Creative Productions, Inc., 958 E. Davies Ave., Littleton, CO 80122 303-794-6482

Crown Ministries, P.O. Box 49, Euclid, MN 56722 218-781-6505

Crowning Touch Films, P.O. Box 425, Durand, MI 48429 517-288-4290

David C. Cook Publishing Co., 850 N. Grove Ave., Elgin, IL 60120 312-641-2400

Day Star Productions, 326 S. Wille Ave., Wheeling, IL 60090 312-541-3547

Del Rey Communications, (Films and Video), P.O. Box 50111, Chicago, IL 60650 312-655-0020

Evangelical Films Inc., 1750 N.W. Hwy., Ste. 250, Garland, TX 75041 214-270-6676

Family Resources, R.R. 1, Box 151G, Aurora, NE 68818 402-694-3969

Films for Christ Association, 2628 W. Birchwood Cir., Mesa, AZ 85202 602-894-1300

Gateway Films, Inc., P.O. Box 540, Worcester, PA 19490 215-584-1893

Glenray Communications, (Films and Video), 1530 Elizabeth St., Pasadena, CA 91104 818-797-5462

Global Films, 319 N. Blanchard, Wheaton, IL 60187 312-682-3444

Good News Productions, Intl., P.O. Box 222, Joplin, MO 64802 417-782-0060

Gospel Light Video, 2300 Knoll Dr., Ventura, CA 93003 805-644-9721

Growth Resources, Intl., P.O. Box 28090, Santa Ana, CA 92799-8090 714-863-9440

Harvest Communications, Inc., 222 N. Kansas, Wichita, KS 67214 316-262-0732

Harvest Productions, (Evangelical Baptist Missions), P.O. Box 2225, Kokomo, IN 46904 317-455-2112; 317-453-4488

Heartland/Mark IV/Mustard Seed Productions, Inc., 5907 Meredith Dr.,

Des Moines, IA 50322 515-278-4737; 800-247-3456; 800-251-3456 (Iowa)

Heinz Fussle Productions, Rt. 3, Lake Sharon 34, Warsaw, IN 46580

Image Associates of Indiana, Inc., Ste. F, 117 Lincolnway East, Mishawaka, IN 46544 219-259-6758

Image Transform Laboratories, 3611 N. San Fernando Blvd., Burbank, CA 91505 213-841-3812

Inspirational Film Distributors, Inc., 2508 Hayes Ct., Burnsville, MN 55337 612-890-1969

Inspirational Media, (Campus Crusade for Christ), (create, produce, market and distribute Christian audio/visual materials), 2700 Little Mountain Dr., P.O. Box 6046, San Bernardino, CA 92412 714-886-5224; 800-392-7542

International Cinema Artist Corporation, 1450 30th, West Des Moines, IA 50265 515-224-0919

John Schmidt Productions, 2300 E. Brookdale Pl., Fullerton, CA 92631 714-871-1993

JRB Motion Graphics Ltd., 4117 Stone Way N., Seattle, WA 98103 206-632-0834

Kuntz Bros., Inc., P.O. Box 8047, Dallas, TX 75205 214-691-4500

Life Productions, Inc., 200 Galleria Pkw., N.W., Ste. 710, Atlanta, GA 30339 404-984-9971

Ligonier Ministries, Inc., 598 S. North Lake Blvd., Ste. 1008, Altamonte Springs, FL 32701 305-834-1633

Lutheran Electronic Media, 3400 N. IH 35, Austin, TX 78705 512-452-7661

3M Co., Building 223-25 E., St. Paul, MN 55144 612-733-0740

Malaga Cove Pictures, 75 Malaga Cove Plaza, Palos Verdes Est., Palos Verdes, CA 90274

Maranatha Productions, Inc., (live drama & TV programming), P.O.

Box 210, Dixon, IL 61021-0210 815-284-4126

Maritz Communication Co., Laboratory Div., 1395 N. Hwy. Dr., Fenton, MO 63026 314-225-1354

Mass Media Ministries, 2116 N. Charles St., Baltimore, MD 21218 301-727-3270

McDougal Films, 350 Adams Ave., Glencoe, IL 60022 312-835-5333

Mel White Productions, 30 North Raymond, Ste. 312, Pasadena, CA 91103

Merit Media International, 1314 Circle Way, Laguna Beach, CA 92651 714-494-1944

Missionary Enterprises, P.O. Box 2127, La Habra, CA 90631 213-697-4617

Moody Institute of Science, 12000 E. Washington Blvd., Whittier, CA 90606 213-698-8256; 800-821-9179

Multnomah Productions, 10209 S.E. Division, Portland, OR 97266 503-256-4528; 800-547-5890; 800-452-6994 (Oregon)

National Religious Broadcasters, P.O. Box 1926, Morristown, NJ 07962-1926. Editorial and Advertising Offices, 299 Webro Rd., Parsippany, NJ 07054 201-428-5400

An affiliate of the National Association of Evangelicals, National Religious Broadcasters (NRB) has more than 1,250 member radio and television stations and evangelical organizations. NRB's goals are two-fold: to ensure (1) that religious broadcasters continue to have access to the radio and television airwaves, and (2) that broadcasters observe a high standard of excellence in their programming to present the gospel clearly.

In 1987, NRB's Board of Directors approved the standards of accreditation for the Ethics and Financial Integrity Commission (EFICOM).

This new self-regulatory commission is designed to insure the highest possible standards in fund raising and financial expenditures in religious broadcasting.

NavPress, (The Navigators), P.O. Box 6000, Colorado Springs, CO 80934 719-598-1212; 800-366-7788

New Liberty Enterprises, Inc., 150 S. Glenoaks Blvd., Ste. 9222, Burbank, CA 91510 818-842-6167

Olive Film Productions, Inc., P.O. Box 9, Madison, AL 35749 205-837-4166; 800-521-7618

Omega Films, P.O. Box 1872, Rancho Santa Fe, CA 92067 619-942-8672

Ormond Organization, 3620 Central Ave., Nashville, TN 37205 615-383-1576

Paulist Productions, 17575 Pacific Coast Hwy., Pacific Palisades, CA 90272 213-454-0688

Paulmar, Inc., 3316 Commercial Ave., Northbrook, IL 60062 312-498-1020

Quadrus Media Ministry, 128 Kishwaukee St., Rockford, IL 61104 815-987-3970; 800-435-4489

Religious Film Corporation, P.O. Box 4029, Westlake Village, CA 91359 818-991-3290; 800-338-3456

Research Technology, Intl., 4700 Chase Ave., Lincolnwood, IL 60646 312-677-3000

Robert Fuqua Productions, P.O. Box 38261, Dallas, TX 75238 214-634-8002

Sacred Cinema, P.O. Box K, Paoli, PA 19301

Seven Star Productions, P.O. Box 17126, Long Beach, CA 90807

Southwest Film Lab, Inc., 3024 Fort Worth Ave., Dallas, TX 75211 214-331-8347

Swartwout Productions, 703 Manzanita Dr., Sedona, AZ 86336 602-282-2270

The Master's Collection, P.O. Box 362, Sta. A, Rexdale, Ontario, Canada M9W 5L3 416-681-2760; 800-263-9116 (Canada only)

The Salvation Army, Office of Media Ministries, 6500 Harry Hines Blvd., P.O. Box 2608, Dallas, TX 75221 214-353-2731; 800-527-4691

Tyndale Christian Video, 336 Gundersen Dr., P.O. Box 80, Wheaton, IL 60189 312-668-8300; 800-243-1839

Vanguard Video, 6535 E. Skelly Dr., Tulsa, OK 74145 918-622-6460

Victory International Productions, P.O. Box 5277, Garden Grove, CA 92645 213-598-7208

Video Dynamics, P.O. Box 20330, Jackson, MS 39209 601-373-7717

Vision Video, 2030 Wentz Church Rd., Box 540, Worcester, PA 19490 215-584-1893

Walk Thru the Bible Ministries, Inc., 61 Perimeter Park, P.O. Box 80587, Atlanta, GA 30366 404-458-9300; 800-554-9300

White Lion Pictograph, 401 ISOM Rd., Ste. 410, San Antonio, TX 78216 512-826-3615

Word, Inc., 5221 N. O'Connor Blvd., Ste. 1000, Irving, TX 75039 214-556-1900

Word Church Services, (a division of Word, Inc.), 7300 Imperial, Waco, TX 76702-2518 817-776-8613; 800-433-3327; 800-792-3210 (Texas)

World Thrust Films, 5930 18th St., N.E., St. Petersburg, FL 33703 813-527-5205

Zoeller Productions, 1104 Linden Way, Brea, CA 92621

RADIO PROGRAM PRODUCERS

Afterglow Productions, 6223 Lochlevin Cove, Memphis, TN 38119 901-682-3028

Alberto Mottesi Evangelistic Association, Inc., P.O. Box 340, Midway City, CA 92655 714-554-6681

Ambassador Advertising Agency, 515 E. Commonwealth Ave., Fullerton, CA 92632 714-738-1501

American Bible Society, 1865 Broadway, New York, NY 10023 212-581-7400

American Indian Hour, Box 4187, Inglewood, CA 90309 213-292-2398

Art of Family Living, The, 1900 Firman Dr., Richardson, TX 75081 214-823-3128

Back to the Bible Broadcast, Box 82808, Lincoln, NE 68501 402-474-4567

Back to God Hour of the Christian Reformed Church in North America, 6555 West College Dr., Palos Heights, IL 60463 312-371-8700

Baptist Missionary Association of America, Radio/TV Department, P.O. Box 6, 535 Enterprize Ave., Conway, AR 72032 501-329-6891

Baptist Radio & TV Commission, Southern Baptist Convention, 6350 W. Freeway, Fort Worth, TX 76150 817-737-4011; 800-433-5757

Bellevue Baptist Church, 70 N. Bellevue Blvd., Memphis, TN 38104 901-725-9777

Ben Haden Evangelical Association, 554 McCallie Rd., Chattanooga, TN 37402; Box 100, Chattanooga, TN 37401 615-267-7959

Bethel Church of Christ Holiness, 4171-1/2 Brighton Ave., Los Angeles, CA 90062 213-292-4310

Bethel Gospel Tabernacle, 110-25 Guy Brewer Blvd., Jamaica, NY 11433

Bible Fellowship Hour/World Scope Ministries, Box 10386, Glendale, CA 91209 213-243-4740

Bible For You, Inc., The, 124 S. Columbia Dr., Decatur, GA 30030 404-377-7321

Bible Study Time, Inc., P.O. Box 1714, Spartansburg, SC 29304 805-583-5967

Bible Way Church, The, 1100 New Jersey Ave. N.W., Washington, D.C. 20001 202-789-0700

Billy Graham Evangelistic Association, 1300 Harmon Pl., Minneapolis, MN 55403 612-338-0500

Biola Hour, The, Biola University, 13800 Biola Ave., La Mirada, CA 90639 213-944-0351 ext. 3332

Bob Harrison Ministries, P.O. Box 3509, Oakland, CA 94609 415-672-0898

Bob Larson Ministries, P.O. Box 36480, Denver, CO 80236 303-980-1511

Breakthrough Radio, 1826 Basse Rd., San Antonio, TX 78213

Brethren Hour, The, First Brethren Church, 150 North Shade Ave., Sarasota, FL 33577 813-366-3316

Calvary Assembly, 1199 Clay St., Winter Park, FL 32789 305-644-1199

Calvary Radio Ministry, 123 W. 57th St., New York, NY 10019 212-975-0170

Campmeeting Ministries, Inc., 3948 Hwy. 90, Pace, FL 32571 904-994-7131

Carl Richardson Ministries, 300 Angela Dr., Brandon, FL 33511 813-684-3300

Cathedral Caravan, Inc., 6550 Mango Ave. S., St., Petersburg, FL 33707 813-347-2463; 813-347-2865

Central Church, 6655 Winchester, Memphis, TN 38115 901-365-4673

Centro Christiano de Bay Ridge, 6324 7th Ave., Brooklyn, NY 11220 718-238-4000

Chapel, The, 895 N. Forest Rd., Buffalo, NY 14221 716-634-4440

Chapel of the Air, Inc., The, Box 30, Wheaton, IL 60189 312-668-7292

Children's Bible Hour, Box 1, Grand Rapids, MI 49501; office: 1331 Plainfield, N.E., Grand Rapids, MI 49505 616-451-2009

Christ Covenant Pulpit, P.O. Box 220774, Charlotte, NC 28222 704-847-3505

Christ for the Nations Institute of Biblical Studies, 1266 N. Country Rd., Stony Brook, NY 11790 516-689-7660

Christian Associated Projects, Inc., Skyview, Cottondale, AL 55453 205-553-8587

Christian Broadcasting Network, Inc., The, CBN Center, Virginia Beach, VA 23463 804-424-7777

Christian Children's Associates, Inc., Box 446, Toms River, NJ 08754 201-240-3003

Christian Church John 3:16, 864 Westchester Ave., Bronx, NY 10455 212-991-4222

Christian Destiny, Inc., P.O. Box C, E Hwy. 56, Hillsboro, KS 67063 316-947-2345

Christian Enterprises, Inc., P.O. Box 272, Ashland, VA 23003 804-798-4711

Christian Evang. Churches of America, 2433 Coolidge Ave., Oakland, CA 94601 415-533-8300

Christian Financial Concepts, Rt. 5, Box 130 Dahlonega, GA 30533 404-864-4570

Christian Jamboree Ministries, Inc., 8181 GSRI Rd., Baton Rouge, LA 70820 504-766-4334

Christian & Missionary Alliance, The, 350 N. Highland Ave., Nyack, NY 10960 914-353-0750

Christian Radio Foundation, P.O. Box 23960, Fort Lauderdale, FL 33307 305-491-8677

Christian Research Institute, Box 500, San Juan Capistrano, CA 92693; 22672 Lambert St., Ste. 615, El Toro, CA 92630 714-855-9926

Christian Retreat, Rt. 2, Box 279, Bradenton, FL 34202 813-747-6481

Christian Tabernacle Church, 10508 Union Ave., Cleveland, OH 44105

Christian Voice, 214 Massachusetts Ave. N.E., Ste. 540, Washington, D.C. 20002 202-544-5202

Christian World Communications, 367 Mt. Paran Rd. N.W., Atlanta, GA 30327 404-252-0300

Christian World Outreach, 1405 N. Main St., Evansville, IN 47711 812-428-7788

Christians' Hour Broadcasting Association, The, 3420 Glenmore Ave., Cincinnati, OH 45211 513-661-4240

Church of God, 1303 E. 5th St., Anderson, IN 46012 317-642-0256

Church of God-Forward in Faith, 1441 Guthrie Dr., Cleveland, TN 37311 615-478-7240

Church of God in Christ, Inc., P.O. Box 6054, Portsmouth, VA 23703 804-484-8903

Church of God of Prophecy, Bible Place, Cleveland, TN 37311 615-479-8511

Clear Creek Baptist Bible College, Pineville, KY 40977 606-337-3196

Columbia Bible College Broadcasting Co., P.O. Box 3122, Columbia, SC 29230 803-754-5400

Comfort and Cheer, Rt. 2, 1580 Crestwood Dr., Toccoa, GA 30577 404-886-6996

Communion Communications, P.O. Box 11582, 515 N. Highland, Memphis, TN 38111 901-323-1919

Community of Jesus, The, Box 1094, 11 Bay View Dr., Orleans, MA 02653 617-255-1094

Contact America, P.O. Box 3777, Washington, D.C. 20013 800-638-3616; 202-546-3444

Contemporary Sounds in Communicating Good News, Box 5, Oceanside, CA 92054 619-722-8284

Coral Ridge Ministries, 5554 N. Federal Hwy., Drexel Bldg., Second Floor, Ft. Lauderdale, FL 33308 305-772-0404

Cornerstone World Outreach Center, 1701 S. Fort, Springfield, MO 65807 417-831-7242

Creative Communications Associates, 876 N. Batavia, Orange, CA 92668 714-997-8450

Cross and Flame Communications, P.O. Box 288, Cleveland, OH 44070 216-779-1953

David Munizzi Ministries, Inc., P.O. Box 1105, Valley Stream, NY 11582 516-872-0591

Dayspring Ministries, P.O. Box 8465, Santa Cruz, CA 95061 408-462-4498

Derek Prince Ministries, Box 300, Ft. Lauderdale, FL 33302 305-763-5202

Domain Communications, 289 Main Pl., P.O. Box 337, Wheaton, IL 60189 312-668-5300

Don Wildmon Report, P.O. Box 2440, Tupelo, MS 38803 601-844-5036

Edward Lubin Productions, 5237 Oaksdale Ave., Woodland Hills, CA 91364 818-715-9555

Elmbrook Church, 777 S. Barker Rd., Waukesha, WI 53186 414-786-7051

Encounter Ministries, Inc., Box 757800, Memphis, TN 38175-7800 901-365-9696

Ernie Wilson Ministries, 4925 Larchwood Ave., Philadelphia, PA 19143 215-474-9217

Evangelistic Outreach, Inc., P.O. Box 56, Pedro, OH 45659 614-532-2105

Evansong Ministries, c/o KNLB, P.O. Box V, Lake Havasu City, AZ 86403

Ever Increasing Faith Ministries, 7901 S. Vermont Ave., Los Angeles, CA 90044 213-758-3777

Fairlane Assembly of God, 22575 Ann Arbor Trail, Dearborn Hts., MI 48127 313-561-3300

Faith America Foundation, Box USA, Scottsdale, AZ 85252

Faith Assembly of God, 254 Spackenkill Rd., Poughkeepsie, NY 12603 914-462-5955

Faith Center, 4700 S. Main St., Rockford, IL 61102 815-964-0600

Faith Gospel Broadcast, P.O. Box 22, St. Petersburg, FL 33731 813-822-7253

Family Life Broadcasting Syste, Inc., Corporate Offices, Box 35300, Tucson, AZ 85740 602-742-6976; 7355 N. Oracle, Ste. 200, Tucson, AZ 85704

Family Life Seminars, 122 C St. N.W., Ste. 850, Washington, D.C. 20001 202-783-1377

Family Station, Inc., 290 Hegenberger Rd., Oakland, CA 94621 415-568-6200

Fellowship Missionary Baptist Church, 45th Place & Princeton Ave., Chicago, IL 60609 312-924-3232

First Assembly of God, P.O. Box 1024, Nicholasville, KY 40356

First Assembly of God, 2100 44th St. S.W., Grand Rapids, MI 49509 616-531-2100

First Baptist Alcoa, 819 Gilbert St., Alcoa, TN 37701 615-982-6221

First Light Ministries, 7401 Katy Freeway, Houston, TX 77024 713-957-6740

First Southern Baptist Church, Box 15039, Del City, OK 73155 405-732-1300

First Things First, 1200 Ninth St., Wichita Falls, TX 76301 817-723-2764

Focus on Faith Productions, P.O. Box 563, Kings Hwy. & Park Ave., Valley Cottage, NY 10989 914-268-3000

Focus on the Family, Pomona, CA 91799 714-620-8500

Forward in Faith, 1441 Gutherie Dr., Cleveland, TN 37311 615-472-3361

Foundation for Christian Living, P.O. Box FCL, Pawling, NY 12564 914-855-9126

Four States Christian Mission, Inc., 125 N. Prospect St., P.O. Box 685, Hagerstown, MD 21740 301-739-1166

Full Gospel A M E Zion Church 4207 Norcross St., Temple Hills, MD 20748 301-899-9411

Full Gospel Business Men's Fellowship, 3150 Bear St., Costa Mesa, CA 92626 714-754-1400

Fuller Evangelistic Association, P.O. Box 989, Pasadena, CA 91102 213-449-0425

Gadela Christian Church, P.O. Box 640405, Miami, FL 33164 305-825-6723

Gateway Cathedral, 200 Clarke Ave., Staten Island, NY 10306 718-667-0300

Good Life Associates, P.O. Box 81803, Lincoln, NE 68501

Good News Communications, Inc., 2876 Mabry Rd. N.E., Atlanta, GA 30319 404-237-0326

Good News Productions, Intl., Box 222, Joplin, MO 64802 417-782-0060

Good News Unlimited, 11710 Education St., Auburn, CA 95603 916-823-9690

Good Tidings Gospel Hall, P.O. Box 588, New York, NY 10008 718-951-8048

Gospel Association for the Blind, Inc., The, P.O. Box 62, Delray Beach, FL 33447 305-499-8900

Gospel Missionary Union, 10000 N. Oak, Kansas City, MO 64155 816-734-8500

Gospel Outreach of New York, 42-26 Little Neck Pkwy., Little Neck, NY 11363 718-428-4090

Gospel Tide Hour, Box 151, Chambersburg, PA 17201 717-264-7288

Grace Conservative Baptist Church, 30 Demarest Ave., Nanuet, NY 10954 914-623-3897

Grace Gospel Fellowship, 1011 Aldon St. S.W., P.O. Box 910, Grand Rapids, MI 49509 616-531-0046

Grace N' Vessels, 77 Grays Bridge Rd., Brookfield, CT 06804 203-775-1990

Grace Presbyterian Church, 114 W. Forrest Hill, Peoria, IL 61604; Box 3452, Peoria, IL 61614 309-688-3641

Grand Old Gospel Fellowship, Inc., 610 E. Mt. Pleasant Ave., Philadelphia, PA 19119 215-242-5550

Greater Holy Temple Church of God in Christ, 1656 Edgewood Ave., Jacksonville, FL 32208 904-768-4891

Greater Pittsburgh Christian Temple, 250 S. Pacific Ave., Pittsburgh, PA 15224

Guidelines, Inc., mailing: Box G, Laguna Hills, CA 92654; location: 26076 Getty Dr., Laguna Niguel, CA 92677 714-582-5001

Guido Evangelistic Association, Inc., Box 508, 600 N. Lewis St., Metter, GA 30439 912-685-2222

Haven of Rest Ministries, 2410 Hyperion Ave., Los Angeles, CA 90027 213-664-2103

Heath Christian Union Church, 152 Pike Ave., Heath, OH 43056 614-522-4845

Heaven and Home Hour, Inc., P.O. Box 100, Glendale, CA 91209 818-241-3415

Heralds of Hope, Inc., Box 3, Breezewood, PA 15533 717-485-4021

Hermano Pablo Ministries, P.O. Box 100, 2080 Placentia, Costa Mesa, CA 92628 714-645-0676

Hope for the Heart, P.O. Box 7, Dallas, TX 75221 615-894-6300

Hope Temple, Inc., 4500 N. Main St., Findlay, OH 45840 419-422-3944

Horizon International, P.O. Box 17480, San Diego, CA 92117 619-277-4991

Hour of Freedom Broadcast, 208 N. Main St., Oberlin, OH 44074 216-774-2283

Impact for Living, P.O. Box 265, Scranton, PA 18501

In Touch Ministries/ITM Inc., 796 W. Peachtree St. N.E., Atlanta, GA 30308 404-881-0550

Insight for Living, P.O. Box 4444, 211 E. Imperial Hwy., Ste. 100, Fullerton, CA 92634 714-870-9161

Inspiration of the Good Shepherd, 183 Merrill St., Brentwood, NY 11717 516-273-1162

Institute for Creation Research, P.O. Box 2667, El Cajon, CA 92021 619-448-0900

Institute of Family Living, 8230 E. Broadway, Ste. W-5, Tucson, AZ 85710 602-886-8108

International American Broadcasting Co., Inc., 3710 Marquis Dr., Garland, TX 75042 214-272-0686

International Christian Center, 701 State St., Garland, TX 75040 214-272-2173

International Christian Media, 2227 Meadow Dr., Carrollton, TX 75007 800-327-3383

International Lutheran Laymen's League, 2185 Hampton Ave., St. Louis, MO 63139 314-647-4900

International Media Service, 333 F St., N.W., Ste. 700, Washington, DC 20005 202-638-5071

International Prison Ministry, P.O. Box 63, Dallas, TX 75221 214-494-2302

Jack Van Impe Ministries, Box J, Royal Oak, MI 48068 313-435-3322

Jewish Voice Broadcast, Inc., P.O. Box 6, Phoenix, AZ 85001 602-971-8501

Jimmy Waters Ministries, P.O. Box A, Macon, GA 31202

J O Patterson Evangelistic Association, 1774 S. Parkway E., Memphis, TN 38114

Joe Lovelady Foundation, P.O. Box 8000, New Orleans, LA 70182 504-288-1461

John Stembridge Ministries, Inc., 545 N.E. 125th St., North Miami, FL 33161 305-893-0866

Joni & Friends, P.O. Box 3333, Agoura Hills, CA 91365 818-706-5664

Joshua's Sword, P.O. Box 331269, Fort Worth, TX 76163 817-292-8341; 205-345-6358

Juventud Evangelica, Inc., P.O. Box 34674, Hudson, FL 34674 813-863-8287

Kenneth Copeland Ministries, Fort Worth, TX 76192 817-535-1920

Kenneth Hagin Ministries P.O. Box 50126, Tulsa, OK 74150 918-258-1588

Kings College, The, Briarcliff Manor, NY 10510 914-941-7200

KJLY-FM Radio, P.O. Box 72, Blue Earth, MN 56013 507-526-3233

KSJB/Church of the Air, P.O. Box 987, Jamestown, ND 58401 701-252-0467

KWKY Radio, Box 662, Des Moines, IA 50303 515-981-0981

La Catedral del Pueblo Church, 441 E. 12th St., Hialeah, FL 33010 305-884-4000

La Hora de la Reforma, 6555 W. College Dr., Palos Heights, IL 60463 312-371-8700

La Voz de Salvacion, Bible Pl., Cleveland, TN 37311 615-479-8511

La Voz Del Pueblo, 807 S. Euclide Ave., Los Angeles, CA 90023 213-268-2919

Last Harvest Ministries, Inc., 9240 Markville Dr., Dallas, TX 75243 214-235-4444

Leawood Baptist Church, 2638 Macon Rd., Memphis, TN 38122 901-324-7169

LeSea Broadcasting Network, P.O. Box 12, South Bend, IN 46624 219-291-8200

Liberty Federation, 2020 Tate Springs Rd., Lynchburg, VA 24501 804-528-5000

Liberty University, Box 20,000, 3765 Candlers Mtn. Rd., Lynchburg, VA 24506 804-582-2235

Lifeline Communications, Union Rescue Mission, P.O. Box 629, Los Angeles, CA 90053-0629 213-628-6103

Lifeline Ministries, Inc., P.O. Box 14, Osprey, FL 34229 813-966-4561

Living Word Ministries, 350 Fifth Ave., New York, NY 10118 212-564-1511

Lloyd Ogilvie Ministries, Inc., 6037 Hollywood Blvd., Hollywood, CA 90028 213-464-7690

Looking Up, 1155 Aurora Ave., P.O. Box 296, Naperville, IL 60540 312-420-1300

Los Gatos Christian Church, 16845 Hicks Rd., Los Gatos, CA 95030 408-268-1411

Love Songs, Inc., 2899 Cordie Lee Ln., Germantown, TN 38138 901-755-9475

Luis Palau Evangelistic Association, P.O. Box 1173, Portland, OR 97207 503-643-0777

Lutheran Gospel Hour, P.O. Box 12, Pasadena, CA 91102 818-798-2784

Macedonian Missionary Service, 631 32nd St. N.W., Winter Haven, FL 33880 813-293-8388

Malcolm Smith Ministries, P.O. Box 29747, 3838 Medical Dr., San Antonio, TX 78229 512-558-3838

Marilyn Hickey Ministries, P.O. Box 17340, Denver, CO 80217 303-777-7302

Mass Communications Board of the Church of God, Inc., P.O. Box 2007, 1303 E. 5th St., Anderson, IN 46018 317-642-0256

Mennonite Media Services, 1251 Virginia Ave., Harrisonburg, VA 22801 703-434-2026

Message to Israel, 1811 Flatbush Ave., P.O. Box 52, Brooklyn, NY 11210 718-377-0744

Messianic Vision, Inc., The, P.O. Box 34444, Bethesda, MD 20817 301-963-4400

Methodist Hour International, P.O. Box 77, Orlando, FL 32802 305-830-0255

Midwest Christian Foundation, 31st & York Rd., Oak Brook, IL 60521 312-654-1882

Minirth-Meier Foundation, P.O. Box 1925, Richardson, TX 75085 214-669-1733

Missionary Gospel Fellowship, Drawer W, Turlock, CA 95381 209-634-8575

Monument of Faith Evangelical Church, 7359 S. Chappel Ave., Chicago, IL 60649

Moody Broadcasting Services, 820 N. LaSalle Dr., Chicago, IL 60610 312-508-6900

Moody Church, 1609 N. LaSalle St., Chicago, IL 60614 312-943-0466

Morning Cheer, Inc., P.O. Box B, North East, MD 21901 301-287-5433

Movimiento Misionero Mundial, Inc., (World-wide Missionary Movement), San Juan, PR & Washington, D.C., GPO Box 3644, San Juan, PR 00936 809-761-8806

Multimedia Ministries International, 18221 Torrence Ave., Lansing, IL 60438 312-895-7000

Myerstown Grace Brethren Church, 430 E. Lincoln Ave., Myerstown, PA 17067 717-866-5704

Narramore Christian Foundation, 1409 N. Walnut Grove Ave., P.O. Box 5000, Rosemead, CA 91770 818-288-7000

National Foundation, Inc., 7617 Little River Trnpk., Ste. 200, Heritage Bldg., Annandale, VA 22003 703-642-8244

Nazarene Communications, 6401 The Paseo, Kansas City, MO 64131 816-333-7000

New Beginning, A, P.O. Box 4424, Riverside, CA 92514 714-781-9991

New Bethel Church of God in Christ, 6440 Piney Branch Rd. N.W., Washington, D.C. 20012 202-829-1523

New Life Mission, P.O. Box 21945, Chattanooga, TN 37421 615-899-3334

Northwestern Productions, 3003 N. Snelling Ave., St. Paul, MN 55113 612-631-5040

Old-Time Gospel Hour, Lynchburg, VA 24514 804-528-4112

On a High Mountain Ministries, Inc., 29 New York Ave., Ocean Grove, NJ 07756 201-776-5715

Pacific Garden Mission, 646 S. State St., Chicago, IL 60605 312-922-1462

Peoples Church of God, 833 W. Pershing Rd., Decatur, IL 62526 217-877-7224

Planned Living Seminars, P.O. Box 400, Yakima, WA 98907; 814 N. 1st St., Yakima, WA 98901 509-457-7677

Polish Gospel Hour, P.O. Box 486, Buffalo, NY 14240 716-895-7454

Power of Pentecost Ministry, 1020 Lippincott, Flint, MI 48503 313-234-0192

Prayer of Faith Ministry, 717 Savannah St., Greensboro, NC 27406 919-373-0219

Precept Ministries of Reach Out Inc., P.O. Box 23000, Chattanooga, TN 37422 615-892-6814

Puertas Abiertas, P.O. Box 27250, Santa Ana, CA 92799 714-751-3333

Radio Bible Class, Box 22, Grand Rapids, MI 49555 616-942-6770

Radio Bible Hour, Inc., 1717 W. Broadway, Western Plaza Center P.O. Box 99, Newport, TN 37821 615-623-3400

Radio Bible Institute, Christian Enterprises Inc., P.O. Box 272, Ashland, VA 23005 804-798-4711

Radio Vision Cristiana, P.O. Box 317, 60 West Castor Pl., Staten Island, NY 10312 718-948-6230

Ralph Neighbour Evangelistic Association, Inc., The, P.O. Box 19888, Houston, TX 77224; 14925 Memorial Dr., Ste. 101, Houston, TX 77079 713-497-7901

Ranch Hope for Boys, P.O. Box 325, Sawmill Rd., Alloway, NJ 08001 609-935-1555

Redeeming Love Christian Center, The, 145 West Rt. 59, Nanuet, NY 10954 914-623-9300

Rehoboth Baptist Church, 2997 Lawrenceville Hwy., Tucker, GA 30084; P.O. Box 451000, Atlanta, GA 30345 404-939-3182

Religion in Media, 3400 Wilshire Blvd., Ste. 50, Los Angeles, CA 90010 213-387-7180

Religious Heritage of America, Inc., 7900 Jerome Ave., St. Louis, MO 63143 314-781-7888

Rev. Antonio Orona Ministries, P.O. Box 779, Bronx, NY 10462 212-863-8138

Revivaltime Media Ministries, General Council of the Assemblies of God, P.O. Box 70, Springfield, MO 65801 417-862-2781

Richard Hatch Ministries, Inc., 705 Liberty Ave., Pittsburgh, PA 15222 412-281-3830

River of Life Church, 661 Rockbridge Rd. N.W., Lilburn, GA 30247 404-925-3005

Rod of God Ministries, The, P.O. Box 240381, Charlotte, NC 28224; 3410 Wilkinson Blvd., Charlotte, NC 28224; office: 704-394-7777; home: 704-527-0780

Romanian Missionary Society, P.O. Box 527, Wheaton, IL 60189-0527 312-665-6503

Roswell Street Baptist Church, 774 Roswell St., Marietta, GA 30060 404-424-9817

Roy Bishop Productions, Inc., 428 Kings Hwy., Swedesboro, NJ 08085 609-467-3026

Rudy Hernandez Evangelism, Inc., 2300 Basse Rd., San Antonio, TX 78213

Russian Christian Radio, P.O. Box 1667, 1732 Mountain View Ct., Estes Park, CO 80517 303-586-8638

Saints Alive in Jesus, P.O. Box 1076, Issaquah, WA 98027 206-392-2077

Salt Shakers Full Gospel Ministries, 727 Cobbs Creek Pkwy., Philadelphia, PA 19143

Sanders Christian Foundation, P.O. Box 2094, South Hamilton, MA 01982 617-468-7306

Sar Shalom Ministries, Inc., P.O. Box 1073, East St. Louis, IL 62204 618-235-9515

Schambach Revivals, Inc., Rt. 4, Box 155, Tyler, TX 75703 214-894-6131

Seed Time Ministries, Inc., P.O. Box 580, Post Falls, ID 83854 208-664-4833

SEMAE Prod., P.O. Box 420006, Miami, FL 33142 305-635-6366

Shadyrest Bible Conference, Inc., R.D. 2, Box 245, Trenton, NJ 06820 609-298-3793

Shalom Fellowship, 27 Congress St., P.O. Box 4464, Salem, MA 01970 617-744-8131

Shalom Israel, P.O. Box 1292, Calgary, Alberta T2P 2L2, Canada 403-262-3723

Showers of Blessing Ministry, Inc., 1137 Avon Ave., Atlanta, GA 30310 404-752-8960

SIM International, P.O. Box 7900, Charlotte, NC 28241 704-529-5300

Songtime, Inc., Box 350, Boston, MA 02101 617-848-7787

Sound Words Communications, Inc., 1000 S. 84th St., Lincoln, NE 68510 402-483-4541

Southland Baptist Temple, 927 Yarbro Ln., P.O. Box 2527, Paducah, KY 42002 502-444-9678

Southwest Radio Church, 901 N.W. 6th, Oklahoma City, OK 73106 405-235-5396; 800-652-1144

Southwestern Union Conference of Seventh Day Adventists, Satellite Trans American Radio, 777 S. Burleson Blvd., P.O. Box 4000, Burleson, TX 76028 817-295-0476

Spanish Eastern District Assemblies of God, 1260 Thierlot Ave., Bronx, NY 10472 212-824-8797

Star Communications, P.O. Box 730, Durant & Turkey Creek Rds., Durant, FL 33530 813-737-1300

Straight Gate Church, 15340 Southfield, Detroit, MI 48223 313-837-3440

Straight Talk Radio, P.O. Box 769, Leander, TX 78641 512-778-5591

Street Meetings, Inc., P.O. Box 724, Dallas, TX 75221 214-327-3052

Sunday Line Communications, 8220 Cowichan Rd., Blaine, WA 98230 206-371-2082

Sweetwater Church of the Valley, 14240 N. 43rd Ave., Glendale, AZ 85306 602-978-5511

Tabernacle Presbyterian Church, 418 E. 34th St., Indianapolis, IN 46205 317-923-5458

Teenagers for Christ, 6223 Lochlevin Cove, Memphis, TN 38119 901-682-3028

Templo Calvario, 2617 W. 5th St., Santa Ana, CA 92703 714-834-9331

The Salvation Army, (National Headquarters), 799 Bloomfield Ave., Verona, NJ 07044 201-239-0606

Thru the Bible Radio Network, P.O. Box 7100, Pasadena, CA 91109 818-795-4145

Time of Deliverance, Deliverance Evangelistic Church, 4732 N. Broad St., Philadelphia, PA 19141 215-456-2162; 215-456-2152

Tips for Teens, 3003 N. Snelling, Roseville, MN 55113 612-636-4900

Traditional Values Coalition, 100 S. Anaheim Blvd., Ste. 320, P.O. Box 940, Anaheim, CA 92805 714-520-0300

Trans World Missions, 4205 Santa Monica Blvd., Los Angeles, CA 90029 213-663-1176

Tri-State Inspirational Broadcasting, Inc., P.O. Box IBC, 3625 Helton Dr., Florence, AL 35630 205-766-6610

Truth for Today Media Messages, 1700 S. Main, Greenville, MS 38701 601-335-3578

Truth on the March, Box 492, E. Stroudsburg, PA 18301

Turning Point, P.O. Box 3838, San Diego, CA 92103 619-440-1802

Twentieth Street Baptist Church, Twentieth St. 5th Ave., Huntington, WV 25703 304-523-0824

Urban Alternative, The, P.O. Box 763008, Dallas TX 75376 214-943-3868

Ventures for Christ, P.O. Box 3463, Fayetteville, AR 72701 501-442-4074

Victory Broadcasting Network, 1416 Larkin Williams Rd., St. Louis, MO 63026 314-343-4359

Victory Gospel Association, The, 103 Richbourg Rd., Greenville, SC 29615 803-268-1308

Visit with the Joneses, Inc., A, Box 575, Erie, PA 16512

Voice of Americanism, P.O. Box 90, Glendale, CA 91209 818-240-4871

Voice of Comfort, P.O. Box 7, Cape Coral, FL 33910 813-549-2279

Voice of Praise, 24 Flower Ln., Levittown, PA 19055 215-946-9558

Voice of Salvation, The, Bible Pl., Cleveland, TN 37311 615-479-8511

Voice of the Bible Tabernacle, P.O. Box 496, Evergreen, AL 36401 205-578-2181

Wesleyan Church, The, Box 50434, Indianapolis, IN 46250 317-842-0444

Wings of Faith, P.O. Box 8001, Canton, OH 44711 216-833-4658

Wings of Healing, Inc., P.O. Box 730, Montebello, CA 90640 213-724-3873; 213-685-8892

Wisdom From the Word, 6400 Ardleigh St., Philadelphia, PA 19119 215-549-8800

WNYK Productions, Nyack College, Nyack, NY 10960 914-358-1710

Women Alive Ministries, Inc., Box 312, Collingswood, NJ 08108 609-858-6750

Women's Lobby, 2311 Capitol Ave., Sacramento, CA 95816 916-447-2633

Word and the World Dedication Evangelism, Inc., The, Box 10, Towaco, NJ 07082 201-334-9081

Word of Faith World Outreach Center, P.O. Box 819000, Dallas, TX 75381 214-620-1586

Word of Grace Broadcast, Inc., P.O. Box 7, San Antonio, TX 78291; 13735 Stoney Hill, San Antonio, TX 78231 512-492-3784; 512-821-5277

Word of Grace Communication, P.O. Box 4000, Panorama City, CA 91412 213-764-5904

Word-TV, Tate Springs Rd., Lynchburg, VA 24506 804-528-2080

Words of Hope, Inc., 700 Ball Ave., N.E., Grand Rapids, MI 49503 616-459-6181

World Bible Society, P.O. Box 5000, Costa Mesa, CA 92646 714-642-7443

World Fellowship Ministry Foundation, 11510 Georgia Ave., Ste. 115, Wheaton, MD 20906 301-942-4443

World Messianic Fellowships, Inc., 57 Edmund St., Box 449, Lynbrook, NY 11563 516-887-2866; 516-593-1724

World Prophetic Ministry, Inc., Box 907, Colton, CA 92324 714-825-2767

World Radio, P.O. Box 2000, 3201 N. 7th St., West Monroe, LA 71294 318-396-6000

Youth for Christ/USA, P.O. Box 419, Wheaton, IL 60189 312-668-6600

FILM PRODUCERS/DISTRIBUTORS & VIDEO PROGRAM PRODUCERS/DISTRIBUTORS

American Bible Society, 1865 Broadway, New York, NY 10023 212-581-7400

American Religious Town Hall, 745 N. Buckner, Dallas, TX 75218 214-328-9828

Assembly of God, 1487 Glen Ave., Wahiawa, HI 96786 808-622-4681

ATS Communications, 7206 Halifax Ave., N., Minneapolis, MN 55429 612-561-0018

Baptist (Southern) Radio & TV Convention, 6350 W. Frwy., Fort Worth, TX 76150 817-737-4011; 800-433-5757

Bellevue Baptist Church, 70 N. Bellevue Blvd., Memphis, TN 38104 901-725-9777

Ben Haden Evangelical Association, 554 McCallie Ave., Chattanooga, TN 37402; P.O. Box 100, Chattanooga, TN 37401 615-267-7959

Bethel Temple of Evansville, Inc., 4400 Lincoln Ave., Evansville, IN 47715 812-477-8888

Billy Graham Evangelistic Association, P.O. Box 9313, Minneapolis, MN 55440 612-338-0500

Black Buffalo's TV Pow Wow, P.O. Box 2607, Hemet, CA 92343 714-925-9083

Breakthrough Radio & TV, 1826 Basse Rd., San Antonio, TX 78213 512-735-4094

Buenos Amigos Inc., P.O. Box 969, Calistoga, CA 94515 707-942-0880

Calvary Assembly of God, 1199 Clay St., Winter Park, FL 32789 305-644-1199

Calvary Church Inc., 4000 Pacific Coast Hwy., Torrance, CA 90505

Campmeeting Ministries Inc., 3948 Hwy. 90, Pace, FL 32571 904-994-7131

Campus Crusade for Christ International, Arrowhead Springs, San Bernardino, CA 92414 714-886-5224

Cathedral Caravan Inc., 6550 Mango Ave. S., St. Petersburg, FL 33707 813-347-2463; 813-347-2865

Chapel, The, 895 N. Forest Rd., Buffalo, NY 14221 716-634-4440

Chapel Hill Harvester Church, P.O. Box 7300, Atlanta, GA 30357 404-243-5020

Chinese Television Co., 2 Waverly Pl., San Francisco, CA 94108 415-433-4880

Christ for the World Inc., P.O. Box 3428, Orlando, FL 32802 305-423-3172

Christian Broadcasting Network, Inc., The, CBN Center, Virginia Beach, VA 23463 804-424-7777

Christian Children's Associates, Inc., P.O. Box 446, Toms River, NJ 08754 201-240-3003

Christian Communications of Chicagoland, Inc./WCFC TV 38, One N. Wacker Dr., 11th Floor, Chicago, IL 60606 312-977-3838

Christian Communications Network, 8691 Echo Dr., La Mesa, CA 92041 619-454-1964

Christian Destiny, Inc., P.O. Box C, E. Hwy. 56, Hillsboro, KS 67063 316-947-2345

Christian Evangelical Churches of America, 2433 Coolidge Ave., Oakland, CA 94601 415-533-8300

Christian Jamboree Ministries, 8181 GSRI Rd., Baton Rouge, LA 70820 504-766-4334

Christian Retreat, Rt. 2, Box 279, Bradenton, FL 34202 813-747-6481

Christian Television Network, P.O. Box 19700, 17405 Lahser, Detroit, MI 48219 313-538-5100

Christian World Communications, 367 Mt. Paran Rd. N.W., Atlanta, GA 30327 404-252-0300

Church of God in Christ, 2416 Orcutt Ave., Newport News, VA 23607 804-245-7200; 804-245-5545

Church of God of Prophecy, Bible Pl., Cleveland, TN 37311 615-479-8511

Community of Jesus, The, P.O. Box 1094, 11 Bay View Dr., Orleans, MA 02653 617-255-1094

Coral Ridge Ministries, 5554 Federal Hwy., Drexel Bldg. 2nd Floor, Ft. Lauderdale, FL 33308 305-722-0404

Cornerstone World Outreach Center, 1701 S. Fort, Springfield, MO 65807 417-831-7242

CRC-TV, Division of Back to God Hour, 6555 W. College Dr., Palos Heights, IL 60463 312-371-8700

Darlene Matthews Ministries/His New Sound, P.O. Box 9880, 320 E. Methvin, Longview, TX 75608 214-236-7958

David Munizzi Ministries, P.O. Box 1105, Valley Stream, NY 11582 516-872-0591

Discovery Broadcasting Network, 15720 Hillcrest, Dallas, TX 75248 214-387-4475

Dove Broadcasting Inc., P.O. Box 1616, 3409 Rutherford Rd., Greenville, SC 29602 803-244-1616

Elmbrook Church, 777 S. Barker Rd., Waukesha, WI 53186 414-786-7051

Evangelistic Outreach, Inc., P.O. Box 56, Pedro, OH 45659 614-532-2116

Ever Increasing Faith Ministries, P.O. Box 90,000, Los Angeles, CA 90009; 7901 S. Vermont Ave., Los Angeles, CA 90044 213-758-3777

Faith America Foundation, Box USA, Scottsdale, AZ 85253

Faith for Today, 1100 Rancho Conejo Blvd., Newbury Park, CA 91320 805-373-7700

Faith Temple, Rt. 2, Taylors, SC 29687 803-895-4142

Family Crusade International, P.O. Box 24561, San Jose, CA 95124 408-978-8622

Family Life Seminars, 122 C St. N.W., Ste. 850, Washington, D.C. 20001 202-783-1377

Features International, P.O. Box 64503, 1801 Delaney St., Virginia Beach, VA 23464 804-363-9700

Fellowship Missionary Baptist Church, 45th Pl. & Princeton Ave., Chicago, IL 60609 312-924-3232

First Assembly of God Church, P.O. Box 11267, Memphis, TN 38111 901-324-3585

First Baptist Alcoa, 819 Gilbert St., Alcoa, TN 37701 615-982-6221

First Baptist Church of Houston, 7401 Katy Frwy., Houston, TX 77024 713-957-6740

First Baptist Church Worship Hour, 1200 Ninth, Wichita Falls, TX 76301 817-723-2764

First Light Ministries, 7401 Katy Frwy., Houston, TX 77024 713-957-6730

First Presbyterian Church at Houston, 5300 Main St., Houston, TX 77004 713-526-2525

First Southern Baptist Church, P.O. Box 15039, Del City, OK 73155 405-732-1300

Focus on Faith Productions, P.O. Box 563, Kings Hwy. & Park Ave., Valley Cottage, NY 10989 914-268-3000

Ford Philpot Evangelistic Association, Box 3000, Lexington, KY 40533 606-276-1479

Forward in Faith, (Church of God), 1441 Guthrie Dr., Cleveland, TN 37311 615-472-3361

Four States Christian Missions, Inc., P.O. Box 685, Hagerstown, MD 21740 301-739-1166

Full Gospel A M E Zion Church, 4207 Norcross St., Temple Hills, MD 20748 301-899-9411

Full Gospel Business Men's Fellowship, 3150 Bear St., Costa Mesa, CA 92625 714-754-1400

Gary Randall Program, P.O. Box 240, Portland, OR 97207 503-636-8126

Gateway Cathedral, 200 Clarke Ave., Staten Island, NY 10306 718-667-0300

God is Good World Evangelistic Association, P.O. Box 422, Oakhurst, NJ 07755 201-922-3278

Good News Communications, Inc., 2876 Mabry Rd. N.E., Atlanta, GA 30319 404-237-0326

Good News Unlimited, 11710 Education St., Auburn, CA 95603 916-823-9690

Gospel Association for the Blind, Inc., The, P.O. Box 62, Delray Beach, FL 33447 305-499-8900

Gospel Films, Inc., P.O. Box 455, 2735 E. Apple, Muskegon, MI 49442 616-773-3361; 800-253-0413; 800-632-0319 (Michigan)

Gospel Graphics, Inc., 288 Gold Rush Rd., Lexington, KY 40503 606-276-4883; 606-276-4884

Grace N' Vessels, P.O. Box 196, Brookfield, CT 06805 203-775-1990

Grace Presbyterian Church, 114 W. Forrest Hill, Peoria, IL 61604; P.O. Box 3452, Peoria, IL 61614 309-688-3641

Greater Holy Temple Church of God in Christ, 1656 Edgewood Ave., Jacksonville, FL 32208 904-768-4891

Grove Avenue Baptist Church, 8701 Ridge Rd., Richmond, VA 23229 804-740-8888

Guidelines, Inc., Box G, Laguna Hills, CA 92653; 26076 Getty Dr., Laguna Niguel, CA 92677 714-582-5001

Guido Evangelistic Association, Inc., P.O. Box 508, Metter, GA 30439 912-685-2222; 912-685-2376

Hanguk Christian Broadcasting, Inc., 545 Eighth Ave. 15-N, New York, NY 10018 212-594-5757; 212-564-7534

Hart Productions, 115 Worden, Ann Arbor, MI 48103 313-761-8870

Hollywood Pacific Studios, 6290 Sunset Blvd., Hollywood, CA 90028 213-463-3189

Hope Temple, Inc., 4500 N. Main St., Findlay, OH 45840 419-422-3944

Hour of Power, Crystal Cathedral, 4201 W. Chapman Ave., Orange, CA 92668 714-971-4101

Impact Productions, 1405 N. Main, Evansville, IN 47711 812-428-7788

Inspirational Concert Series, 545 N.E. 125th St., N. Miami, FL 33161 305-893-0800

In Touch Ministries/ITM, Inc., 796 W. Peachtree St. N.E., Atlanta, GA 30308 404-881-0550

International American Broadcasting Co., Inc., 3720 Marquis, Garland, TX 75042 214-272-0686

International Broadcasting Network, P.O. Box 73313, Houston, TX 77273 713-376-9582

International Correspondence Institute, P.O. Box 50848, Ft. Worth, TX 76105 817-496-5033

International Lutheran Laymen's League, 2185 Hampton Ave., St. Louis, MO 63139 314-647-4900

International Media Service, 1333 F St. N.W., Ste. 700, Washington, D.C. 20005 202-638-5071

Jack Van Impe Ministries, Box J, Royal Oak, MI 48068 313-435-3322

James Robison Evangelistic Association, P.O. Box 18489, Fort Worth, TX 76118 817-267-4211

Jewish Voice Broadcast, Inc., Box 6, Phoenix, AZ 85001 602-971-8501

Jimmy Waters Ministries, P.O. Box A, Macon, GA 31202

Joe Lovelady Foundation, P.O. Box 8000, New Orleans, LA 70182 504-288-1461

John Ankerberg Show, The, P.O. Box 8977, Chattanooga, TN 37411 615-892-7722

John Hagee Ministries, P.O. Box 1400, San Antonio, TX 78295 512-342-8510

Joy of Music, The, 2809 Wayzata Blvd., Minneapolis, MN 55407 612-377-3730

Jubilee Communications, P.O. Box 22815, Chattanooga, TN 37422

Kansas City Youth for Christ, KYFC-TV 50, 4715 Rainbow Blvd., Shawnee Mission, KS 66205 913-262-1700

Ken Anderson Films, P.O. Box 618, Winona Lake, IN 46590 219-267-5774

Kenneth Copeland Ministries, Fort Worth, TX 76192 817-535-1920

La Catedral del Pueblo Church, 441 E. 12th St., Hialeah, FL 33010 305-884-4000

La Hora de la Reforma, Reforma TV, 6555 W. College Dr., Palos Heights, IL 60463 312-371-8700

Larry Jones International Ministries/Feed the Children, P.O. Box 36, Oklahoma City, OK 73101 405-942-0228

LBC Productions, 4851 Lanier Dr., Baton Rouge, LA 70812 504-355-5605

Leawood Baptist Church, 3638 Macon Rd., Memphis, TN 38122 901-324-7169

LeSea Broadcasting Network, Box 12, South Bend, IN 46614 219-291-8200

Liberty University, P.O. Box 20,000, Candler's Mtn. Rd., Lynchburg, VA 24506 804-582-2235

Lifeline Ministries Inc., P.O. Box 14, Osprey, FL 34229 813-966-4561

Living Way Ministries, 14300 Sherman Way, Van Nuys, CA 91405 818-786-7090

Lloyd Ogilvie Ministries Inc., 6037 Hollywood Blvd., Hollywood, CA 90028 213-464-7690

Look and Live Ministries, 1201 S. Charles St., Baltimore, MD 21230 301-539-7322

Los Gatos Christian Church, 11845 Hicks Rd., Los Gatos, CA 95030 408-268-1411

Lowell Lundstrom Ministries, Inc., E. Hwy. 10, Sisseton, SD 57262 605-698-3937

Luis Palau Evangelistic Team, P.O. Box 1173, Portland, OR 97207 503-643-0777

Lutheran Ministries Media, 3425 Crescent Ave., Ft. Wayne, IN 46805 219-483-3173

Lutheran Television, 2185 Hampton Ave., St. Louis, MO 63139 314-647-4900

Malcolm Neal Productions, 46 Park Ln., McKinney, TX 75069 214-727-1466

Maranatha Ad Agency, 2230 Anne St., Santa Ana, CA 92704 714-546-9211

March of Faith TV Ministry, 5440 Oakman Blvd., Detroit, MI 48204

Marilyn Hickey Ministries, P.O. Box 17350, Denver, CO 80217 303-698-1155

Mark IV Pictures, Inc., Box 3810, Urbandale Station, 5907 Meredith Dr., Des Moines, IA 50322 515-278-4737

Mennonite Media Services, 1251 Virginia Ave., Harrisonburg, VA 22801 703-434-2026

Midwest Christian Foundation, 31st & York Rd., Oak Brook, IL 60521 312-654-1882

Minirth-Meier Foundation, P.O. Box 1925, Richardson, TX 75085; 2100 N. Collins Blvd., Richardson, TX 75080 214-669-1733

Mission Service Supply, P.O. Drawer 2957, West Monroe, LA 71294 318-325-8674

Monument of Faith Evangelical Church, 7359 S. Chappel Ave., Chicago, IL 60649

Myerstown Grace Brethren Church, 430 E. Lincoln Ave., Myerstown, PA 17067 717-866-5704

Narramore Christian Foundation, P.O. Box 5000, 1409 N. Walnut Grove Ave., Rosemead, CA 91770 818-288-7000

Nason Media Corporation, 777 S. Main, #206, Orange, CA 92668 714-978-8112

National Association of Evangelicals, 1023 15th St., N.W., Ste. 500, Washington, D.C. 20005 202-789-1011

Nazarene Communications, 6401 The Paseo, Kansas City, MO 64131 816-333-7000

New Life Assembly of God, 28 Hedgehog Rd., Trumbull, CT 06611 203-261-2728

Old-Time Gospel Hour, 701 Thomas Rd., Lynchburg, VA 24502 804-239-9281

Oscar Canales Evangelistic Ministries Inc., P.O. Box 540 14244 Ingleside Ave., Dolton, IL 60419 312-841-6967

Park Plaza Church of Christ, 5925 E. 51st St., Tulsa, OK 74135 918-627-3201

Penn Wood Bible Church, Rt. 1, Box 75, Everett, PA 15537 814-623-9444

Precept Ministries of Reach Out Inc., 7324 Noah Reid Rd., Chattanooga, TN 37421 615-892-6814

Radio Bible Class, Box 22, Grand Rapids, MI 49555 616-942-6770

Radio Revival, Inc. of Birmingham, Ala., P.O. Box 10684, Birmingham, AL 35202 205-845-4254

Redwood TeleMedia, 20200 Redwood Rd., Castro Valley, CA 94546 415-886-8448

Rehoboth Baptist Church, 2997 Lawrenceville Hwy., Tucker, GA 30084; P.O. Box 451000, Atlanta, GA 30345 404-939-3182

Religion in Media, 3400 Wilshire Blvd., Ste. 50, Los Angeles, CA 90010 213-387-7180

Religious Heritage of America, Inc., 7900 Jerome Ave., St. Louis, MO 63143 800-325-3016

Religious Roundtable, The, 3295 Poplar Ave., P.O. Box 11467, Memphis, TN 38111 901-458-3795

Revival Fire Ministries, P.O. Box 1707, Joplin, MO 64802 417-624-0749

Richard Hatch Ministries, 705 Liberty Ave., Pittsburgh, PA 15222 412-281-3830

Rock Church, 640 Kempsville Rd., Virginia Beach, VA 23464-2794 804-495-5200

Rod of God Ministries, The, P.O. Box 240381, Charlotte, NC 28224; 3410 Wilkinson Blvd., Charlotte, NC 28724 704-394-7777

Roswell Street Baptist Church, 774 Roswell St., Marietta, GA 30060 404-424-9817

Roy Bishop Productions, Inc., 428 Kings Hwy., Swedesboro, NJ 08085 609-467-3026

Rudy Hernandez Evangelism, Inc., 2300 Basse Rd., San Antonio, TX 78213 512-525-8811

Santa Fe Communications Inc., 7700 W. Blue Mound Rd., Milwaukee, WI 53213 414-259-6504

Schambach Revivals, Inc., Rt. 4, Box 155, Tyler, TX 75703 214-894-6131

SEMAE Productions, P.O. Box 420006, Miami, FL 33142 305-635-6366

Shalom Fellowship, The, Box 4464, Salem, MA 01970 603-352-0938

Showers of Blessing Ministry, Inc., 1137 Avon Ave., Atlanta, GA 30310 404-752-8960

Soul's Harbor, Calvary Temple, 230 Nicollet Mall, Minneapolis, MN 55401 612-338-0771

Sound Words Communications, Inc., 1000 S. 84th St., P.O. Box 5949, Lincoln, NE 68510 402-483-4541

Spanish Eastern District Assemblies of God, 1260 Thierlot Ave., Bronx, NY 10472 212-824-8797

Star Communications, P.O. Box 730, Durant & Turkey Creek Rds., Durant, FL 33530 813-737-1300

Straight Gate Church, 15340 Southfield, Detroit, MI 48223 313-837-3440

Sunday Line Communications, 8220 Cowichan Rd., Blaine, WA 98230 206-371-2082

Sweetwater Church of the Valley, 14240 N. 43rd Ave., Glendale, AZ 85306 602-978-5511

Tabernacle Presbyterian Church, 418 E. 34th St., Indianapolis, IN 46205 317-923-5458

Tel-All Corporation, 16905 S.W. 90 Ave., Miami, FL 33157

Templo Calvario, 2617 W. 5th St., Santa Ana, CA 92703 714-834-9331

Time of Deliverance, Deliverance Evangelistic Church, 4732 N. Broad St., Philadelphia, PA 19141 215-456-2162; 215-456-2152

Traditional Values Coalition, P.O. Box 940, 100 S. Anaheim Blvd., Ste. 320, Anaheim, CA 92805 714-520-0300

Trinity Broadcasting Network, 2442 Michelle Dr., Tustin, CA 92680 714-832-2950

TVSC/Group W Productions, 310 Parkway View Dr., Pittsburgh, PA 15205 412-348-4709

Valley Chapel, Assemblies of God, 300 Valley Rd., Clifton, NJ 07013 201-278-0953

Valley Forge Films Inc., Box K, Paoli, PA 19301 215-647-7730

Ventures for Christ, P.O. Box 3463, Fayetteville, AR 72701 501-442-4074

Victory Broadcasting Network, 1416 Larkin-Williams, St. Louis, MO 63026 314-343-4359

Vive Productions, Box 1511, Allentown, PA 18105 215-433-4563; 215-261-1726

Voice of Salvation, The, Bible Pl., Cleveland, TN 37311 615-479-8511

W V Grant Evangelistic Association, 4447 Brass Way, Dallas, TX 75236 214-333-2176

Wallace & Associates, 3715 Woodlands Dr., Smyrna, GA 30080 404-431-9309

WORD-TV, Lynchburg General-Marshall Lodge Hospitals, Tate Springs Rd., Lynchburg, VA 24506 804-528-2080

Word Alive Ministries, P.O. Box 545, 113 Lighthouse Dr., Manahawkin, NJ 08050 201-240-WORD

Word of Faith World Outreach Center, P.O. Box 819099, Dallas TX 75381 214-620-1586

World Fellowship Ministry Foundation, 1150 Georgia Ave., Wheaton, MD 20906 202-488-4442; 301-942-1564

World Prophetic Ministry, Inc., Box 907, Colton, CA 92324 714-825-2767

World Vision, 919 W. Huntington Dr., Monrovia, CA 91016 818-357-7979

World Wide Pictures Inc., (Billy Graham Film Ministry), 1201 Hennepin Ave., Minneapolis, MN 55403 612-338-3335; 800-328-4318

WRDG TV 16, P.O. Box 16, Burlington, NC 27216 919-376-6016

Media: Print Organizations

BIBLE/LITERATURE AGENCIES

American Bible Society, 1865 Broadway, New York, NY 10023 212-581-7400

American Scripture Gift Mission, Inc., (ASGM), (publishers & distributors of Scripture portions), 241 Fairfield Ave., P.O. Box 2126, Upper Darby, PA 19082-2126 215-734-2040

Augsburg Fortress Publishers, (Evangelical Luth. Ch. in Am.), 426 S. Fifth St., P.O. Box 1209, Minneapolis, MN 55440 612-330-3300

Barclay Press, (Northwest Yearly Meeting of Friends), P.O. Box 232, Newberg, OR 97132 503-538-7345

Barnabas Foundation, 15127 S. 73rd Ave., Ste. G, Orland Park, IL 60462 312-532-3444

B.B. Kirkbride Bible Co., Inc., 335 W. 9th St., Indianapolis, IN 46202; mailing: P.O. Box 606, Indianapolis, IN 46206 317-634-3252; 800-428-4385

Berea Publications, P.O. Box 100, Powhatan, VA 23139

Bible League, The, 16801 Van Dam Rd., South Holland, IL 60473 312-331-2094

Bible Literature International, P.O. Box 477, 625 E. North Broadway, Columbus, OH 43216 614-267-3116

Bibles for India, (affiliate of The Bible League), 4221 Richmond N.W., Grand Rapids, MI 49504 616-453-8855

Bibles for Mexico, (affiliate of The Bible League), 4221 Richmond N.W., Grand Rapids, MI 49504 616-453-8855

Canyonview Press, 12730 Finlay Rd. N.E., Silverton, OR 97381 503-873-8296

Chosen People Ministries, 1300 Cross Beam Dr., Charlotte, NC 28217-2800 704-357-9000

Christian Literature Crusade, Inc., P.O. Box 1449, Fort Washington, PA 19034 215-542-1242

Christian Publications, (C&MA), 3825 Hartzdale Dr., Camp Hill, PA 17011 717-761-7044; 800-233-4443

Church Bible Studies, 191 Mayhew Way, Walnut Creek, CA 94596 415-937-7286

Crista Ministries, 19303 Fremont N., Seattle, WA 98133 206-546-7200

David C. Cook Foundation, 850 N. Grove, Elgin, IL 60120 312-741-2400

Evangelical Church Library Assoc., P.O. Box 353, Glen Ellyn, IL 60138 312-668-0519

Every Home for Christ/World Literature Crusade, 20232 Sunburst St., Chatsworth, CA 91311 818-341-7870

Family Life Institute, (Bible stories for kids & the family), P.O. Box 244, Nordland, WA 98358 206-385-0234

Gideons International, 2900 Lebanon Rd., Nashville, TN 37214 615-883-8533

Gospel Literature International, (GLINT), 1409 Walnut Grove, Rosemead, CA 91770 818-288-2812

Harvest Publications, (Bapt. Gen. Conf.), 2002 S. Arlington Hgts. Rd., Arlington Heights, IL 60005 312-228-0200

Here's Life Publishers, Inc., P.O. Box 1576, San Bernardino, CA 92402 714-886-7981

Holman Bible Publishers, 127 Ninth Ave., N., Nashville, TN 37234 615-251-2510; 800-251-3225

India Rural Evangelical Fellowship, (church planting, orphanage, Christian school), 8915 A Robin Dr., Des Plaines, IL 60016 312-297-6414

International Bible Society, P.O. Box 62970, Colorado Springs, CO 80962-2970 719-528-1900; 800-524-1588

InterVarsity Press, P.O. Box 1400, Downers Grove, IL 60515 312-964-5700

Jews for Jesus, 60 Haight St., San Francisco, CA 94102 415-864-2600

John Milton Society for the Blind, 475 Riverside Dr., #455, New York, NY 10115 212-870-3335

Living Bibles International, 1979 Mill St., Naperville, IL 60540 312-369-0100

Logoi, Inc., 4100 W. Flagler St., Ste. B-3, Miami, FL 33134 305-446-8297

Lutheran Braille Evangelism Assoc., 1740 Eugene St., White Bear Lake, MN 55110 612-426-0469

Mott Media, 1000 E. Huron St., Milford, MI 48042 313-685-8773

National Publishing Co., P.O. Box 8386, Philadelphia, PA 19101 215-732-1863

Success with Youth Publications, Inc., P.O. Box 2789, LaJolla, CA 92038 619-578-4700

The Pocket Testament League, P.O. Box 368, 117 Main St., Lincoln Park, NJ 07035 201-696-1900

Walk Thru the Bible Ministries, Inc., 61 Perimeter Park, P.O. Box 80587, Atlanta, GA 30366 404-458-9300; 800-554-9300

William Carey Library, 1705 N. Sierra Bonita Ave., Pasadena, CA 91104 213-798-4067

Wycliffe Bible Translators, 19891 Beach Blvd., Huntington Beach, CA 92648 714-536-9346

Zondervan Bible Publishers, 1415 Lake Dr., S.E., Grand Rapids, MI 49506 616-698-6900; 800-253-1309 (order processing & customer service)

BOOK/MUSIC PUBLISHERS AND DISTRIBUTORS

Abingdon Press, P.O. Box 801, Nashville, TN 37202 615-749-6451 Toll Free for orders: 1-800-251-3320

Accent Books, P.O. Box 15337, Denver, CO 80215 303-988-5300; 800-525-5550

American Bible Society, 1865 Broadway, New York, NY 10023 212-581-7400

Augsburg Fortress Publishers, (Evang. Luth. Ch. in Am.), 426 S. Fifth St., P.O. Box 1209, Minneapolis, MN 55440 612-330-3300

Baker Book House Company, P.O. Box 6287, Grand Rapids, MI 49506 616-676-9185

Baptist Spanish Publishing House, (South. Bapt.), 7000 Alabama, P.O. Box 4255, El Paso, TX 79914-4255 915-566-9656

Barbour & Company, Inc., 164 Mill St., Westwood, NJ 07675 201-664-6460

Barclay Press, (Northwest Yearly Meeting of Friends), P.O. Box 232, Newberg, OR 97132 503-538-7345

B.B. Kirkbride Bible Co., P.O. Box 606 Indianapolis, IN 46206 317-634-3252; 800-428-4385

Beacon Hill Press of Kansas City, (Ch. of the Nazarene), P.O. Box 527, Kansas City, MO 64141 816-931-1900

Bethany House Publishers, (a div. of Bethany Fellow. Inc.), 6820 Auto Club Rd., Minneapolis, MN 55438 612-829-2258

Board for Media Ministries of the Brethren in Christ Church, 301-305 N. Elm St., P.O. Box 189, Nappanee, IN 46550-0189 219-773-3164

Brethren Press, (Ch. of the Breth.), 1451 Dundee Ave., Elgin, IL 60120 312-742-5100; 800-323-8039

Bridge Publishing, Inc., 2500 Hamilton Blvd., South Plainfield, NJ 07080 201-754-0745

Broadman Press, Inc., (South. Bapt.), 127 Ninth Ave., N., Nashville, TN 37234 615-251-2544; 800-251-3225; 800-342-0021 (Tenn.)

Brownlow Publishing Co., Inc., 6309 Airport Freeway, Fort Worth, TX 76117 817-831-3831

Canyonview Press, 12730 Finlay Rd. N.E., Silverton, OR 97381 503-873-8296

Cambridge University Press, 32 E. 57th St., New York, NY 10022 212-688-8885; 800-221-4512, ext. 413

CBP Press, (Christian Ch.), P.O. Box 179, St. Louis, MO 63166 314-371-6900; 800-351-2665; 800-451-2665 (Mo)

Childrens Press (Goldencraft), 5440 N. Cumberland Ave., Chicago, IL 60656 312-693-0800

Chosen Books Publishing Co., Ltd., c/o Fleming H. Revell Co., 184 Central Ave., Old Tappan, NJ 07675 201-768-8060

Christian Education Publishers, P.O. Box 2789, LaJolla, CA 92038 619-578-4700

Christian Library, (a div. of Barbour & Co. Inc.), 164 Mill St., Westwood, NJ 07675 201-664-6460

Christian Light Bookstores, (a div. of Brd. for Media Mins. of the Breth. in Christ Ch.), 301-305 N. Elm St.,

P.O. Box 189, Nappanee, IN 46550-0189 219-773-3164

Christian Publications, (C&MA), 3825 Hartzdale Dr., Camp Hill, PA 17011 717-761-7044; 800-233-4443

Churches Alive!, P.O. Box 3800, San Bernardino, CA 92413 714-886-5361

Concordia Publishing House, (Luth. Ch. Mo. Synod), 3558 S. Jefferson Ave., St. Louis, MO 63118 314-664-7000

C.R. Gibson Co., Knight St., Norwalk, CT 06856 203-847-4543

C.S.S. Publishing Company, 628 S. Main St., Lima, OH 45804 419-227-1818

David C. Cook Publishing Co., 850 N. Grove Ave., Elgin, IL 60120 312-741-2400

Doubleday-Galilee, 245 Park Ave., New York, NY 10167 212-984-7235

Evangel Press, (a div. of Brd. for Media Mins. of the Breth. in Christ Ch.), 301-305 N. Elm St., P.O. Box 189, Nappanee, IN 46550-0189 219-773-3164

Evangel Publishing House, (a div. of Brd. for Media Mins. of the Breth. in Christ Ch.), 301-305 N. Elm St., P.O. Box 189, Nappanee, IN 46550-0189 219-773-3164

Evangelical Christian Publishers Association, 950 W. Southern Ave., Ste. 102, Tempe, AZ 85282 602-966-3998

Fleming H. Revell Co., 184 Central Ave., Old Tappan, NJ 07675 201-768-8060

Fortress Press, 2900 Queen Ln., Philadelphia, PA 19129 215-848-6800

Friends Book Store, (Evang. Friends Ch., Eastern Region), 145 S. Broadway, Salem, OH 44460 800-537-0269 (for orders)

Good News Publishers/Crossway Books, 9825 W. Roosevelt Rd., Westchester, IL 60153 312-345-7474

Gospel Light Publications, P.O. Box 3875, Ventura, CA 93006 805-644-9721

Gospel Publishing House, (A/G), 1445 Boonville Ave., Springfield, MO 65802 417-862-2781

Green Leaf Press, P.O. Box 6880, Alhambra, CA 91802 818-289-4106

Harold Shaw Publishers, P.O. Box 567, 388 Gundersen Dr., Wheaton, IL 60189 312-665-6700; 800-SHAW-PUB

HarperSanFrancisco, 151 Union St., San Francisco, CA 94111 415-477-4400

Harvest House Publishers, Inc., 1075 Arrowsmith, Eugene, OR 97402 503-343-0123

Harvest Publications, (Bapt. Gen. Conf.), 2002 S. Arlington Hgts. Rd., Arlington Heights, IL 60005 312-228-0200

Herald Press, (Menn.), 616 Walnut Ave., Scottdale, PA 15683 412-887-8500

Here's Life Publishers, Inc., P.O. Box 1576, San Bernardino, CA 92402 714-886-7981

Holman Bible Publishers, 127 Ninth Ave., N., Nashville, TN 37234 615-251-2510; 800-251-3225

International Bible Publishing Co., Inc., P.O. Box 814091, Dallas, TX 75381 214-620-9190

InterVarsity Press, P.O. Box 1400, Downers Grove, IL 60515 312-964-5700

Judson Press, P.O. Box 851, Valley Forge, PA 19482 215-768-2123

Keats Publishing Co., P.O. Box 876, New Canaan, CT 06840 203-966-8721

Kindred Press, 4-168 Riverton Ave., Winnipeg, Manitoba R2L 2E5, Canada

Kregel "Out of Print" Bookstore, (nondenom. Christian Bookstores),

525 Eastern Ave., S.E., Grand Rapids, MI 49503 616-459-9444

Kregel Publications, (nondenom.), P.O. Box 2607, Grand Rapids, MI 49501 616-451-4775

Leadership Dynamics, Intl., (church training curriculum), 6666 Powers Ferry Rd., Ste. 120, Atlanta, GA 30339 404-980-0626; 800-843-1262

Living Word Curriculum, (Gospel Light Publications), P.O. Box 3875, Ventura, CA 93006 805-644-9721

Loizeaux Brothers, Inc., P.O. Box 277, Neptune, NJ 07753 201-774-8144

Master Book Publishers, 10946 Woodside Ave. N., Santee, CA 92071 619-448-1121

Meriwether Publishing, Ltd./Contemporary Drama Service, (interdenom. publisher), P.O. Box 7710, Colorado Springs, CO 80933 719-594-4422

Moody Press, 820 N. LaSalle Dr., Chicago, IL 60610 312-508-6850

Mott Media, 1000 E. Huron St., Milford, MI 48042 313-685-8773

Multnomah Press, 10209 S.E. Division St., Portland,OR 97266 503-257-0526

NavPress, (The Navigators), P.O. Box 6000, Colorado Springs, CO 80934 719-598-1212; 800-366-7788

Nazarene Publishing House, (Ch. of the Nazarene), 2923 Troost Ave., Kansas City, MO 64109; P.O. Box 419527, Kansas City, MO 64141 816-931-1900

North American Liturgy Resources, (music book/hymnal publishers), 10802 N. 23rd Ave., Phoenix, AZ 85029 602-864-1980; 800-528-6043

OMF Books, (publishers & distributors of books on mission work in East Asia), 404 S. Church St., Robesonia, PA 19551 215-693-5881

Omega Publications, P.O. Box 4130, Medford, OR 97501 503-826-9279

Oxford University Press, 200 Madison Ave., New York, NY 10016 212-679-7300

Paideia Press Ltd., P.O. Box 770, Lewiston, NY 14092

Paraclete Press, P.O. Box 1568, Orleans, MA 02653 617-255-4685

Pentecostal Publishing House, (United Pent. Ch.), 8855 Dunn Rd., Hazelwood, MO 63042 314-837-7300

Presbyterian Publishing House, (Pres. Ch./U.S.A.), 341 Ponce de Leon Ave., N.E., Atlanta, GA 30365 404-873-1549

Presbyterian & Reformed Publishing Co., P.O. Box 817, Phillipsburg, NJ 08865 201-454-0505

Regal Books, (Gospel Light Publications) P.O. Box 3875, Ventura, CA 93006 805-644-9721

Roper Press, Inc., 915 Dragon St., Dallas, TX 75207 214-742-6696; 800-331-2502

Rushwin Publishing (BMI), (Gibson Davidsong Publishing [ASCAP]), (music publisher); contact: James Gibson, manager, P.O. Box 1150, Buna, TX 77612 409-423-2521

Scripture Press Publications Inc. 1825 College Ave., Wheaton, IL 60187 312-668-6000

Servant Publications P.O. Box 8617, 840 Airport Blvd., Ann Arbor, MI 48107 313-761-8505

Standard Publishing Co., 8121 Hamilton Ave., Cincinnati, OH 45231 513-931-4050; 800-543-1353; 800-582-1385 (Ohio)

Thom Schultz Publications Inc., (The Youth Ministry Publisher) P.O. Box 481, 2890 N. Monroe Ave. Loveland, CO 80539 303-669-3836

Thomas Nelson Publishers, P.O. Box 141000, Nashville, TN 37214 615-889-9000

Troika Ministries, 6927 N.W. 78th St., Kansas City, MO 64152

Tyndale House Publishers, Inc., 336 Gundersen Dr., P.O. Box 80, Wheaton, IL 60189 312-668-8300; 800-243-1839; 800-323-9400 (orders only)

Upper Room, P.O. Box 189, Nashville, TN 37202-0189 615-340-7200

Victor Books, P.O. Box 1825, Wheaton, IL 60189 312-668-6000

Warner Press, Inc., P.O. Box 2499, Anderson, IN 46018 317-644-7721; 800-428-6427

Westminster Press/John Knox Press, (Pres. Ch./U.S.A.), 925 Chestnut St., Philadelphia, PA 19107 215-928-2700; 800-523-1631

Whitaker House, Pittsburgh and Colfax Sts., Springdale, PA 15144 412-274-4440

Wm. B. Eerdmans Publishing Co., 255 Jefferson Ave. S.E., Grand Rapids, MI 49503 616-459-4591; 800-253-7521

Word, Inc., 5221 N. O'Connor Blvd., Ste. 1000, Irving, TX 75039 214-556-1900

Word Publishing, (a division of Word, Inc.), 5221 N. O'Connor Blvd., Ste. 1000, Irving, TX 75039 214-556-1900

Worthy Publishing, 3934 Sandshell, Fort Worth, TX 76137 817-232-3166; 800-527-5489

Zondervan Corporation, 1415 Lake Dr., S.E., Grand Rapids MI 49506 616-698-6900

MAGAZINE AND MISCELLANEOUS PUBLISHING ORGANIZATIONS

American Tract Society, 1624 N. First St., Garland, TX 75040 214-276-9408

Evangelical Press Association, P.O. Box 4550, Overland Park, KS 66204 913-381-2017

Since its formation in 1949, the Evangelical Press Association has sought to enhance the professional stature and spiritual influence of Christian journalism. Members are asked to subscribe to a seven-point doctrinal statement which is NAE's own statement of faith. To be listed in *National Evangelical Directory* under the Evangelical Press Association a publication is produced by a member of EPA, a member of NAE, or an NAE member denomination.

Faith Prayer & Tract League, 2627 Elmridge Dr. N.W. 49504, Grand Rapids, MI 616-453-7695

God and Country Creations, Dept. 272, P.O. Box 22555, Tempe, AZ 85282 602-967-6209

Good News, Forum for Scriptural Christianity, 308 E. Main St., P.O. Box 150, Wilmore, KY 40390 606-858-4661; 800-451-READ (for ordering subscriptions & books)

Manuscriptures, Inc., 336 E. Forest Ave., Wheaton, IL 60187 312-668-1293

Publishing Directions, Inc., (magazines, newsletters, brochures, annual reports, publishing consulting), 1223 Potomac St., N.W., Washington, D.C. 20007 202-337-0800

Actionline, P.O. Box 203, Prospect Hts. IL 60070-0203 312-870-3800

Adult Focus, (Randall House Publications), P.O. Box 17306, Nashville, TN 37217 615-361-1221

Advance, (General Council of A/G), 1445 Boonville Ave., Springfield, MO 65802 417-862-2781

Advent Christian Witness, (Adv. Christian Gen. Conf.) P.O. Box 23152, Charlotte, NC 28212 704-545-6161

Advocate, (Chs. of Christ in Christian Union), P.O. Box 30, Circleville, OH 43113 614-474-8856

Again, (Antiochian Orthodox Archdiocese), P.O. Box 106, Mt. Hermon, CA 95041 408-338-3644

Aglow, Box 1, Lynnwood, WA 98046-1557 206-775-7282

Alliance Life, (C&MA), 350 N. Highland, Nyack, NY 10960-1497 914-353-0750

APU Life, (Azusa Pacific University), P.O. Box APU, APU, Citrus & Alosta, Azusa, CA 91702-7000 818-969-3434

Asbury Herald, The, (Asbury Theological Seminary), 204 N. Lexington Ave. Wilmore, KY 40390-1199 606-858-3581

Associate Reformed Presbyterian, The, (Assoc. Ref. Pres. Ch.), 1 Cleveland St., Greenville, SC 29601 803-232-8297

Atlantic Baptist, (Atlantic Bapt. Conv.), P.O. Box 756, Kentville, Nova Scotia B4N 3X9, Canada 902-678-6868

Australian Evangel, (A/G in Australia), P.O. Box 95, St. Agnes, S. Australia 5097 Phone: 6-8-336-5005

Banner, The, (Christian Reformed Ch. Publications), 2850 Kalamazoo Ave., S.E. Grand Rapids, MI 49560 616-246-0732

Baptist Herald, (N. Am. Bapt. Inc.), 1 S. 210 Summit Ave. Oakbrook Terrace, IL 60181 312-495-2000

Berean Statesman, (Berean League), 2875 Snelling Ave. N., St. Paul, MN 55113 612-633-0654

Between Times, (Warner Press, Inc.) P.O. Box 2499, Anderson, IN 46018 317-644-7721

Beyond, (JAARS), P.O. Box 248, Waxhaw, NC 28173 704-843-6000

Bible-in-Life-Friends, (David C. Cook Pub. Co.), 850 N. Grove Ave.,

Elgin, IL 60120 312-741-0800 ext. 422

Bible-in-Life-Pix, (David C. Cook Pub. Co.), 850 N. Grove Ave., Elgin, IL 60120 312-741-0800 ext. 422

Bibles for the World News, (Bibles for the World, Inc.), P.O. Box 805, Wheaton, IL 60189 312-668-7733

Bread, (Nazarene Publishing House), 6401 The Paseo, Kansas City, MO 64131 816-333-7000

Breakthrough, (Slavic Gospel Assoc.), P.O. Box 1122, Wheaton, IL 60189 312-690-8900

Brethren Evangelist, The, (Breth. Publishing House), 524 College Ave., Ashland, OH 44805 419-289-1708

Bridegroom's Messenger, The, (Intl. Pent. Ch. of Christ), Box 439, London, OH 43140 614-852-0348

Bridgebuilder, (Evangel Temple, Inc.), 610 Rhode Island Ave., N.E., Washington, D.C. 20002-1292 202-269-2082

Build, (Evang. Menn. Ch.), 1420 Kerrway Ct., Ft. Wayne, IN 46805 219-423-3649

Bulletin, (Church of God Intl. Offices), P.O. Box 2430, Cleveland, TN 37320 615-472-3361

Businessgram, P.O. Box 21, Bowling Green, OH 43402 419-352-8483

Call to Prayer, (World Gospel Mission) P.O. Box WGM, Marion, IN 46952-0948 317-664-7331

Called Out, (Div. of Christian Fellow. of Columbia), 4600 Christian Fellowship Rd., Columbia, MO 65203 314-445-8567

Campus Life, (Christianity Today, Inc.), 465 Gundersen Dr., Carol Stream, IL 60188 312-668-2477

CBMC Contact, (Christian Business Men's Committee of USA), P.O. Box 3308, Chattanooga, TN 37404 615-698-4444

Channels, (Renewal Fellow. within the Pres. Ch. in Canada), c/o 2130 Wesbrook Mall, Vancouver, British Columbia V6T 1W6, Canada 604-224-3245

Charisma, (Stephen Strang), 190 N. Westmonte Dr., Altamonte Springs, FL 32730 305-869-5005

Chosen People, The, (Chosen People Ministries), 1300 Cross Beam Dr., Charlotte, NC 28217-2800 704-357-9000

Christ for the Nations, (Christ for the Nations), P.O. Box 769000, Dallas, TX 75376-9000 214-376-1711

Christian Cause, The, (Great Commission Inc.), P.O. Box 1300, Laurel, MD 20707 301-725-5914

Christian Contender, The, (Christian Chamber of Commerce), P.O. Box 840555, Houston, TX 77284 713-855-3357

Christian Education Journal, (Scripture Press Ministries), P.O. Box 513, Glen Ellyn, IL 60138 312-668-6000

Christian Education Today, (Jerry A. Wilke), P.O. Box 15337, Denver, CO 80215 303-988-5300

Christian Educators Journal, Dan Diephouse, sec., 12322 S. 69th Ct., Palos Heights, IL 60463

Christian Essence, (Christian Resource Center of Washington), P.O. Box 62, Ferndale, WA 98248 206-671-1871

Christian Herald (Christian Herald Assoc.), 40 Overlook Dr., Chappaqua, NY 10514 914-769-9000

Christian History Magazine, (Christian History Inst.), P.O. Box 540, Worcester, PA 19490 215-584-1893

Christian Home and School, (Christian Schools Intl.), 3350 East Paris Ave., S.E., Grand Rapids, MI 49508 616-957-1070

Christian Leader, The, (Menn. Breth. Ch. USA), P.O. Box L, Hillsboro, KS 67063 316-947-3966

Christian Living for Senior Highs, (David C. Cook Pub. Co.), 850 N. Grove Ave., Elgin, IL 60120 312-741-2400

Christian Management Report, (Christian Ministries Management Assoc.), P.O. Box 4638, Diamond Bar, CA 91765 714-861-8861

Christian Management Review, (J. Alan Youngren), 1243 Hawthorne Ln., Downers Grove, IL 60515 312-969-8584

Christian Medical & Dental Society Journal, P.O. Box 830689, Richardson, TX 75083-0689 214-783-8384

Christian Mission, (Christian Aid), Rt. 10, Box 1, Charlottesville, VA 22901 804-977-5650

Christian Newspaper, The, (James Beeler/Ed Neely Management), 136 Twenty-Third St., Knoxville, TN 37916 615-637-0673

Christian Observer, The, (The Christian Observer Inc.), 9400 Fairview Ave., Ste. 200, Manassas, VA 22110 703-335-2844

Christian Psychology for Today, (Minirth-Meier Clinic), 2100 N. Collins, Richardson, TX 75080 214-669-1733

Christian Reader, The (Tyndale House Publishers Inc.), P.O. Box 220, Wheaton, IL 60189 312-668-8300

Christian Research Journal, (CRI), P.O. Box 500, San Juan Capistrano, CA 92693 714-855-9926

Christian School, (LS Publishers), 1308 Santa Rosa, Wheaton, IL 60187 312-653-4588

Christian Standard, (Standard Publishing) (Chs. of Christ in Christian Union), 8121 Hamilton Ave., Cincinnati, OH 45231 513-931-4050

Christian Union Witness, (Christian Union), 106 W. Broadway, P.O. Box 397, Excelsior Springs, MO 64024 816-637-4668

Christianity Today, (Christianity Today, Inc.), 465 Gundersen Dr., Carol Stream, IL 60188 312-260-6200

Christians in Photojournalism, (Gary Fong), 1610 35th St., Sacramento, CA 95816 916-455-5429

II Chronicles Magazine, (Mack Lloyd Lewis), 228 E. Main, Stes. 3 & 4, Medford, OR 97501 503-779-4704

Church Advocate, The, (Chs. of God, Gen. Conf.), P.O. Box 926, Findlay, OH 45839 419-424-1961

Church Herald, The, (The Church Herald, Inc., Ref. Ch. Am.), 6157 28th St. S.E., Grand Rapids, MI 49506-6999 616-957-1351

Church Herald and Holiness Banner, The, (Herald & Banner Press), P.O. Box 4060, Overland Park, KS 66204 913-432-0331

Church of God Evangel, (Ch. of God), 1080 Montgomery Ave., Cleveland, TN 37311 615-476-4512

Church of God Missions, (Missions Education), P.O. Box 2337, Anderson, IN 46018-2337 317-649-7597

Closer Walk, (Walk Thru the Bible Ministries, Inc.), P.O. Box 80587, Atlanta, GA 30366 404-458-9300

Co-Laborer, (Woman's National Auxiliary Conv.), P.O. Box 1088, Nashville, TN 37202 615-361-1010

Command, (Officer's Christian Fellow.), P.O. Box 1177, Englewood, CO 80150 303-761-1987

Commonlife, (Alliance for Renewal), Rt. 10, Woodville Rd., Mansfield, OH 44903 419-526-4699

Communicator, (Western Cons. Bapt. Sem.), 5511 S.E. Hawthorne Blvd. Portland, OR 97220 503-233-8561

Compassion Update, (Compassion Intl.), 3955 Cragwood Dr., P.O. Box 7000, Colorado Springs, CO 80903 303-594-9900

Confident Living, (Good News Broadcasting Assoc.), 301 South 12th, Lincoln, NE 68501 402-474-4567

Connection, The, (Dove Christian Fellow.), R.D. 4 Box 149E, Lititz, PA 17543 717-627-6000

Connections, (Biola University), Biola University, 13800 Biola Ave., La Mirada, CA 90639 213-944-0351

Conservative Baptist, (Cons. Bapt. Assoc. of Am.), P.O. Box 66, Wheaton, IL 60189 312-653-5350

Contact, (National Assoc. of Free Will Bapt.) P.O. Box 1088, Nashville, TN 37202 615-361-1010

Conviction, (Fellowship Press) 4909 East Buckeye Rd., Madison, WI 53716 608-221-1528

Cornerstone, (Jesus People USA), 4747 N. Malden, Chicago, IL 60640 312-561-2450

Counselor, (Scripture Press), P.O. Box 632, Glen Ellyn, IL 60138 312-668-6000

Covenant Companion, The, (The Evan. Cov. Ch.), 5101 N. Francisco Ave., Chicago, IL 60625 312-784-3000

Covenanter Witness, (Ref. Pres. Ch. of N. Am.), 7418 Penn Ave., Pittsburgh, PA 15208 412-241-0436

Crusade News, (World Gospel Crusades), P.O. Box 3, Upland, CA 91785 714-982-1564

Crusader, (Calvinist Cadet Corps), P.O. Box 7529, Grand Rapids, MI 49507 616-241-5616

Crux, (Regent College), 2130 Wesbrook Mall, Vancouver, British Columbia V6T 1W6, Canada 604-224-3245

Daily Walk, The, (Walk Thru the Bible Ministries, Inc.), P.O. Box 80587, Atlanta, GA 30366 404-458-9300

Dallas Insider, (Dallas Theo. Sem.), 3909 Swiss Ave., Dallas, TX 75204 214-824-3094

Decision, (Billy Graham Evang. Assoc.), 1300 Harmon Pl., Minneapolis, MN 55403 612-338-0500

271

Design, (The Wesleyan Ch.), P.O. Box 50434, Indianapolis, IN 46250 317-842-0444

Discipleship Journal, (The Navigators), P.O. Box 6000, Colorado Springs, CO 80934 719-598-1212

Discovery Digest, (Radio Bible Class), P.O. Box 22, Grand Rapids, MI 49555 616-942-6770

Door of Hope, P.O. Box 10460, Glendale, CA 91209 818-956-7500

Doorways, P.O. Box C, Colorado Springs, CO 80901 719-576-2700

Elim Bell Tower, (Elim Fellow.), 7245 College St., Lima, NY 14485 716-582-2790

Elmbrook, (Elmbrook Church), 777 S. Barker Rd., Waukesha, WI 53186 414-786-7051

EMC Today, (Evangelical Menn. Ch.), 1420 Kerrway Ct., Ft. Wayne, IN 46805 219-423-3649

Emphasis on Faith and Living (Missionary Ch.), 3901 S. Wayne Ave., Fort Wayne, IN 46801 219-456-4502

End Times Messenger, (Apostolic Ch. of Pent.), 85 E. 10th Ave., Vancouver, British Columbia V5T 1Y9, Canada 604-874-1817

EPC Reporter, (Evang. Pres. Ch.), 26049 Five Mile Rd., Detroit, MI 48239 313-532-9555

EP News Service, (Official weekly news service of EPA), 1619 Portland Ave. S., Minneapolis, MN 55404 612-339-9579

Equipping the Saints, (Vineyard Ministries Intl.), P.O. Box 65004, Anaheim, CA 92805 714-533-9281

Eurovision Advance, P.O. Box 1136, Claremont, CA 91711-1136 714-621-1070

Evangel, (Free Meth. Dept. of C.E.), 901 College Ave., Winona Lake, IN 46590 219-267-7656

Evangelical Baptist Herald, (Russian-Ukranian Evang. Bapt. Union, U.S.A.), P.O. Box 1743, Union, NJ 07083 201-964-4784

Evangelical Beacon, (Evang. Free Ch. of Am.), 1515 E. 66th St., Minneapolis, MN 55423 612-866-3343

Evangelical Friend, (Evang. Friends Al.), P.O. Box 232 Newburg, OR 97132 503-538-7345

Evangelical Missions Quarterly, (Evang. Missions Infor. Service), P.O. Box 794, Wheaton, IL 60189 312-653-2158

Evangelical Visitor, (Breth.in Christ Ch.), P.O. Box 166, 301 N. Elm St., Nappanee, IN 46550 219-773-3164

Evangelical World, (WORLD EVANGELICAL FELLOWSHIP), P.O. Box WEF, Wheaton, IL 60189-8003 312-668-0440

Evangelicals Today, The, (Philippine Council of Evang. Chs.), Box 10121, Quezon City (Main), Philippines 3008; Phone: 922-98-22

Evangelizing Today's Child, (Child Evangelism Fellow., Inc.), P.O. Box 348, Warrenton, MO 63383 314-456-4321

Faith Today, (Evang. Fellow. of Canada), P.O. Box 8800, Station B, Willowdale, Ontario M2K 2R6, Canada 416-479-5885

Family Walk, (Walk Thru the Bible Ministries, Inc.), P.O. Box 80587, Atlanta, GA 30366 404-458-9300

FEBC News, (Far East Broadcasting Co.), P.O. Box 1, La Mirada, CA 90637 213-947-4651

Focus, (Nazarene Publishing House), 6401 The Paseo, Kansas City, MO 64131 816-333-7000

Focus, CBN University, Virginia Beach, VA 23464 804-424-7000

Focus on the Family, (Focus on the Family, Inc.), 801 Corporate Center Dr., Pomona, CA 91768 714-620-8500

Focus on the Family Clubhouse, (Focus on the Family, Inc.), 801 Corporate Center Dr., Pomona, CA 91768 714-620-8500

Focus on the Family Clubhouse, Jr., (Focus on the Family, Inc.), 801 Corporate Center Dr., Pomona, CA 91768 714-620-8500

Food for the Hungry, (Food for the Hungry), P.O. Box E, Scottsdale, AZ 85252 602-998-3100

Footprints, (Morris Cerullo World Evangelism), P.O. Box 700, San Diego, CA 92138 619-239-4300 ext. 261

Foresee, (Conserv. Cong. Christian Conf.), 7582 Currell Blvd., Suite 108, St. Paul, MN 55125 612-739-1474

Foursquare World Advance, (Intl. Ch. of the Foursq. Gospel), 1100 Glendale Blvd., Los Angeles, CA 90026 213-484-1100

Freeway, (Scripture Press), P.O. Box 632, Glen Ellyn, IL 60138 312-668-6000

Fulness Magazine, 120 McLeroy, Saginaw, TX 76179 817-232-9171

Fundamentalist Journal, (Old Time Gospel Hour), 2220 Langhorne Rd., Lynchburg, VA 24514 804-528-4112

Gem, The, (Chrs. of God, Gen. Conf.), P.O. Box 926, Findlay, OH 45839 419-424-1961

GEM's Europe Report, (Greater Europe Mission), P.O. Box 668, Wheaton, IL 60189 312-462-8050

General Baptist Messenger, (Gen. Assoc. of Gen. Bapts.), 100 Stinson Dr., Poplar Bluff, MO 63901 314-285-7746

Good News, (Forum for Scriptural Christianity, Inc.), 308 E. Main St., P.O. Box 150, Wilmore, KY 40390 606-858-4661; 800-451-READ (for ordering subscriptions & books)

Gospel Herald, (Ch. of God of the Mountain Assembly), P.O. Box 157, Jellico, TN 37762 615-784-8260

Gospel Message, The, (GMU), 10000 North Oak, Kansas City, MO 64155 816-734-8500

Gospel Tidings, (Fellow. of Evang. Bible Chs.), 5800 S. 14th St., Omaha, NE 68107-3598 402-731-4780

Grace Chronicle, The, (Grace World Outreach Ch.), 2695 Creve Coeur Mill Rd., Maryland Heights, MO 63043 314-291-6647

Grace Tidings, (Grace College of the Bible), 1515 South 10th St., Omaha, NE 68108 402-449-2828

Grace Today, (Grace Community Ch.), 13248 Roscoe Blvd., Sun Valley, CA 91352 818-909-5771

Group Magazine, (Thom Schultz Publications, Inc.), P.O. Box 481, 2890 N. Monroe Ave., Loveland, CO 80539 303-669-3836

Happenings, (Free Will Bapt. Board of Retirement), P.O. Box 1088, Nashville, TN 37202 615-361-1010

Harvestnews, (Grace Breth. Home Missions), P.O. Box 587, Winona Lake, IN 46590 219-267-5161

Heartbeat, (Nat'l Assoc. Free Will Bapt.), P.O. Box 1088, Nashville, TN 37202 615-361-1010

Helping Hand, The, (Pent. Holiness Women's Ministries), P.O. Box 12609, Oklahoma City, OK 73157 405-787-7110

Herald of Holiness, (Ch. of the Nazarene), 6401 The Paseo, Kansas City, MO 64131 816-333-7000

High Adventure, (A/G Royal Rangers), 1445 Boonville Ave., Springfield, MO 65802 417-862-2781 ext. 4181

Horizon International Magazine, P.O. Box 17480, San Diego, CA 92117 619-268-2948

IL Faro, (Christian Ch. of N. Am.), Box 141A, R.D. 1, Transfer, PA 16154-9005 412-962-3501

Illustrated Bible Life, (Ch. of the Nazarene), 6401 The Paseo, Kansas City, MO 64131 816-333-7000

Image, 115 Warren Dr., Ste. D., West Monroe, LA 71291 318-396-4366

Impact, (Cons. Bapt. Foreign Miss. Soc.), P.O. Box 5, Wheaton, IL 60189 312-665-1200

Impact, 12-B East Coast Rd., Singapore 1542, Republic of Singapore Phone: 345-0444

In Other Words, (Wycliffe Bible Translators), 19897 Beach Blvd., Huntington Beach, CA 92638 714-536-9346

In Touch, (Wesley Press), P.O. Box 50434, Indianapolis, IN 46250 317-674-3301

Increase Magazine, (Bible Christian Union), P.O. Box 410, Hatfield, PA 19440 215-361-0500

India Journal, (The Bible League) 4221 Richmond N.W., Grand Rapids, MI 49504 616-453-8855

Indian Life, (Intertribal Christian Comm.), P.O. Box 3765, Station B, Winnipeg, Manitoba R2W 3R6, Canada 204-661-9333

Inside the Mission, (Young Life), P.O. Box 520, Colorado Springs, CO 80901 719-473-4262

Insight, (Advent Christian Gen. Conf.), P.O. Box 23152, Charlotte, NC 28212 704-545-6161

Insight, (Seventh-day Adventist Ch.), 55 W. Oak Ridge Dr., Hagerstown, MD 21740 301-791-7000

Interest, (Letters of Interest), 218 W. Willow, Wheaton, IL 60187 312-653-6573

Interlit, (David C. Cook Found.), Cook Square, Elgin, IL 60120 312-741-2400

International Faith Report, 3840 S. 103 E. Ave., Ste. 132, Tulsa, OK 74146 918-665-2773

International Journal of Frontier Missions, (Intl. Student Leaders Coalition for Frontier Missions), P.O. Box 40638, Pasadena, CA 91104 818-398-2323

International Pentecostal Holiness Advocate, (Intl. Pent. Hol. Ch.), P.O. Box 12609, Oklahoma City, OK 73157 405-787-7110

InterVarsity, 6400 Schroeder Rd., Box 7895, Madison, WI 53707-7895 608-274-9001

Journal of Christian Camping, (Christian Camping Intl.), P.O. Box 646, Wheaton, IL 60189 312-462-0300

Journal of Christian Nursing, (InterVarsity Christian Fellow.), P.O. Box 1650, Downers Grove, IL 60515 312-964-4809

Joyful Woman, The, (Joyful Christian Ministries), 118 Shannon Lake Circle, Greenville, SC 29615 803-297-1625

Jubilee, (Prison Fellow. Ministries), P.O. Box 17152, Washington, DC 20041 703-478-0100

Jubilee International, (Prison Fellowship Intl.), P.O. Box 17434, Washington, DC 20041 703-481-0000

Kindred Spirit, (Dallas Theo. Sem.), 3909 Swiss Ave., Dallas, TX 75204 214-824-3094

Latin America Evangelist, (Latin America Mission), P.O. Box 52-7900, Miami, FL 33152-7900 305-884-8400

Leadership, (Christianity Today, Inc.), 465 Gundersen Dr., Carol Stream, IL 60188 312-260-6200

Leaves of Healing, (Christian Catholic Ch., Evang. Prot.), Dowie Memorial Dr., Zion, IL 60099 312-746-1411

Librarian's World, (Evang. Ch. Library Assoc.), P.O. Box 353, Glen Ellyn, IL 60138-0353 312-668-0519

Lifechangers, (Bob Mumford), 50 Mitchell Blvd., San Rafael, CA 94913 415-499-8314

Lifeline, (Union Rescue Mission), P.O. Box 629, Los Angeles, CA 90053-9983 213-628-6103

Light and Life, (Free Meth. Ch. of N.A.), 901 College Ave., Winona Lake, IN 46590 219-267-7656

Lighted Pathway, (Pathway Press), 1080 Montgomery Ave., Cleveland, TN 37311 615-476-4512

Live, (Gospel Publishing House, A/G), 1445 Boonville Ave., Springfield, MO 65802 417-862-2781

LPEA Heartbeat, (Luis Palau Evangelistic Assoc.), P.O. Box 1173, Portland, OR 97207 503-643-0777

Luke Society News, The, (Luke Society, Inc.), 1121 Grove St., Vicksburg, MS 39180 601-638-1629

Lutherans Alert, (Conserv. Luth. Assoc.), P.O. Box 7186, Tacoma, WA 98407 206-383-5653

Magazine for Christian Youth!, The, (The United Meth. Pub. House), P.O. Box 801, Nashville, TN 37202 615-749-6463

MAP International Report, (MAP Intl.), 2200 Glynco Pkwy., Brunswick, GA 31520 912-265-6010

Maranatha, (Maranatha Assembly of God), P.O. Box 936, Newark, NJ 07101 201-589-3830

Maranatha Manna, (WOLC Radio), P.O. Box 528, Berlin, MD 21811 301-641-3953

Marketplace, The, (Menn. Economic Development Associates), 402-280 Smith St., Winnipeg, Manitoba, R3C 1K2, Canada 204-944-1995

Marriage Partnership, The, (Christianity Today, Inc.), 465 Gundersen Dr., Carol Stream, IL 60188 312-260-6200

Media Update, (Menconi Ministries), P.O. Box 306, Cardiff, CA 92007 619-436-8676

Memos, (Gospel Publishing House A/G), 1445 Boonville Ave., Springfield, MO 65802 417-862-2781

Mennonite, The, (Gen. Conf. Menn. Ch.), P.O. Box 347, Newton, KS 67114 316-283-5100

Mennonite Brethren Herald, (Menn. Breth. Ch. of Canada) 3-169 Riverton Ave., Winnipeg, Manitoba R2L 2E5, Canada 204-669-6575

Message, (Multnomah School of the Bible) 8435 N.E. Glisan St., Portland, OR 97220 503-255-0332

Message of the Cross, The, (Bethany Fellow.), 6820 Auto Club Rd., Minneapolis, MN 55438 612-944-2121

Message of the Open Bible, (Open Bible Stan. Chs.), 2020 Bell Ave., Des Moines, IA 50315-1096 515-288-6761

Messenger, (Pent. Free Will Bapt. Ch.), P.O. Box 1568, Dunn, NC 28334 919-892-4161

Ministries Today, (Strang Comm.Co.), 190 N. Westmonte Dr., Altamonte Springs, FL 32714 305-869-5005

Miracle Living Magazine, P.O. Box 5640-14240, Glendale, AZ 85312 602-978-5511

Mission America Newsletter, (General Council of A/G), 1445 Boonville Ave., Springfield, MO 65802 417-862-2781 ext. 3264

Mission Frontiers, (U.S. Center for World Mission), 1605 Elizabeth St., Pasadena, CA 91104 818-797-1111

Missionary Monthly, (Missionary Monthly Inc.), P.O. Box 6181, Grand Rapids, MI 49516-6181 616-235-7347

Missionary Tidings, The, (Women's Missionary Fellow. Intl., Free Meth. Ch.), 901 College Ave., Winona Lake, IN 46590 219-267-7657

Moments With God, (N. Am. Bapt. Conf.), 1 South 210 Summit Ave., Oakbrook Terrace, IL 60181 213-495-2000

Moody Alumni Magazine, (Moody Bible Institute), 820 N. LaSalle Dr., Chicago, IL 60610 312-329-4412

Moody Monthly, (Moody Bible Institute), 2101 W. Howard St., Chicago, IL 60645 312-508-6820

Mountain Movers, (A/G), 1445 Boonville Ave., Springfield, MO 65802 417-862-2781

NAE Washington Insight, (NATIONAL ASSOCIATION OF EVANGELICALS), 1023 15th St., N.W., Ste. 500 Washington, DC 20005 202-789-1011

National & International Religion Report, Wike Associates, Inc., P.O. Box 21433, Roanoke, VA 24018 703-989-1330

Native Reflections, (Wesleyan Indian Ministries), P.O. Box 891, Hot Springs, SD 57747 605-745-4077

Navlog, The, (The Navigators), P.O. Box 6000, Colorado Springs, CO 80934 303-598-1212

Neighbourly Good News, (Creative Christian Comm., Inc.), 28 Arthur St. South, Ste. 201, Elmira, Ontario N3B 2M5, Canada 519-669-8180

New England Church Life, (Evangelistic Assoc. of New England), 88 Tremont St., Ste. 600, Boston, MA 02108 617-523-3579

New Horizons in the Orthodox Presbyterian Church, (Orthodox Pres. Ch.), 7401 Old York Rd., Philadelphia, PA 19126 215-635-1131

News Network International (NNI) P.O. Box 28001, Santa Ana, CA 92799 714-775-4900; TELEX 910-593-1332; FAX 714-531-6228

Newswire, (Slavic Gospel Assoc.), P.O. Box 1122, Wheaton, IL 60189 312-690-8900

OMS Outreach, (OMS Intl. Inc.), P.O. Box A, Greenwood, IN 46142 317-881-6751

Open Doors News Brief & Magazine, (Open Doors), 16520 Harbor Blvd., Fountain Valley, CA 92706 714-531-6000

Open Letter, The, (Covenant Fellow. of Pres.), P.O. Box 8307, Chattanooga, TN 37411 615-855-0709

Other Side, The, (The Other Side), 300 W. Apsley St., Philadelphia, PA 19144 215-849-2178

Overcomer, The, (Open Bible Stan. Chs.), 2020 Bell Ave., Des Moines, IA 50315 515-288-6761

Overseas Council, (Overseas Council Team, Inc.), P.O. Box 751, Greenwood, IN 46142 317-882-4174

Overseas Crusades, (OC Ministries), 25 Corning Ave., Milpitas, CA 95035 408-263-1101

Overview, (Evangelical Ch. of N. Am.), 7525 SE Lake Rd., Ste. 7, Milwaukie, OR 97267 503-652-1029

Partners, P.O. Box 15025, San Jose, CA 95115-0025 408-298-0965

Partnership Update, (WORLD RELIEF OF NAE), P.O. Box WRC, Wheaton, IL 60189 312-665-0235

Pastoral Renewal, (Servant Ministries, Inc.), P.O. Box 8617, Ann Arbor, MI 48107 313-761-8505

PCA Messenger, The, (Pres. Ch. in Am.), 1852 Century Place, Ste. 101, Atlanta, GA 30345 404-320-3388

Pentecostal Evangel, (Gospel Publishing House, A/G), 1445 Boonville Ave., Springfield, MO 65802 417-862-2781

Pentecostal Holiness Advocate, (Intl. Pent. Hol. Ch.), P.O. Box 12609, Oklahoma City, OK 73157 405-787-7110

Pentecostal Messenger, The, (Pent. Ch. of God), P.O. Box 850, Joplin, MO 64802 417-624-7050

Pentecostal Minister, The, (Ch. of God Intl. Offices), P.O. Box 2430, Cleveland, TN 37320 615-472-3361

Pentecostal Testimony, The, (Pent. Assem. of Canada), 10 Overlea Blvd., Toronto, Ontario M4H 1A5, Canada 416-425-1010

People of Destiny Magazine, (People of Destiny Intl.), 7781-B Beechcraft Ave., Gaithersburg, MD 20879 301-948-4890

Perspective, (Pioneer Clubs), P.O. Box 788, Wheaton, IL 60189 312-293-1600

Perspectives, (Ref. Ch. Press), 6157 28th St. S.E., Grand Rapids, MI 49506-6999 616-957-1351

Perspectives on Science and Christian Faith, (American Scientific Affiliation), P.O. Box 668, Ipswich, MA 01938 617-356-5656

Plough, The, (Woodcrest Service Committee, Inc.), Hutterian Brethren, Ulster Park, NY 12487 914-339-6680

Plus, (Foundation for Christian Living), P.O. Box FCL, Pawling, NY 12564 914-855-5000

Possibilities, (Robert Schuller Ministries), 1223 Potomac St. N.W., Washington, DC 20007 202-337-0800

Power for Living, (Scripture Press Publications, Inc.), P.O. Box 632, Glen Ellyn, IL 60138 312-668-6000

Prayer Line, The, (Prayer by Mail Society, Inc.), P.O. Box 55146, Seattle, WA 98155 206-363-3586

Preacher's Magazine, The, (Nazarene Publishing House), 6401 The Paseo, Kansas City, MO 64131 816-333-7000

Primitive Methodist Journal, (Primitive Meth. Ch., USA), 40 E. Northampton St., Wilkes-Barre, PA 18702 717-823-4527

Promoter, The, (OK State Assoc. of Free Will Bapts.), P.O. Box 7527, Moore, OK 73153 405-799-8933

Psychology for Living, (Narramore Christian Found.), 1409 N. Walnut Grove Ave., Rosemead, CA 91770 818-288-7000

Quarterly, (Christian Legal Society), P.O. Box 1492, Merrifield, VA 22116 703-560-7314

Quiet Miracle, The, (Bible Lit. Intl.), 625 E. North Broadway, Columbus, OH 43214 614-267-3116

Quiet Revolution, A, (Voice of Calvary Ministries), P.O. Box 10562, Jackson, MS 39209 601-353-1635

Railroad Evangelist, The, (Railroad Evang. Assoc., Inc.), Rt. 4, Box 97, Spencer, IN 47460 812-829-4667

Rainbow Graphics, (Bethany Christian Services), 901 Eastern Ave. N.E., Grand Rapids, MI 49503 616-459-6273

Real Issue, The, (Campus Crusade for Christ), 14679 Midway, Ste. 100, Dallas, TX 75244 214-490-7770

Record, The, (The Christian Civic League of Maine), P.O. Box 5459, Augusta, ME 04330 207-622-7634

Reformed Journal, The, (Wm. B. Eerdmans Publishing Co.), 255 Jefferson St. S.E., Grand Rapids, MI 49503 616-459-4591

Reformed Worship, (CRC Publications), 2850 Kalamazoo S.E., Grand Rapids, MI 49560 616-246-0752

Resource, (Nazarene Publishing House), 6401 The Paseo, Kansas City, MO 64131 816-333-7000

Response, (Seattle Pacific University), 3307 Third Ave. W., Seattle, WA 98119 206-281-2051

Salt and Light, (Christian Career Women), 1523 Silver Strand Circle, Palatine, IL 60074 312-359-5073

Save Our World, (Ch. of God World Missions), P.O. Box 2430, Cleveland, TN 37320-2430 615-478-7200

Second Look Magazine, (Radio Bible Class), 290 North D St., Ste. 602, San Bernardino, CA 92401 714-885-2622

Sharing the Victory, (Fellow. of Christian Athletes), 8701 Leeds Rd., Kansas City, MO 64129 816-921-0909

SIM Now, (SIM Intl.), 10 Huntingdale Blvd., Scarborough, Ontario M1W 2S5, Canada 416-497-2424

Single Adult Ministries Journal, (Jerry D. Jones), P.O. Box 3010, Colorado Springs, CO 80934 303-549-6471

Sojourners, (Sojourners), P.O. Box 29272, Washington, DC 20017 202-636-3637

Sound the Lord's Trumpet, (Jim Fitzpatrick), P.O. Box 1495, Largo, FL 34649 813-581-8944

Spiritual Counterfeits Project Journal/Newsletter, P.O. Box 4308, Berkeley, CA 94704 415-540-0300

Spiritual Fitness in Business, (Probe Ministries Intl.), 1900 Firman Dr., Ste. 100, Richardson, TX 75081 214-480-0240

Sprint, (David C. Cook Pub. Co.), 850 N. Grove Ave., Elgin, IL 60120 312-741-2400

Standard, (Nazarene General Ch.), 6401 The Paseo, Kansas City, MO 64131 816-333-7000 ext. 344

Standard, The, (Bapt. Gen. Conf.), 2002 S. Arlington Heights Rd., Arlington Heights, IL 60005 312-228-0200

Student Venture News, 17150 Via Del Campo, Ste. 200, San Diego, CA 92127 619-487-2717

Sunday Digest, (David C. Cook Pub. Co.), 850 N. Grove Ave., Elgin, IL 60120 312-741-2400

Sunday School Counselor, (General Council of A/G), 1445 Boonville Ave., Springfield, MO 65802 417-862-2781

Swinging Bridge, The, (Messiah College Student Assoc.), Messiah College, P.O. Box 1313, Grantham, PA 17027 717-766-1800

Tabletalk, (Ligonier Ministries), 598 S. North Lake Blvd., Ste. 1008, Altamonte Springs, FL 32701 305-834-1633

TEAM Horizons, (The Evangelical Alliance Mission), 400 South Main Pl., Carol Stream, IL 60188; mailing:

P.O. Box 969, Wheaton, IL 60189 312-653-5300

Teen Missions Control, (Teen Missions Intl.), P.O. Box 542468, Merritt Island, FL 32952 305-453-0350

Teen Power, (Scripture Press Publications), P.O. Box 632 Glen Ellyn, IL 60138 312-668-6000

Teens Today, (Nazarene Publishing House), 6401 The Paseo, Kansas City, MO 64131 816-333-7000

The War Cry, (The Salvation Army), 799 Bloomfield Ave., Verona, NJ 07044 201-239-0606

Threefold Advocate, (John Brown University), John Brown University, Siloam Springs, AR 72761 501-524-3131

Today's Christian Woman, (Christianity Today, Inc.), 465 Gundersen Dr., Carol Stream, IL 60188 312-260-6200

Today's Man, (General Council of A/G), 1445 Boonville Ave., Springfield, MO 65802 417-862-2781 ext. 4176

Touch, (Calvinettes) P.O. Box 7259, Grand Rapids, MI 49510 616-241-5616

Touching, (WORLD RELIEF OF NAE), P.O. Box WRC, Wheaton, IL 60189 312-665-0235

TQ Magazine (Good News Broadcasting Assoc.), P.O. Box 82808, Lincoln, NE 68501 402-474-4567

Trim Tab, The, (Fellow. of Christian Airline Personnel), 136 Providence Rd., Fayetteville, GA 30214 404-461-9320

Twin Cities Christian, (Leonard and JoAnne Jankowski, 1619 Portland Ave. S., Minneapolis, MN 55404 612-339-9579

United Brethren, The, (Ch. of the United Breth. in Christ), 302 Lake St., Huntington, IN 46750 219-356-2312

United Evangelical, (Evang. Cong. Ch.), 100 W. Park Ave., Myerstown, PA 17067 717-866-7581

United Evangelical ACTION, (NATIONAL ASSOCIATION OF EVANGELICALS), P.O. Box 28, Wheaton, IL 60189 312-665-0500

Urban Mission, (Westminster Sem.), 7090 Eldred N.E., Rockford, MI 49341 616-246-0832

Venture Magazine, (Christian Service Brigade), P.O. Box 150, Wheaton, IL 60189 312-665-0630

Vineyard Newsletter, The, (Assoc. of Vineyard Chs.), P.O. Box 9590, Anaheim, CA 92802-9590 714-778-6757

Virtue, (Virtue Ministries), P.O. Box 850, Sisters, OR 97759 503-549-8261

Vision, (Young Calvinist Federation), P.O. Box 7259, Grand Rapids, MI 49510 616-241-5616

Vista, (Wesley Press), P.O. Box 50434, Indianapolis, IN 46250 317-576-8144

Vital Christianity, (Ch. of God, Anderson, Ind.), P.O. Box 2499, Anderson, IN 46018 317-644-7721

Voice, (Dordt College), Dordt College, Sioux Center, IA 51250 712-722-3771

Voice, (Full Gospel Business Men), 3150 Bear St., Costa Mesa, CA 92626 714-754-1400

Voice of Evangelical Methodism, (Evang. Meth. Ch.), 3000 W. Kellogg, Wichita, KS 67213 316-943-3278

Voice of Prophecy News, (The Voice of Proph.), P.O. Box 2525, 1100 Rancho Conejo Blvd., Newbury Park, CA 91320 805-373-7657

Voice of Renewal International, (Voice of Renewal Intl.), Box 1145, 7443 Frickenhausen, West Germany; Phone: 07022-49-700

Wesleyan Advocate, The, (The Wesleyan Ch.), P.O. Box 50434, Indianapolis, IN 46250-0434 317-576-1313

Wesleyan World, (Wesleyan Ch.), P.O. Box 50434, Indianapolis, IN 46250-0434 317-842-0444

Wheaton Alumni Magazine, (Wheaton Alumni Assoc.), Wheaton College, Wheaton, IL 60187 312-260-5025

Wherever, (The Evangelical Alliance Mission), 400 South Main Pl., Carol Stream, IL 60188; mailing: P.O. Box 969, Wheaton, IL 60189 312-653-5300

Wittenburg Door, The, (Youth Specialties), 1224 Greenfield Dr., El Cajon, CA 92021 619-440-2333

Woman's Touch, (General Council of A/G), 1445 Boonville Ave., Springfield, MO 65802 417-862-2781

Women Alive, (Daniel Hinthorn, M.D.), P.O. Box 4683, Overland Park, KS 66204 913-649-8583

Word and Way, (Mo. Bapt. Conv.), 400 E. High St., Jefferson City, MO 65101 314-635-7931

Word of Faith, The, (Kenneth Hagin Ministries), P.O. Box 50126, Tulsa, OK 74150-0126 918-258-1588

World, (God's World Publications), P.O. Box 2330, Asheville, NC 28802 704-253-8063

World Concern Loveline, (World Concern), 19303 Fremont Ave. N., Seattle, WA 98133 206-546-7287

World Harvest, (Lester Sumrall), P.O. Box 12, South Bend, IN 46624 219-291-3292

World Mission, (Ch. of the Nazarene), 6401 The Paseo, Kansas City, MO 64131 816-333-7000

World Vision, (World Vision), 919 W. Huntington Dr., Monrovia, CA 91016 818-357-7979

Worldorama, (Pent. Holiness Ch.), P.O. Box 12609, Oklahoma City, OK 73157 405-787-7110

Worldteam Today, (Worldteam, Inc.), 1607 Ponce de Leon Blvd., P.O. Box 143038, Coral Gables, FL 33114 305-446-0861

279

Worldwide Challenge, (Campus Crusade for Christ), P.O. Box 6710, San Bernardino, CA 92412 714-886-5224 ext. 1207

Worldwide News, (The Pocket Testament League), 117 Main St., P.O. Box 368, Lincoln Park, NJ 07035 201-696-1900

Worldwide Thrust, (WEC Intl.), P.O. Box 1707, Fort Washington, PA 19034-8707 215-646-2322

Writer's Inspirational Market News, (Dobbs Publishing Group), P.O. Box 5650, Lakeland, FL 33807 813-644-3548

Young Life, P.O. Box 520, Colorado Springs, CO 80901 719-473-4262

Young Missionary, (Wesley Press), P.O. Box 50434, Indianapolis, IN 46250-0434 317-576-1312

Your Church Magazine, (Bill Berry), SMS Publications, Inc., 1418 Lake St., Evanston, IL 60201 312-328-3386

Youth and Christian Education Leadership, (Ch. of God), 1080 Montgomery Ave., Cleveland, TN 37311 615-478-7599

Youth Leader, The, (General Council of A/G), 1445 Boonville Ave., Springfield, MO 65802 417-862-2781

Youth Walk, (Walk Thru the Bible Ministries), P.O. Box 80587, Atlanta, GA 30366 404-459-9300

Youthworker Journal, (Youth Specialties), 1224 Greenfield Dr., El Cajon, CA 92021 619-440-2333

BUSINESS AFFILIATE MEMBERS

American Tract Society, 1624 N. First St., Garland, TX 75040 214-276-9408

Banta Publications Group, 2340 Des Plaines Ave., Ste. 211, Des Plaines, IL 60018 312-699-3390

Don Stewart Association, P.O. Box 2960, Phoenix, AZ 85062 602-866-1665

Evangel Press, (Breth. in Christ Ch.), 301 N. Elm St., Nappanee, IN 46550 219-773-3164

Heritage Printers and Publishers, 9029 Directors Row, Dallas, TX 75247 214-630-4300

Parthenon Press, 201 Eighth Ave. S., Nashville, TN 37202

Press of Ohio Inc., The, 3765 Sunnybrook Rd., Brimfield, OH 44240 216-678-5868

United Litho, 2818 Fallfax Dr., Falls Church, VA 22042 703-560-5700

Missions/Relief Organizations

Evangelical Foreign Missions Association, 1023 15th St. N.W., Ste. 500, Washington, D.C. 20005 202-789-1011

Founded in 1945, the Evangelical Foreign Missions Association (EFMA), an NAE affiliate, is the largest missions association in the world, with 93 member mission boards and more than 13,343 missionaries from North America serving in every part of the world. EFMA provides diplomatic contact, government representation and information services through its Washington, D.C., office and defends the religious liberty of minority groups in foreign lands.

United States

Action International Ministries, P.O. Box 490, Bothell, WA 98011 206-485-1967

Advent Christian General Conference, Dept. of World Missions, P.O. Box 23152, Charlotte, NC 28212 704-545-6161

Africa Inter-Mennonite Mission, 224 W. High St., Elkhart, IN 46516 219-295-3711

American Leprosy Missions, One Broadway, Elmwood Park, NJ 07407 201-794-8650

Assemblies of God, Division of Foreign Missions, 1445 Boonville Ave., Springfield, MO 65802 417-862-2781

Associate Reformed Presbyterian Church, World Witness, 1 Cleveland St., Greenville, SC 29601 803-233-5226

Baptist General Conference, World Missions, 2002 S. Arlington Heights Rd., Arlington Heights, IL 60005 312-228-0200

Bethany Fellowship Missions (a division of Bethany Fellowship Inc.), 6820 Auto Club Rd., Minneapolis, MN 55438 612-829-2492

Bible League, The, 16801 Van Dam Rd., South Holland, IL 60473 312-331-2094

Bible Literature International, P.O. Box 477, 625 E. North Broadway, Columbus, OH 43216 614-267-3116

Brethren Church Missionary Board, 530 College Ave., Ashland, OH 44805 419-289-1708

Brethren in Christ Missions, P.O. Box 390, Mount Joy, PA 17552-0027 717-653-8067

Calvary Evangelistic Mission, WIVV Missionary Radio Station, P.O. Box A, San Juan, PR 00936 809-724-2727

Campus Crusade for Christ International, Arrowhead Springs, San Bernardino, CA 92414 714-886-5224

Christian Church of North America, Missions Dept., Box 141-A, R.D. #1, Transfer, PA 16154 412-962-3501

Christian Literature Crusade, P.O. Box 1449, Fort Washington, PA 19034 215-542-1242

Christian & Missionary Alliance, Division of Overseas Ministries, 350 N. Highland, Nyack, NY 10960 914-353-0750

Christian Reformed World Ministries, 2850 Kalamazoo Ave., S.E., Grand Rapids, MI 49560 616-241-1691

Christian Reformed World Missions, 2850 Kalamazoo Ave. S.E., Grand Rapids, MI 49560 616-241-1691

Christian Reformed World Relief Committee, 2850 Kalamazoo Ave. S.E., Grand Rapids, MI 49560 616-241-1691

Church of God World Missions, P.O. Box 2430, Cleveland, TN 37320-2430 615-472-3361

Churches of Christ in Christian Union, Foreign Missionary Dept., P.O. Box 30, Circleville, OH 43113 614-474-8856

Compassion International, P.O. Box 7000, Colorado Springs, CO 80933 303-594-9900

Conservative Baptist Foreign Mission Society, P.O. Box 5, Wheaton, IL 60189 312-665-1200

Conservative Baptist Home Mission Soc., P.O. Box 828, Wheaton, IL 60189 312-653-4900

Eastern European Bible Mission, P.O. Box 110, Colorado Springs, CO 80901 719-577-4450; 800-227-2979

Evangelical Congregational Church, Division of Missions, P.O. Box 186, Myerstown, PA 17067 717-866-7581

Evangelical Free Church, Overseas Missions Dept., 1515 E. 66th St., Minneapolis, MN 55423 612-866-3343

Evangelical Friends Missions, P.O. Box 671, Arvada, CO 80001 303-421-8100

Evangelical Mennonite Church, Commission on Overseas Missions, 1420

281

Kerrway Ct., Fort Wayne, IN 46805 219-423-3649

Evangelistic Faith Missions, P.O. Box 609, Bedford, IN 47421 812-275-7531

Every Home for Christ/World Literature Crusade, 20232 Sunburst St., Chatsworth, CA 91311 818-341-7870

Far East Broadcasting, Co., P.O. Box 1, La Mirada, CA 90637 213-947-4651

Foursquare Missions International, 1100 Glendale Blvd., Los Angeles, CA 90026 213-484-2400

Free Methodist Church, General Missionary Board, 901 College Ave., Winona Lake, IN 46590 219-267-7656

Free Will Baptist Board of Foreign Missions, P.O. Box 1088, Nashville, TN 37202 615-361-1010

Friends Church Southwest, P.O. Box 1607, Whittier, CA 90609 213-947-2883

General Baptist Foreign Mission Society, 100 Stinson Dr., Poplar Bluff, MO 63901 314-785-7746

Grace Ministries International, 2125 Martindale Ave. S.W., Grand Rapids, MI 49509 616-241-5666

International Students, Inc., P.O. Box C, Colorado Springs, CO 80901 303-576-2700

International Teams, P.O. Box 203, Prospect Heights, IL 60070 312-870-3800

InterVarsity Missions, 6400 Schroeder Rd., P.O. Box 7895, Madison, WI 53707-7895 608-274-9001

Latin America Mission, P.O. Box 52-7900, Miami, FL 33152-7900 305-884-8400

Link Care Center, 1734 West Shaw Ave., Fresno, CA 93711 209-439-5920

Literacy & Evangelism International, 1800 S. Jackson Ave., Tulsa, OK 74107 918-585-3826

Logoi, Inc., 4100 W. Flagler St., Miami, FL 33134 305-446-8297

Luis Palau Evangelistic Association, P.O. Box 1173, Portland, OR 97207 503-643-0777

Lutheran Brethren World Missions, P.O. Box 655, Fergus Falls, MN 56537 218-739-3336

Media Associates International, Inc., 130 N. Bloomingdale Rd., Ste. 101, Bloomingdale, IL 60108 312-893-1141; 312-893-1977

Mennonite Brethren Missions/Services, 315 S. Lincoln St., Hillsboro, KS 67063 316-947-3151

Mission Aviation Fellowship, P.O. Box 3202, Redlands, CA 92373-0998 714-794-1151

Mission Possible, P.O. Box 2014, Denton, TX 76202 817-382-1508

Missionary Church (World Partners), Overseas Ministries, 3901 S. Wayne Ave., Fort Wayne, IN 46807 219-456-4502

Missionary Internship, P.O. Box 457, Farmington, MI 48024 313-474-9110

Navigators, The, P.O. Box 6000, Colorado Springs, CO 80934 719-598-1212

Nazarene Division of World Mission, 6401 The Paseo, Kansas City, MO 64131 816-333-7000

North American Baptist Conference, Missions Dept., 1 S. 210 Summit Ave., Oakbrook Terrace, IL 60181 312-495-2000

OMS International, P.O. Box A, Greenwood, IN 46142 317-881-6751

Open Bible Standard Missions, 2020 Bell Ave., Des Moines, IA 50315 515-288-6761

Open Doors With Brother Andrew, 16520 Harbor Blvd., Ste. G, Fountain Valley, CA 92708 714-531-6000

Overseas Crusades, 25 Corning Ave., Milpitas, CA 95035 408-263-1101

Partners International, (formerly CNEC), 1470 N. Fourth St., San Jose, CA 95115 408-298-0965

Pentecostal Holiness Church, World Missions Dept., P.O. Box 12609, Oklahoma City, OK 73157 405-787-7110

Presbyterian Church in America, Mission to the World, 1852 Century Pl., Ste. 201, Atlanta, GA 30345 404-320-3373

Primitive Methodist International Mission Board, 7872 Glenwood Ave., Youngstown, OH 44512 216-758-2282

Reformed Presbyterian Church of N. America, Board of Foreign Missions, Rt. 1, Box 1-A, Winchester, KS 66097 913-774-4585

Trans World Radio, P.O. Box 98, Chatham, NJ 07928 201-966-2700

U.S. Center for World Mission, 1605 E. Elizabeth St., Pasadena, CA 91104 818-797-1111

United Brethren in Christ, Board of Missions, 302 Lake St., Huntington, IN 46750 219-356-2312

United World Mission, P.O. Box 8000, St. Petersburg, FL 33738 813-391-0195

WEC International, P.O. Box A, Fort Washington, PA 19034 215-646-2323

Wesleyan Church, General Dept. of World Missions, P.O. Box 50434, Indianapolis, IN 46250 317-576-8160

World Concern, Box 33000, Seattle, WA 98133 206-546-7201

World Gospel Crusades, P.O. Box 3, Upland, CA 91786 714-982-1564

World Gospel Mission, P.O. Box WGM, Marion, IN 46952 317-664-7331

World Mission Prayer League, 232 Clifton Ave., Minneapolis, MN 55403 612-871-6843

World Opportunities International, 1415 N. Cahuenga Blvd., Hollywood, CA 90028 213-466-7187

World Vision, 919 W. Huntington Dr., Monrovia, CA 91016 818-357-1111

Youth for Christ/USA, P.O. Box 419, Wheaton, IL 60189 312-668-6600

Zwemer Institute of Muslim Studies, P.O. Box 365, Altadena, CA 91001 818-794-1121

Canada

Brethren in Christ Missions, 2519 Stevensville Rd., Stevensville, Ontario L0S 1S0, Canada 416-382-3144

Evangelical Mennonite Conference, Board of Missions, Box 1268, Steinbach, Manitoba R0A 2A0, Canada 204-326-6401

Mennonite Brethren Missions/Services, 2-169 Riverton Ave., Winnipeg, Manitoba R2L 2E5, Canada 204-669-6575

Pentecostal Assemblies of Canada, Overseas Missions Dept., 10 Overlea Blvd., Toronto, Ontario M4H 1A5, Canada 416-425-1010

Candidate Missions

Christians in Action, P.O. Box 728, 37721 Rd. 200, Woodlake, CA 93286-9998 209-564-3762

Church Resource Ministries, P.O. Box 5189, Fullerton, CA 92635 714-879-5540

Harvesting in Spanish, 245 S. Benton, Denver, CO 80226 303-232-3030

International Bible Society, P.O. Box 62970, Colorado Springs, CO 80962-2970 719-528-1900; 800-524-1588

International Discipleship Mission, P.O. Box 2120, Orange, CA 92669 213-697-0756

LeTourneau Ministries International, P.O. Box 489, Rockwall, TX 75087 214-771-8325

Medical Ambassadors International, P.O. Box 6645, Modesto, CA 95355 209-524-0600

283

Operation Mobilization, P.O. Box 2277, Peachtree City, GA 30269 404-487-0480

Teen Missions International, P.O. Box 542468, Merritt Island, FL 32954-2468 305-453-0350

World-Wide Missions, 1593 E. Colorado Blvd., Pasadena, CA 91109-7125 818-449-4313

Interdenominational Foreign Mission Association of North America, Inc., P.O. Box 395, Wheaton, IL 60189-0395 312-682-9270

Since 1917 IFMA has served as an independent association of conservative, evangelical, nondenominational mission agencies.

United States

Africa Evangelical Fellowship, P.O. Box 2896, Boone, NC 28607 704-264-6036

Africa Inland Mission, P.O. Box 178, Pearl River, NY 10965 914-735-4014

American Missionary Fellowship, P.O. Box 368, Villanova, PA 19085 215-527-4439

Arab World Ministries (formerly North Africa Mission), P.O. Box 96, Upper Darby, PA 19082 215-352-2003

Back to the Bible, P.O. Box 82808, Lincoln, NE 68501 402-474-4567

BCM International, Inc., 237 Fairfield Ave., Upper Darby, PA 19082 215-352-7177

Berean Mission, Inc., 3536 Russell Blvd., St. Louis, MO 63104 314-773-0110

Bible Christian Union, P.O. Box 410, Hatfield, PA 19440 215-361-0500

CAM International, 8625 La Prada Dr., Dallas, TX 75228 214-327-8206

Chosen People Ministries, 1300 Cross Beam Dr., Charlotte, NC 28217-2800 704-357-9000

Every Home for Christ/World Literature Crusade, 20232 Sunburst St., Chatsworth, CA 91311 818-341-7870

Far East Broadcasting Company, P.O. Box 1, La Mirada, CA 90637 213-947-4651

Frontiers, Inc., P.O. Box 40159, Pasadena, CA 91104 818-798-0807

Global Outreach Mission, P.O. Box 711, Buffalo, NY 14240 716-842-2220

Gospel Missionary Union, 10000 N. Oak, Kansas City, MO 64155 816-734-8500

Gospel Recordings, 122 Glendale Blvd., Los Angeles, CA 90026 213-250-0207

Greater Europe Mission, P.O. Box 668, Wheaton, IL 60189 312-462-8050

Helps International Ministries, Inc., Rt. 1, Box 171-D, Harlem, GA 30814 404-556-3408

InterAct Ministries, (formerly Arctic Missions), 31000 S.E. Kelso Rd., Boring, OR 97009 503-668-5571

Intercristo, (div. of Crista Ministries, Inc.), Seattle, WA 98133 206-546-7330; 800-426-1342

International Christian Fellowship, P.O. Box 986, 213 Naperville St., Wheaton, IL 60187 312-668-8569

International Missions, Inc., Box 14,866, Reading, PA 19612-4866 215-375-0300

InterServe, U.S.A. (BMMF), P.O. Box 418, Upper Darby, PA 19082 215-352-0581

Island Missionary Society, P.O. Box 8971, Greensboro, NC 27419 919-288-7692

Janz Team Ministries, Box 711, Buffalo, NY 14240

Jews for Jesus, 60 Haight St., San Francisco, CA 94102 415-864-2600

Kids Alive International, 2507 Cumberland Dr., Valparaiso, IN 46383 219-464-9035

Liebenzell Mission of the U.S.A., 26 Heath Ln., Schooley's Mountain, NJ 07870 201-852-3044

LIFE Ministries, P.O. Box 200, San Dimas, CA 91773 714-599-8491

Media Associates International, Inc., 130 N. Bloomingdale Rd., Ste. 101, Bloomingdale, IL 60108 312-893-1141; 312-893-1977

Mexican Mission Ministries, P.O. Box 636, Pharr, TX 78577 512-787-3543

Mission Aviation Fellowship, P.O. Box 202, Redlands, CA 92373 714-794-1151

Mission: Moving Mountains, Box 986, Burnsville, MN 55337 612-432-5929

Missionary Internship, P.O. Box 457, Farmington, MI 48332 313-474-9110

Missionary TECH Team, 25 FRJ Dr., Longview, TX 75602 214-757-4530

Missions Outreach, P.O. Box 73, Bethany, MO 64424 816-425-2277

NAIM Ministries, P.O. Box 151, Point Roberts, WA 98281

Navajo Gospel Mission, P.O. Box 2803, Flagstaff, AZ 86003 602-526-0875

Open Air Campaigners, P.O. Box 2440, Plainfield, NJ 07060-0740 201-757-8427

Overseas Christian Servicemen's Centers, P.O. Box 1268, Englewood, CO 80150 303-762-1400

Overseas Missionary Fellowship, 404 S. Church St., Robesonia, PA 19551 215-693-5881

Partners International (formerly CNEC), 1470 N. Fourth St., P.O. Box 15025, San Jose, CA 95115 408-298-0965

Pioneers, P.O. Box 527 Sterling, VA 22170 703-450-4770

PRM International (Portable Recording Ministries), 760 Waverly Rd., Holland, MI 49423 616-396-5291

Ramabai Mukti Mission, P.O. Box 4912, Clinton, NJ 08809 201-735-8770

RBMU International, 8102 Elberon Ave., Philadelphia, PA 19111 215-745-0680

Romanian Missionary Society, P.O. Box 527, Wheaton, IL 60189-0527 312-665-6503

SEND International, P.O. Box 513 Farmington, MI 48332 313-477-4210

SIM USA, P.O. Box 7900, Charlotte, NC 28241 704-529-5100

Slavic Gospel Association, P.O. Box 1122, Wheaton, IL 60189 312-690-8900

South America Mission, P.O. Box 6560, Lake Worth, FL 33466 305-965-1833

South American Crusades, P.O. Box 2530, Boca Raton, FL 33427 305-487-6080

Spiritual Overseers Service, 4362 Vale St., Irvine, CA 92714 714-852-1002

The Evangelical Alliance Mission (TEAM), P.O. Box 969, Wheaton, IL 60189 312-653-5300

The Pocket Testament League, P.O. Box 368, 117 Main St., Lincoln Park, NJ 07035 201-696-1900

Trans World Radio, P.O. Box 98, Chatham, NJ 07928 201-966-2700

UFM International, P.O. Box 306, Bala-Cynwyd, PA 19004 215-667-7660

United World Mission, P.O. Box 8000, St. Petersburg, FL 33738 813-391-0195

U.S. Center for World Mission, 1605 E. Elizabeth St., Pasadena, CA 91104 818-797-1111

World Missions Fellowship, P.O. Box 5148, Oregon City, OR 97045-8148 503-655-5152

World Radio Missionary Fellowship, P.O. Box 553000, Opa Locka, FL 33055 305-624-4252

World Reach, P.O. Box 26155, Birmingham, AL 35226 205-979-2400

Worldteam, P.O. Box 143038, Coral Gables, FL 33114 305-446-0861

Zwemer Institute of Muslim Studies, P.O. Box 365, Altadena, CA 91001 818-794-1121

Canada

Africa Evangelical Fellowship, 470 McNicoll Ave., Willowdale, Ontario M2H 2E1, Canada 416-491-0881

Africa Inland Mission, 1641 Victoria Park Ave., Scarborough, Ontario M1R 1P8, Canada 416-751-6077

Arab World Ministries (formerly North Africa Mission), P.O. Box 3398, Cambridge, Ontario N3H 4T3, Canada 519-653-3170

Berean Mission, P.O. Box 448, Rothesay, New Brunswick E0G 2W0, Canada 506-847-3815

Bible Christian Union, 845 Upper James St., Ste. 206, Hamilton, Ontario L9C 3A3, Canada 416-389-0335

Bible Club Movement of Canada, 798 Main St. E., Hamilton, Ontario L8M 1L4, Canada 416-549-9810

CAM International, 52 John Murray St., Stoney Creek, Ontario L8J 1C8, Canada 416-573-9373

Chosen People Ministries, P.O. Box 4400, Station D, Hamilton, Ontario L8V 4L8, Canada 416-545-9066

Canadian South America Mission, P.O. Box 1599, Guelph, Ontario N1H 6R7, Canada 519-824-6453

Christian Nationals Evangelism Commission, 2110 Argentia Rd., Mississauga, Ontario L5N 2K7, Canada 416-826-8680

Far East Broadcasting Associates of Canada, P.O. Box 2233, Vancouver, British Columbia V6B 9Z9, Canada 604-278-2848

Global Outreach Mission, Box 1210, Saint Catharines, Ontario L2R 7A7, Canada 416-684-1401

Gospel Missionary Union of Canada, 2121 Henderson Hwy., Winnipeg, Manitoba R2G 1P8, Canada 204-338-7831

Gospel Recordings of Canada, 391 Aberdeen Ave., Hamilton, Ontario L8P 2R8, Canada 416-528-2421

Greater Europe Mission, P.O. Box 984, Oshawa, Ontario L1H 7N2, Canada 416-728-8222

InterAct Ministries, (formerly Arctic Missions), Box 250, Station G, Calgary, Alberta T3A 2G2, Canada 403-239-6188

International Christian Fellowship, P.O. Box 3077, Station F, Scarborough, Ontario M1W 3P5, Canada 416-499-1596

International Missions, P.O. Box 2064, St. Catharines, Ontario L2M 6P5, Canada 416-646-0228

InterServe Canada (BMMF), 4028 Sheppard Ave. East-Ste. 200, Agincourt, Ontario M1S 1S6, Canada 416-293-9832

Janz Team Ministries, 2121 Henderson Hwy., Winnipeg, Manitoba R2G 1P8, Canada 204-334-0055

Jews for Jesus, 4801 Keele #45, Downsview, Ontario M3J 3A4, Canada 416-736-8811

Latin America Mission, 4030 Sheppard Ave. East, Scarborough, Ontario M1S 1S6, Canada 416-291-2805

Liebenzell Mission, R.R. #1, Moffat, Ontario L0P 1J0, Canada 519-822-9748

Mission Aviation Fellowship, P.O. Box 368 Guelph, Ontario N1H 6K5, Canada 519-821-3914

Missions Outreach, P.O. Box 100, Caronport, Saskatchewan S0H 0S0, Canada 306-756-2224

NAIM Ministries, P.O. Box 39, Delta, British Columbia V4K 3N5, Canada 604-943-6125

Navigators of Canada, 270 Esna Park Dr., Unit 12, Markham, Ontario L3R 1H3, Canada 416-475-0300

Northern Canada Evangelical Mission, P.O. Box 3030, Prince Albert, Saskatchewan S6V 7V4, Canada 306-764-3388

Overseas Missionary Fellowship, 1058 Avenue Rd., Toronto, Ontario M5N 2C6, Canada 416-485-0427

Ramabai Mukti Mission, Canada, 306-543 Granville St., Vancouver, British Columbia V6C 1X8, Canada 604-685-5028

RBMU International, 2110 Argentia Rd., Mississauga, Ontario L5N 2K7, Canada 416-858-8004

SEND International, 1111 Finch Ave., W #309, Downsview, Ontario M3J 2E5, Canada 416-665-2047

SIM Canada, 10 Huntingdale Blvd., Scarborough, Ontario M1W 2S5, Canada 416-497-2424

Slavic Gospel Association, P.O. Box 2, Station K, Toronto, Ontario M4P 2G1, Canada 416-292-2258

The Evangelical Alliance Mission (TEAM), P.O. Box 980, Regina, Saskatchewan S4P 3B2, Canada 306-525-5444

The Pocket Testament League, P.O. Box 3020, Station F, Scarborough, Ontario M1W 2K0, Canada

Trans World Radio, P.O. Box 310, London, Ontario N6A 4W1, Canada 519-672-6510

UFM International, 1020 Matheson Blvd. East, #11, Mississauga, Ontario L4W 4J9, Canada 416-238-0904

Venture Teams International, P.O. Box 7430, Station E., Calgary, Alberta T3C 3M2, Canada 403-286-3422

World Missions Fellowship, 9301 93rd St., Edmonton, Alberta T6C 3T7, Canada 403-466-5091

World Radio Missionary Fellowship, 2110 Argentia Rd., Mississauga, Ontario L5N 2K7, Canada 416-858-7660

Worldteam Canada, P.O. Box 2424, Mississauga, Ontario L5M 2X3, Canada 416-821-8366

Candidate Missions

Ambassadors for Christ, P.O. Box 0280, Paradise, PA 17562 717-687-8564

American Messianic Fellowship, P.O. Box 5470, Lansing, IL 60438 312-418-0020

European Christian Mission, 1077 56th St., Ste. 226, Delta, British Columbia V4L 2A2, Canada 604-943-0211

InterDev, P.O. Box 30945, Seattle, WA 98103-0945 206-789-8330

Rio Grande Bible Institute, 4300 South Business 281, Edinburgh, TX 78539 512-383-3806

World Outreach Fellowship, P.O. Box 585603, Orlando, FL 32858-5603 305-425-5552

Home Missions (United States) Association of North American Missions, P.O. Box 9710, Madison, WI 53715 608-835-5489

Formerly the National Home Missions Fellowship, this voluntary association of conservative, evangelical, non-denominational home mission agencies awakens Christians to the spiritual needs in the homeland.

American Mission for Opening Churches, Inc., P.O. Box 130, Olcott, NY 14126 716-778-8568

American Missionary Fellowship, 672 Conestoga Rd., Box 368, Villanova, PA 19085 215-527-4439

Appalachian Bible Fellowship, Inc., Bradley, WV 25818 304-877-6428

Berean Mission, Inc., 3536 Russell Blvd., St. Louis, MO 63104 314-773-0110

Bethel Bible Village, Inc., P.O. Box 500, Hixson, TN 37343 615-842-5757

Bethel Ministries, P.O. Box 390, Wise, VA 24293 703-328-3161

Campsite Evangelism, Inc., Box 5587, Hudson, FL 34674 813-869-1389

Carver Bible Institute and College, P.O. Box 4335, Atlanta, GA 30302 404-524-0291

Cedine Bible Mission, Inc., R.R. 1, Box 2390, Spring City, TN 37381 615-365-9565

Children's Bible Fellowship of New York, Inc., P.O. Box 92, Plainview, NY 11803 516-938-4161

Drive-in Ministries, P.O. Box 12345, St. Petersburg, FL 33733 813-577-6922

Flagstaff Mission to the Navajos, Inc., P.O. Box AA, Flagstaff, AZ 86002 602-774-2802

Frontier School of the Bible, 705 - 5th Ave., P.O. Box 217, LaGrange, WY 82221 307-834-2215

Grace and Truth Evangelistic Assoc., Camp of the Nations, South Gibson, PA 18842 717-756-2701

Helps International Ministries, Inc., Rt. 1, Box 171-D, Harlem, GA 30814 404-556-3408

Inner City Impact, 2704 W. North Ave., Chicago, IL 60647 312-384-4200

Kentucky Mountain Mission, Inc., Box 588, Beattyville, KY 41311 606-464-2445

Latin Evangelical Outreach, Inc., P.O. Box 549, 188 Union Ave., Irvington, NJ 07111 201-372-7648

The Mailbox Club, Inc., 404 Eager Rd., Valdosta, GA 31602 912-244-6812

Missionary Tech Team, 25 FRJ Dr., Longview, TX 75602 214-757-4530

The North Arkansas Gospel Mission, Hasty, AR 72640 501-429-5845

Open Air Campaigners, P.O. Box 2440, Plainfield, NJ 07060-0740 201-757-8427

"Open Door" Ministries, Inc., P.O. Box 13619, St. Louis, MO 63137 314-868-2203

RBM Ministries, Inc., 5325 W. "F" Ave., Kalamazoo, MI 49009 616-342-9879

Rural American Mission Society, Rt. 1, Box 231, Kermit, WV 25674 304-393-3565

Rural Home Missionary Assoc., P.O. Box 300, 309 N. Main St., Morton, IL 61550 309-263-2350

Scripture Memory Mountain Mission, P.O. Drawer 129, Emmalena, KY 41740 606-251-3231

Source of Light Ministries International, Inc., Madison, GA 30650 404-342-0397

Southern Highland Evangel, Inc., R.R. 1, Box 115, Pounding Mill, VA 24637 703-964-2398

Southland Bible Institute, 238 W. Southland Dr., Ashland, KY 41101 606-928-5127

Southwestern School of Missions, P.O. Box A, 2918 N. Haris, Flagstaff, AZ 86002 602-774-3890

The Pocket Testament League, P.O. Box 368, 117 Main St., Lincoln Park, NJ 07035 201-696-1900

UIM International, 2920 N. 3rd St., P.O. Box U, Flagstaff, AZ 86002 602-774-0651

INTERNATIONAL RELIEF AND DEVELOPMENT ORGANIZATIONS

Christian Reformed World Relief Committee, (Christian Reformed Ch. in No. Am.), 2850 Kalamazoo Ave. S.E., Grand Rapids, MI 49560 616-246-0740

David Livingstone Missionary Foundation, P.O. Box 232, Tulsa, OK 74102 918-494-9902

Food for the Hungry, 7729 E. Greenway Rd., Scottsdale, AZ 85260 602-998-3100; 800-2-HUNGER

Friends Disaster Service, Inc., (Evang. Friends Ch., Eastern Region), 241 Keenan St., Peninsula, OH 44264 216-650-4975

International Aid, Inc., 17011 W. Hickory, Spring Lake, MI 49456 616-846-7490

Mennonite Central Committee, 21 S. 12th St., Akron, PA 17501 717-859-1151

Samaritan's Purse, P.O. Box 3000, Boone, NC 28607 704-262-1980

World Concern, Box 33000, Seattle, WA 98133 206-546-7201

World Relief Corporation, (NAE subsidiary), P.O. Box WRC, Wheaton, IL 60189 312-665-0235; 1-800-535-LIFE; Telex: 910-497-1827; Fax: 312-653-8023

World Vision, 919 W. Huntington Dr., Monrovia, CA 91016 818-357-1111

MISSION SUPPORT SERVICE ORGANIZATIONS

Association of Church Missions Committees, P.O. Box ACMC, Wheaton, IL 60189 312-260-1660; 800-798-ACMC

Bible Memory Association (BMA Intl.), P.O. Box 12,000, Ringgold, LA 71068-2000 318-894-9154

Christian Counselors Training Center, Inc., 101 Berrington Ct., P.O. Box 14558, Richmond, VA 23221 804-358-1343

Correll Missionary Ministries, P.O. Box 1269, Springfield, VA 22151 704-527-1195 (Corrells)

Evangelical Missions Information Service (EMIS), P.O. Box 794, Wheaton, IL 60189 312-653-2158

Great Commission Foundation, Inc., P.O. Box 160, Eclectic, AL 36024 205-541-3348

Haggai Institute, P.O. Box 13, Atlanta, GA 30370 404-449-8869

Interaction, Inc., P.O. Box 950, Fillmore, NY 14735-0950 716-567-4308

International Aid Inc., 17011 W. Hickory, Spring Lake, MI 49456 616-846-7490

LeTourneau Ministries International, P.O. Box 489, Rockwall, TX 75087 214-722-8325

MAP International, 2200 Glynco Prkwy., Box 50, Brunswick, GA 31521-0050 912-265-6010; 800-225-8550; 800-242-8550 (Ga.)

Ministering in Missions, P.O. Box 336, Fort Collins, CO 80522 303-493-6491

Mission to the World (PCA), P.O. Box 29765, Atlanta, GA 30359-0765; 1852 Century Pl., Ste. 201, Atlanta, GA 30345 404-320-3373

Missionary Crusade for Christ, Inc., 301 Monceaux Rd., West Palm Beach, FL 33405 305-478-7987

Missionary World Service and Evangelism, Inc., P.O. Box 123, 408 Talbott Dr., Wilmore, KY 40390 606-858-3171

Missions Advanced Research Center, 919 W. Huntington Dr., Monrovia, CA 91016 818-303-8811

Mobile Missionary Assistance Program, 1736 N. Sierra Bonita, Pasadena, CA 91104 818-791-8663

Navajo Brethren in Christ Mission, (Breth. in Christ Ch.), Star Rt. 4, Box 6000, Bloomfield, NM 87413 505-632-1212

Open Doors With Brother Andrew, P.O. Box 27001, Santa Ana, CA 92799; 16520 Harbor Blvd., Ste. G, Fountain Valley, CA 92708 714-531-6000

Operation Concern, Inc., (evangelical mission working with migrant farmworkers and their families in Palm Beach County), P.O. Box 2149, West Palm Beach, FL 33402; 8543 W. Boynton Blvd., Boynton Beach, FL 33437 305-737-7842

Overseas Ministries Study Center, 490 Prospect St., New Haven, CT 06511-2196 203-624-6672

Presbyterians United for Mission Advance of Northern California, Box 2095, Danville, CA 94526 415-540-6456

Proclamation International, 3 W. Garden St., Ste. 370, P.O. Box 13367, Pensacola, FL 32591 904-438-2878

Tentmakers International, (Tentmaking agencies), P.O. Box 33836, Seattle, WA 98133 206-546-8411

World Missionary Press, P.O. Box 120, New Paris, IN 46553 219-831-2111

World Prayer, (evangelical & inter-denom. mission · organization; challenges Christians to pray for evangelization of the world; publishes World Prayer magazine), 33-37 Farrington St., Flushing, NY 11354 718-762-6565; 718-762-6370

World Servants, Inc., 8233 Gator Lane #6, West Palm Beach, FL 33411 305-790-0800

Worldwide Dental Health Service, (Missionary Dentists), P.O. Box 7002, Seattle, WA 98133 206-546-1200; 206-771-3241

Worldwide Prayer & Missionary Union, 6821 N. Ottawa, Chicago, IL 60631 312-763-2553

Wycliffe Bible Translators, 19891 Beach Blvd., Huntington Beach, CA 92648 714-536-9346

Zook Mission Farm, (Breth. in Christ Ch.), Morrison, IL 61270

RESCUE, INNER-CITY MISSIONS

The Salvation Army, Central Territorial Hdqrtrs., 860 N. Dearborn St., Chicago, IL 60610-3392 312-440-4600

The Salvation Army, Eastern Territorial Hdqrtrs., 120 West 14th St., New York, NY 10011 212-337-7312

The Salvation Army, National Hdqrtrs., 799 Bloomfield Ave., Verona, NJ 07044 201-239-0606

The Salvation Army, Southern Territorial Hdqrtrs., 1424 Northeast Expressway, Atlanta, GA 30329-2088 404-728-1300

The Salvation Army, Western Territorial Hdqrtrs., 30840 Hawthorne Blvd., Rancho Palos Verdes, CA 90274 213-541-4721

International Union of Gospel Missions (IUGM), An Association of Rescue Ministries, P.O. Box 10780, Kansas City, MO 64118-0780 816-436-6334

The International Union of Gospel Missions (IUGM) is an association of rescue ministries. Its purposes include promoting cooperation among missions and developing higher standards of gospel and relief work as well as rehabilitation of persons. Included in the many services rendered by IUGM on a regular basis are alcohol/drug programs; women's ministry: shelters, abused women shelters, residences for unwed mothers, crisis pregnancy centers; family ministries; children and youth ministries; and residences for the elderly.

Member Ministries

Alabama

Bessemer Rescue Mission, 608 N. 18th St.; for mail use: P.O. Box 824, Bessemer, AL 35021 205-428-8449; Rev. Gerald G. Price, dir.

Christian Service Mission, 1149 16th Ave. S., Birmingham, AL 35256 205-252-9949; Ed Cutshall, exec. dir.

Dothan Rescue Mission, 205 E. Washington/214 S. Appletree; for mail use: P.O. Box 6691, Dothan, AL 36302 205-794-4637; Rev. Harry T. Culbreth, exec. dir.

Downtown Jimmie Hale Mission, 2403 3rd Ave. N.; for mail use: P.O. Box 10472, Birmingham, AL 35202 205-323-5878; Rev. Leo Shepura, supt.

Faith Rescue Mission, 108 Camden St., Montgomery, AL 36104 205-262-6024; Tom Newman, exec. dir.

Mission of Hope, 14970 Mission Rd.; for mail use: P.O. Box 8504, Mobile, AL 36689 205-649-0830; Rev. Lonnie L. Miller, exec. dir.

Mobile Rescue Mission, P.O. Box 1095, Mobile, AL 36633; Rev. Ian Lamont

Alaska

Anchorage Rescue Mission, 537 W. 7th Ave.; for mail use: P.O. Box 201689, Anchorage, AK 99520 907-227-5602; John P. Wojciechowski, exec. dir.

Fairbanks Rescue Mission, 506 Gaffney; for mail use: P.O. Box 1345, Fairbanks, AK 99707 907-452-5343; Rev. Ralph E. Pike, exec. dir.

Arizona

Gospel Rescue Mission, 312 W. 28th St., Tucson, AZ 85713 602-622-3495; Jack Grover, exec. dir.

Phoenix Gospel Mission, 440 W. Washington, Phoenix, AZ 85003 602-252-4501; Rev. Carl Spacone, exec. dir.

Sunshine Rescue Mission, 124 S. San Francisco; for mail use: P.O. Box 634, Flagstaff, AZ 86002 602-744-3512; Alan F. Strand, exec. dir.

Arkansas

Gospel Rescue Mission, Inc., P.O. Box 405, Van Buren, AR 72956; John F. Turner

Union Rescue Mission, 3000 Confederate Blvd.; for mail use: P.O. Box 2176, Little Rock, AR 72203 501-375-4459; Denis Hamilton, exec. dir.

California

Bakersfield Rescue Mission, 830 Beale Ave.; for mail use: P.O. Box 2222, Bakersfield, CA 93303 805-325-0863; Jack Swan, supt.

Bethany, 6062 Lake Murray, Ste. 106, La Mesa, CA 92042 619-462-5966; Mrs. Sharon Masek, exec. dir.

Bethel Haven, 1317 Alvardo Terr., Los Angeles, CA 90006 213-387-7899; Mrs. Jo Etta Bennett

Christian Help Center, 2166 Sacramento St.; for mail use: P.O. Box 4040, Vallejo, CA 94590 707-553-8192; Rev. Rey Bernardes, exec. dir.

City Team Ministries, 275 N. First St.; for mail use: P.O. Box 143, San Jose, CA 95103 408-998-4770; Rev. Pat Robertson, dir.

Coachella Valley Rescue Mission, 47-518 Van Buren; for mail use: P.O. Box 514, Indio, CA 92202-0514 619-347-3512; Rev. Robert McMillan, exec. dir.

Eureka Rescue Mission, 110 2nd St.; for mail use: P.O. Box 76, Eureka,

CA 95501-0076 707-443-4551; Rev. William Thomas, Jr., exec. dir.

Evangel Home, 137 N. Yosemite Ave., Fresno, CA 93701 209-264-4714; Miss Gerre Brenneman, exec. dir.

Fresno Rescue Mission, 310 G. St.; for mail use: P.O. Box 1422, Fresno, CA 93716 209-268-0839; Rev. James Taylor, exec. dir.

Good News Rescue Mission, 3100 S. Market; for mail use: P.O. Box 1626, Redding, CA 96099 916-241-5754; Jesse F. Miller, Sr., supt.

Gospel Center, 229 E. Church St.; for mail use: P.O. Box 816, Stockton, CA 95201 209-466-2138; Rev. Jim Porteous, exec. dir.

Green Oak Ranch Boys & Girls Camp, 1237 Green Oak Rd., Vista, CA 92083 714-727-0251; John E. Dunham

Haven of Peace, 7070 Harlan Rd., French Camp; for mail use: P.O. Box 724, Stockton, CA 95201 209-982-0396; Mrs. Jeannete Roos, president of board

Heaven's Gate Ministries, 422 Guerrero; for mail use: P.O. Box 410217, San Francisco, CA 94141 415-861-4422; Ms. Leslie Harvel, exec. dir.

Long Beach Rescue Mission, 1335 Pacific Ave.; for mail use: P.O. Box 1969, Long Beach, CA 90801 213-591-1292; Rev. Wayne A. Teuerle, exec. dir.

Modesto Gospel Mission, 1417 De Harro St.; for mail use: P.O. Box 1203, Modesto, CA 95353-1203 209-529-8259; Rev. Richard Hewitt, exec. dir.

Orange County Rescue Mission, 1901 W. Walnut; for mail use: P.O. Box 1833, Santa Ana, CA 92702 714-835-0499; John F. Lands, exec. dir.

Oroville Rescue Mission, 4250 Lincoln Blvd.; for mail use: P.O. Box 2481,

Oroville, CA 95965 916-533-9120; Rev. C. W. McComas, exec. dir.

Pajaro Rescue Mission, 111 Railroad Ave.; for mail use: P.O. Box 245, Watsonville, CA 95077 408-724-9576; Rev. George Pielenz, exec. dir.

Prison Mission Association, Inc., 3698 Rubidoux Blvd.; for mail use: P.O. Box 3397, Riverside, CA 92519 714-686-2613; Rev. Joe B. Mason, exec. dir.

Redwood Gospel Mission, 101 6th St.; for mail use: P.O. Box 493, Santa Rosa, CA 95402-0493 707-542-4817; Rev. Richard Cross, exec. dir.

Richmond Rescue Mission, 200 MacDonald Ave.; for mail use: P.O. Box 1112, Richmond, CA 94802 415-233-5333; Dr. Malcolm C. Lee, exec. dir.

San Diego Life Ministries, Inc., 1150 J. St.; for mail use: P.O. Box 611, San Diego, CA 92112 619-234-2109; Rev. James E. Flohr, exec. dir.

San Diego Rescue Mission, Inc., 1150 J. St.; for mail use: P.O. Box 611, San Diego, CA 92112 619-234-2109; Rev. James E. Flohr, exec. dir.

Santa Barbara Rescue Mission, 535 E. Yanonali; for mail use: P.O. Box 1049, Santa Barbara, CA 93102 805-966-1316; Charles W. Pope, exec. dir.

Shepherd's Gate, 1639 Portola Ave.; for mail use: P.O. Box 894, Livermore, CA 94550 415-449-0163; Mrs. Alice Ann Cantelow, exec. dir.

Twin Cities Rescue Mission, 940 14th St.; for mail use: P.O. Box 748, Marysville, CA 95901 916-742-8666; Rev. Robert Ash, exec. dir.

Union Rescue Mission, 226 S. Main St.; for mail use: P.O. Box 629, Los Angeles, CA 90053 213-628-6103; Rev. George Caywood, exec. dir.

Visalia Rescue Mission, 322 N.E. 1st St.; for mail use: P.O. Box 109,

Visalia, CA 93279 209-733-2231; Jim Mainord, exec. dir.

Colorado

Denver Rescue Mission, 23rd & Lawrence Sts.; for mail use: P.O. Box 5206, Denver, CO 80217 303-294-0157; Rev. Delbert Maxfield, exec. dir.

Wayside Cross Gospel-Rescue Mission, The, 728 W. 4th St.; for mail use: P.O. Box 4039, Pueblo CO 81003 303-545-5744; Rev. Thomas S. Bond, exec. dir.

District of Columbia

Central Union Mission, 1350 R St., N.W., Washington, D.C. 20009 202-745-7118; Dr. Robert R. Rich, exec. dir.

Gospel Mission, The, 810-5th St., N.W., Washington, D.C. 20001 202-842-1731; Rev. Lincoln Brooks, Jr., exec. dir.

Florida

City Rescue Mission, Inc., The, 1714 Main St.; for mail use: P.O. Box 114, Jacksonville, FL 32201 904-353-5565; Rev. Kaleel Ellison, exec. dir.

Gospel Rescue Mission of the Palm Beaches, 629 Ninth St.; for mail use: P.O. Box 1588, West Palm Beach, FL 33402 305-655-2204; Rev. R. D. Witherow, exec. dir.

Jacksonville New Life Inn, 234 W. State St.; for mail use: P.O. Box 114, Jacksonville, FL 32201 904-353-5565; Rev. Kaleel Ellison, exec. dir.

Lighthouse Ministries, Inc., 117 E. Magnolia St.; for mail use: P.O. Box 3112, Lakeland, FL 33802 813-687-3705; Rev. Lee D. Schmookler, exec. dir.

Miami City Mission, Inc., 1112 N. Miami Ave.; for mail use: P.O. Box 381674, Miami, FL 33238-1674 305-371-3124; Mrs. Constance Ash

Miami Rescue Mission, Inc., 2250 NW 1st Ave.; for mail use: P.O. Box 420620, Miami, FL 33142 305-573-4390; Dr. Franklin M. Jacobs, exec. dir.

Orlando Union Rescue Mission, Inc., 410 W. Central Blvd.; for mail use: P.O. Box 2791, Orlando, FL 32802 305-422-4855; Don Moody, exec. dir.

Waterfront Rescue Mission, The, 16 W. Main St.; for mail use: P.O. Box 854, Pensacola, FL 32594 904-438-4027; Dr. Edmond L. Gray, exec. dir.

Georgia

Anchorage, The, Rt. 2, Box 56, Leesburg, GA; for mail use: P.O. Box 112 Albany, GA 31702 912-435-5692; Rev. Roy Hatfield, exec. dir.

Atlanta Union Mission, 165 Alexander St.; for mail use: P.O. Box 1850, Atlanta, GA 30301 404-897-1621; Thurman Chambers, exec. dir.

Brother Charlie Rescue Center, 326 Beech St.; for mail use: P.O. Box 783, Tifton, GA 31793 912-382-0577; Rev. John S. Gibbs, Sr., exec. dir.

Potter's House, The, (Rehab. home for alcoholics & home for aged men), Rt. 2, Jefferson, GA 30549 404-543-8338; Rev. Jack Lindsay, dir.

Valley Rescue Mission, Inc., 2903 Second Ave.; for mail use: P.O. Box 1232, Columbus, GA 31902-1232 404-322-8267; Howard H. Mott, Sr., exec. dir.

Idaho

Boise Rescue Mission, 520 Front St.; for mail use: P.O. Box 1494, Boise, ID 83701 208-343-2389; Rev. John R. Drzewiecki, exec. dir.

Illinois

Chicago Christian League, 123 S. Green St.; for mail use: P.O. Box 5542, Chicago, IL 60680 312-666-2474; Ed Perrine, acting exec. dir.

Christian Family Care Center, 210 3rd Ave.; for mail use: P.O. Box 1176, Rock Island, IL 61204 309-788-2273; Mrs. Pamela S. Crome, co-dir.

Galesburg Rescue Mission, 435 E. Third St.; for mail use: P.O. Box 591, Galesburg, IL 61401 309-343-4151; David Scholl, exec. dir.

Home Sweet Home Mission, 300 Mission Dr., Bloomington, IL 61701 309-828-7356; Mike Krippel, exec. dir.

Mount Vernon Rescue Mission, 811 S. 10th St., Mount Vernon, IL 62864 618-242-3756; Robert West, supt.

Olive Branch Mission, The, 1047-41 W. Madison St., Chicago, IL 60607; Lawrence P. Davis

Pacific Garden Mission, 646 S. State St., Chicago, IL 60605 312-922-1462; David G. Saulnier, exec. dir.

Peoria Rescue Mission, 601 S.W. Adams; for mail use: P.O. Box 822, Peoria, IL 61652 309-676-6416; Rev. Jerry J. Trecek, exec. dir.

Rockford Rescue Mission, 121 S. Madison St.; for mail use: P.O. Box 4083, Rockford, IL 61110 815-965-5332; Perry D. Pitney, exec. dir.

Wayside Cross Rescue Mission, 215 E. New York St., Aurora, IL 60505; Rev. Wayne Greenawalt, Jr., supt.

Indiana

Christian Center, The, 625 Main St.; for mail use: P.O. Box 743, Anderson, IN 46015 317-649-4264; Rev. Lloyd L. Lambert, exec. dir.

Evansville Rescue Mission, Inc., 300 SE Seventh St., Evansville, IN 47713 812-423-5244; Richard A. Alvis, exec. dir.

Fort Wayne Rescue Mission, 301 W. Superior St.; for mail use: P.O. Box 11116, Fort Wayne, IN 46855 219-426-7357; Rev. Gus Parris, exec. dir.

Grant County Rescue Mission, 423 S. Gallatin St.; for mail use: P.O. Box 63, Marion, IN 46952-0063 219-662-0988; Paul F. Dornes, Jr., exec. dir.

Hope Rescue Mission, 532 S. Michigan St., South Bend, IN 46601 219-288-4842; Bert M. Harrison, exec. dir.

Kokomo Rescue Mission, Inc., 300 W. Mulberry; for mail use: P.O. Box 263, Kokomo, IN 46903-0263 317-456-3838; Rev. Robert Cox, exec. dir.

Light House Mission, Inc., 1200 Eagle St., Terre Haute, IN 47807 812-232-7001; Richard Conners, exec. dir.

Lighthouse Mission, 520 E. Market St., Indianapolis, IN 46204 317-636-0209; Dr. Mike Fishback, exec. dir.

Muncie Mission, 520 S. High St., Muncie, IN 47305 317-288-9122; Rev. Ray Raines, exec. dir.

Shepherd Community, Inc., 1621 E. Washington St., Indianapolis, IN 46201; Dean Cowles

Wayside Mission, 2428 S. Walnut; for mail use: P.O. Box 2309, Muncie, IN 47302 317-288-4674; Rev. Lucille M. Sanders, supt.

Wheeler Rescue Mission, Inc., 245 N. Delaware St., Indianapolis, IN 46204 317-635-3575; William R. Brown, exec. dir.

Iowa

Bethel Rescue Mission, 1310 6th Ave.; for mail use: P.O. Box 4872, Des Moines IA 50306 515-244-5445; Rev. Ralph Huff, exec. dir.

Dubuque Rescue Mission, 398 Main St.; for mail use: P.O. Box 147,

Dubuque, IA 52001-0147 319-583-1394; Rev. Robert R. Williams, exec. dir.

Sioux City Gospel Mission, 301 W. Eighth St., Sioux City, IA 51103 712-255-1769; Rev. Harry Walker

Kansas

Topeka Rescue Mission, Inc., 605 N. Kansas Ave.; for mail use: P.O. Box 1397, Topeka, KS 66601 913-354-1744; Rev. Barry Feaker, exec. dir.

Union Rescue Mission, 130 N. St. Francis, Wichita, KS 67202 316-265-0132; Gene Price, dir.

Kentucky

Fairhaven Rescue Mission, 260 Pike St.; for mail use: P.O. Box 761, Covington, KY 41012-0761 606-491-1027; Rev. Paul D. Kaiser, exec. dir.

Wayside Christian Mission, 822 E. Market, Louisville, KY 40206 502-584-3711; Rev. Timothy Moseley, exec. dir.

Louisiana

Good News Mission, P.O. Box 6102, Lake Charles, LA 70606; William Lee Brown

Shreveport-Bossier Rescue Mission, 2033 Texas Ave.; for mail use: P.O. Box 3949, Shreveport, LA 71103 318-227-2868; Rev. Warren H. Barnes, supt.

Maine

Hope Haven Gospel Mission, 209 Lincoln St.; for mail use: P.O. Box 7228, Lewiston, ME 04240 207-783-6086; Rev. George C. Nickerson, exec. dir.

Maryland

Baltimore Rescue Mission, Inc., 4 N. Central Ave.; for mail use: P.O. Box 735, Baltimore, MD 21203 301-342-2533; Charles E. Buettner, exec. dir.

Christian Shelter, Inc. 325 Barclay St., Salisbury, MD 21801 301-742-6649; Skip Grant, exec. dir.

Four States Christian Missions, Inc., 125 N. Prospect St.; for mail use: P.O. Box 685, Hagerstown, MD 21741 301-739-1165; James M. Resh, exec. dir.

Frederick Union Rescue Mission, 419 W. South St.; for mail use: P.O. Box 3389, Frederick, MD 21701 301-695-6633; Rev. Charles C. Shell, exec. dir.

Helping Up Mission, Inc., 1029 E. Baltimore St., Baltimore, MD 21202 301-675-5003; Rev. Louis H. Redd, exec. dir.

Maryland Suburban Rescue Ministries, 1611 Marlboro; for mail use: P.O. Box 47530, District Heights, MD 20747 301-627-8718; Henry Studer, exec. dir.

Union Rescue Mission of Western Maryland, Inc., 16 Queen City Pavement; for mail use: P.O. Box 1614, Cumberland, MD 21502 301-724-1585; Rev. Cecil L. Taylor, exec. dir.

Westminster Rescue Mission, 658 Lucabaugh Mill Rd.; for mail use: P.O. Box 285, Westminster, MD 21157 301-848-2222; Rev. Warren Davis, exec. dir.

Massachusetts

Kingston House of Merrimac Mission, 39 Kingston St.; for mail use: P.O. Box 69, Essex Sta., Boston, MA 02112-0069 617-482-8819; Rev. Milton Friesen, exec. dir.

Springfield Rescue Mission, 19 Bliss St.; for mail use: P.O. Box 2424, Springfield, MA 01101 413-732-0808; Ron Willoughby, exec. dir.

Michigan

Carriage Town Mission, 605 Garland St.; for mail use: P.O. Box 214, Flint, MI 48501 313-233-8787; Rev. Jerry L. Peaster, exec. dir.

City Rescue Mission of Muskegon, 400 W. Laketon Ave., Muskegon, MI 49441 616-722-2313; Rev. Thomas L. Culp, exec. dir.

City Rescue Mission of Saginaw, Inc., 1021 Burt St.; for mail use: P.O. Box 548, Saginaw, MI 48606 517-752-6051; Ken Streeter

Detroit Rescue Mission Ministries, 150 Stimson; for mail use: P.O. Box 2087, Detroit, MI 48231 313-993-4700; William Broadwick, exec. dir.

Haven of Rest Rescue Mission, 148 E. Michigan; for mail use: P.O. Box 52, Battle Creek, MI 49016 616-965-1148; Rev. Donald Chalfant, exec. dir.

Kalamazoo Gospel Mission, 448 N. Burdick St., Kalamazoo, MI 49007 616-345-2974; John Schuring, exec. dir.

Mel Trotter Ministries, 225 Commerce, S.W., Grand Rapids, MI 49503 616-454-8249; Harold Koning, exec. dir.

Pontiac Rescue Mission, 90 University; for mail use: P.O. Box 3590, Pontiac, MI 48059 313-334-2187; Rev. James Taulbee, exec. dir.

Minnesota

Marie Sandvik Center, Inc., 1112 E. Franklin Ave.; for mail use: P.O. Box 81, Minneapolis, MN 55440 612-870-9617; Rev. Marie Sandvik & Doris K. Nye, co-supts.

New Hope Center, 212 11th Ave. S., Minneapolis, MN 55415 612-333-1589; Terry Hemsworth, exec. dir.

Union Gospel Mission, 435 University Ave., E., St. Paul, MN 55101 612-292-1721; Rev. George Verley, exec. dir.

Mississippi

Gateway Rescue Mission, 328 S. Gallatin, St.; for mail use: P.O. Box 3763, Jackson, MS 39207 601-353-5864; Rev. George Roberson, exec. dir.

Homes of Grace, 14200 Jericho Rd., Vancleave, MS 39564 601-826-5283; Rev. William Barton, exec. dir.

Missouri

City Union Mission, 1108 E. 10th, Kansas City, MO 64106 816-474-9380; Rev. Maurice Vanderberg, exec. dir.

Sunshine Mission, 1919 Olive St., St. Louis, MO 63103 314-231-8209; Joel Montgomery, exec. dir.

United Gospel Rescue Mission, 508 Cherry St.; for mail use: P.O. Box 924, Poplar Bluff, MO 63901 314-785-4683; Rev. James E. Dunn, exec. dir.

Victory Mission, Inc., 203 W. Commercial St.; for mail use: P.O. Box 2884, Springfield, MO 65803 417-831-6387; Rev. Kevin Gleason, exec. dir.

Montana

Butte Rescue Mission, 1204 E. 2nd St.; for mail use: P.O. Box 4192, Butte, MT 59702 406-782-0925; Rev. Dallas Doyle, exec. dir.

Great Falls Rescue Mission, 326 2nd Ave. S.; for mail use: P.O. Box 127, Great Falls, MT 59403 406-761-2653; Joe E. Thompson, exec. dir.

Montana Rescue Mission, 2822 Minnesota Ave.; for mail use: P.O. Box 3232, Billings, MT 59103 406-259-3800; Rev. Tommy Thomas, exec. dir.

Nebraska

Open Door Mission, 2706 N. 21st St., E.; for mail use: P.O. Box 3413, Omaha, NE 68103 402-422-1131; Rev. Robert Timberlake, exec. dir.
People's City Mission, 110 'Q' St.; for mail use: P.O. Box 80636, Lincoln, NE 68501 402-475-1303; Steven R. Janovec, exec. dir.

Nevada

Las Vegas Rescue Mission, 405 W. Wilson Ave.; for mail use: P.O. Box 384, Las Vegas, NV 89101 702-382-5924; Rev. Edward H. Compton, exec. dir.
Reno-Sparks Gospel Mission/World Gospel Mission Crusade, 145 W. 3rd; for mail use: P.O. Box 5956, Reno, NV 89513-5956 702-323-0386; Rev. Howard P. Cooper, dir.

New Jersey

America's Keswick, Keswick Grove, Whiting, NJ 08759 201-350-1187; Rev. William A. Raws, gen. dir.
Atlantic City Rescue Mission, 2009 Bacharach Blvd.; for mail use: P.O. Box 5358, Atlantic City, NJ 08404 609-641-2525; Rev. D. Rex Whiteman, exec. dir.
Goodwill Home and Missions, Inc., 79 University Ave., Newark NJ 07102 201-621-9560; Robert Hough, Jr., exec. dir.
Market Street Mission, Inc., 9 Market St., Morristown, NJ 07960 201-538-0431; John Pinajian, exec. dir.

New Mexico

Albuquerque Rescue Mission, 509-2nd St. S.W.; for mail use: P.O. Box 331, Albuquerque, NM 87103 505-242-3171; Rev. Stanley A. Gourd, exec. dir.
Gospel Rescue Mission, 334 Griggs Ave.; for mail use: P.O. Box 386, Las Cruces, NM 88004 505-523-7691; Rev. Julius Martin
Silver City Gospel Mission, P.O. Box 5798, Silver City, NM 88062; John F. Pershing

New York

Bowery Mission, 227 Bowery, New York, NY 10002 212-674-3456; Rev. John Willock, admin. dir.
Capital City Rescue Mission, Inc., 50 Hudson Ave.; for mail use: P.O. Box 1662, Albany, NY 12201 518-462-0459; Perry T. Jones, exec. dir.
City Mission, 425 Hamilton St.; for mail use: P.O. Box 760, Schenectady, NY 12301 518-372-9311; Randall Tabor, exec. dir.
City Mission Society, Inc., 100 E. Tupper St.; for mail use: P.O. Box 496, Buffalo, NY 14205 716-854-8181; Dr. Darwin Overholt, exec. dir.
Community Missions, Inc., 1570 Buffalo Ave.; for mail use: P.O. Box 1013, Niagara Falls, NY 14302 716-285-3403; Rev. Calvin Babcock, exec. dir.
Gospel Tabernacle, 388 Tremont St., Rochester, NY 14608 716-436-7523; Rev. Richard Cowley, exec. dir.
McAuley Water Street Mission, 90 Lafayette St.; for mail use: P.O. Box 296, New York, NY 10013 212-226-6214; Charles W. Ross, exec. dir.
Missionary Workers of New York, 460 Bergen St., Brooklyn, NY 11217

718-783-3849; Ms. Dale Belli, gen. dir.

Open Door Mission/Samaritan House, 210 W. Main St.; for mail use: P.O. Box 4236, Rochester, NY 14614-0236 716-454-6696; Rev. Kenneth S. Fox, pastor/exec. dir.

Rescue Mission Alliance, Inc., 120 Gifford St., Syracuse, NY 13202 315-472-6251; Dr. Clarence L. Jordan, exec. dir.

St. Paul's House, Inc., 335 W. 51st St., New York, NY 10019 212-265-5433; Rev. H. Creighton Dunlap, dir.

Union Gospel Mission, Inc., 7 W. First St.; for mail use: P.O. Box 297, Jamestown, NY 14701 716-484-1092; Rev. John W. Steinhauser, exec. dir.

Utica Rescue Mission, 203-05 Rutger St., Utica, NY 13501 315-735-1645; Rev. David L. Sanders, exec. dir.

Yonkers Gospel Mission Home, 191 N. Broadway; for mail use: P.O. Box 1491, Yonkers, NY 10702 914-968-6577; G. David Scott, exec. dir.

North Carolina

Cape Fear Gospel Rescue Mission, 411 North 4th St.; for mail use: P.O. Box 1175, Wilmington, NC 28402 919-763-0134; Rev. Duane Cook, exec. dir.

Christian Rehabilitation Center, Inc., ("REBOUND"), 907 W. First St.; for mail use: P.O. Box 33000, Charlotte, NC 28233 704-334-4635; Rev. Gordon Weekley, exec. dir.

Raleigh Rescue Mission, Inc., 314 E. Hargett St.; for mail use: P.O. Box 27391, Raleigh, NC 27611 919-828-2003; Rev. Waymon E. Pritchard, exec. dir.

Smithfield Rescue Mission, P.O. Box 681, Smithfield, NC 27577; Rev. Paul Olsen

Western Carolina Rescue Mission, 225 Patton Ave.; for mail use: P.O. Box 909, Asheville, NC 28802 704-254-0471; Rev. H. Norb May, exec. dir.

Winston-Salem Rescue Mission, 717 Oak St., Winston-Salem, NC 27101 919-723-1848; Rev. Neal Wilcox, exec. dir.

North Dakota

Grand Forks Gospel Mission, P.O. Box 1323, Grand Forks, ND 56206; Rev. Dwain Steinkuehler

New Life Center, 1902 3rd Ave. N.; for mail use: P.O. Box 1067, Fargo, ND 58107 701-235-4453; Dan Danielson, exec. dir.

Ohio

City Gospel Mission, 1419 Elm St., Cincinnati, OH 45210 513-241-5525; Rev. Carl Marcotte, exec. dir.

City Mission, 408 St. Clair Ave., N.W., Cleveland, OH 44113 216-621-1801; Rev. Harry Banfield, exec. dir.

Faith Rescue Mission, Inc., 181 E. Long St., Columbus, OH 43215 614-224-6617; Rev. Norman R. Wittschen, exec. dir.

Haven of Rest Ministries, Inc., P.O. Box 1758, Akron, OH 44309-1758; Rev. Curtis Thomas, exec. dir.

Haven of Rest Rescue Mission, 175 E. Market St., Akron, OH 216-535-1563; for mail use: see Haven of Rest Ministries, Inc.; Rev. Curtis Thomas, exec. dir.

Marjorie Ruth Thomas Harvest Home, 24 N. Prospect St., Akron, OH 216-434-1149; for mail use: see Haven of Rest Ministries, Inc.; Rev. Curtis Thomas, exec. dir.

Rescue Ministries, 962 W. Federal; for mail use: P.O. Box 298, Youngstown, OH 44501 216-744-5485; Rev. Timothy Lowe, exec. dir.

Oklahoma

City Rescue Mission, Inc., 501-523 S. Robinson; for mail use: P.O. Box 25264, Oklahoma City, OK 73125 405-232-2709; Rev. Milton J. Kalman, exec. dir.

John 3:16 Mission, 506 N. Cheyenne; for mail use: P.O. Box 1477, Tulsa, OK 74101 918-587-1186; Rev. Billy Fox, exec. dir.

Oregon

Astoria Rescue Mission, 62 W. Bond; for mail use: P.O. Box 114, Astoria, OR 97103 503-325-6243; Rev. John Bergeman, exec. dir.

Eugene Mission, Inc., 1542 W. 1st Ave.; for mail use: P.O. Box 1149, Eugene, OR 97440 503-344-3251; Ernest M. Unger, exec. dir.

Gospel Rescue Mission of Grants Pass, 244 N.E. E St.; for mail use: P.O. Box 1371, Grants Pass, OR 97526 503-479-8869; Walter Fikso, supt.

Klamath Falls Gospel Mission, 823 Walnut; for mail use: P.O. Box 87, Klamath Falls, OR 97601 503-882-4895; Nick Thompson, exec. dir.

Medford Gospel Mission, 409 N. Front St.; for mail use: P.O. Box 1172, Medford, OR 97501 503-779-1597; Rev. William Gourley, exec. dir.

Portland Rescue Mission Ministries, 111 W. Burnside St.; for mail use: P.O. Box 3713, Portland, OR 97208 503-227-0421; Rev. Ronnie Morris, exec. dir.

Roseburg Rescue Mission, 526 S.E. Lane, Roseburg, OR 97470 503-673-3004; James Teel, exec. dir.

Union Gospel Ministries, 3212 S.E. Ankeny St., Portland, OR 97214

503-235-3551; Dr. R. J. Newsom, exec. dir.

Union Gospel Mission, 345 Commercial N.E.; for mail use: P.O. Box 461, Salem, OR 97308 503-362-3983; George Simonka, exec. dir.

Pennsylvania

Adams Rescue Mission, 2515 York Rd. East, Gettysburg, PA 17325 717-334-7502; James McGlaughlin, exec. dir.

Allentown Rescue Mission, 355 Hamilton St.; for mail use: P.O. Box 748, Allentown, PA 18105 215-437-3529; Rev. Blair Nixdorf, exec. dir.

American Charity Workers, 400 Center St.; for mail use: P.O. Box 238, Conneautville, PA 16406 814-587-2541; Capt. John R. Wilson, exec. dir.

Bethesda Mission, 611 Reily St.; for mail use: P.O. Box 3041, Harrisburg, PA 17105 717-257-4442; Sherburne P. Hill, exec. dir.

City Mission/New Life Center, 1023 French; for mail use: P.O. Box 407, Erie, PA 16512 814-452-4452; Jerry Marshall, exec. dir.

City Rescue Mission, 319 Croton Ave.; for mail use: P.O. Box 965, New Castle, PA 16103 412-652-4321; Dr. F. Dickson Marshall, exec. dir., pastor

Hope Rescue Mission, 645 N. 6th St., Reading, PA 19601 215-375-4224; Rev. George T. Davis, Jr., supt.

Lebanon Rescue Mission, S. 6th & Elm Sts.; for mail use: P.O. Box 5, Lebanon, PA 17042 717-372-2301; William C. Coleman, exec. dir.

Light of Life Rescue Mission, 100 E. North Ave.; for mail use: P.O. Box 6823, Pittsburgh, PA 15212 412-321-4716; Duane Gartland, exec. dir.

Sunday Breakfast Association, 302 N. 13th St.; for mail use: P.O. Box 296,

Philadelphia, PA 19105 215-922-6400; James Campbell, exec. dir.

Washington City Mission, Inc., 84 W. Wheeling St., Washington, PA 15301 412-222-8530; Rodney Rochelle, supt.

Water Street Rescue Mission, 210-230 S. Prince St., Lancaster, PA 17603 717-393-1745; Richard J. McMillen, exec. dir.

Whosoever Gospel Mission, 101 E. Chelten Ave., Philadelphia, PA 19144 215-438-3094; Rev. John P. Baldwin, exec. dir.

York Union Rescue Mission, Inc., 367 W. Market St.; for mail use: P.O. Box 321, York, PA 17405-0321 717-845-7662; Rev. Paul Gorog, exec. dir.

South Carolina

Haven of Rest Rescue Mission, 219 W. Whitner; for mail use: P.O. Box 466, Anderson, SC 29622 803-226-6193

Star Gospel Mission, 474 Meeting St.; for mail use: P.O. Box 2235, Charleston, SC 29403 803-722-2473; Walter McDade Smith, exec. dir.

South Dakota

Union Gospel Mission, 200 N. Weber, Sioux Falls, SD 57102-0498 605-334-6732; Fran Stenberg, exec. dir.

Tennessee

Dyersburg-Dyer County Union Mission, 213 West Cedar; for mail use: P.O. Box 179, Dyersburg, TN 38025-0179 901-285-0726 Rev. Jerry L. Edmundson, exec. dir.

Haven of Rest Rescue Mission, 624 Anderson St.; for mail use: P.O. Box 372, Bristol, TN 37621 615-968-2011; Ronald D. Moore, exec. dir.

Knoxville Union Rescue Mission, Inc., 511 Broadway; for mail use:

P.O. Box 3352 Knoxville, TN 37927-3352 615-522-8167; Rev. F. Monroe Free, exec. dir.

Maranatha Rescue Mission, P.O. Box 3624, Chattanooga, TN 37404; Walter Wendelken

Memphis Union Mission, Inc., 383 Poplar; for mail use: P.O. Box 330, Memphis, TN 38101 901-526-8403; Mrs. Verla Pettit, exec. dir.

Nashville Union Mission, 129 7th Ave. S.; for mail use: P.O. Box 22157, Nashville, TN 37202 615-255-2475; Rev. Carl R. Resener, exec. dir.

Union Gospel Mission, 16 E. Main St.; for mail use: P.O. Box 983, Chattanooga, TN 37404 615-266-3466; Rev. J. Mack Lehigh, exec. dir.

Texas

Door of Hope Mission, 111 N. Lee; for mail use: P.O. Box 1789, Odessa, TX 79760 915-337-8294; Rev. David Pistone, exec. dir.

Faith City Mission, 401 S.E. 2nd St.; for mail use: P.O. Box 804, Amarillo, TX 806-373-6402; Rev. Don L. Prescott, admin., vice pres.

New Hope Ministries, P.O. Box 5087, Waco, TX 76708; Gary Hollomon

Rescue Mission of El Paso, 604 San Francisco Ave.; for mail use: P.O. Box 286, El Paso, TX 79902 915-532-2575; Rev. Wayne Thornton, exec. dir.

Star of Hope, 407 LaBranch St.; for mail use: P.O. Box 4052, Houston, TX 77210 713-227-8900; Donald Johnson, exec. dir., pres.

Twin City Mission, 500 N. Main; for mail use: P.O. Box 3490, Bryan, TX 77801 409-822-7511; Bob Good, exec. dir.

Union Gospel Mission, 922 Park Ave., Dallas, TX 75201; John Gardner

Wichita Falls Faith Mission, Inc., 402 Lamar; for mail use: P.O. Box 965,

Wichita Falls, TX 76307 817-723-5663; Rev. Gordon (Pete) Smith, exec. dir.

Utah

Ogden Rescue Mission, 2781 Wall Ave.; for mail use: P.O. Box 625, Ogden, UT 84402 801-621-4360; Rev. James T. Stanford, exec. dir.

Union Gospel Mission, 118 S. Main St.; for mail use: P.O. Box 448, Helper, UT 84526 801-472-5518; Ed Abel, dir./chaplain

Virginia

City Rescue Mission, 402 4th St. S.E.; for mail use: P.O. Box 525, Roanoke, VA 24003 703-344-9610; Mrs. Lois Johnson Bettis, exec. dir.

Good Samaritan Inn, 2307 Hull St., Richmond, VA 23224 804-231-9995; Rev. Michael McClary, dir.

Peninsula Rescue Mission, Inc., 3700 Huntington Ave.; for mail use: P.O. Box 377, Newport News, VA 23607 804-380-6909; Rev. Lindsay Poteat, supt.

Union Mission, Inc., 130 Brooke Ave.; for mail use: P.O. Box 3203, Norfolk, VA 23514 804-627-8686; Rev. Theodore A. Bashford, exec. dir.

Washington

Life House Gospel Mission, 506 W. 16th, Kennewick, WA 99337 509-586-7336; Larry Groom, exec. dir.

Light House Mission, 910 W. Holly St.; for mail use: P.O. Box 548, Bellingham, WA 98227 206-733-5120; Rev. Al Archer, exec. dir.

Tri-City Union Gospel Mission, Inc., 112 N. 2nd Ave.; for mail use: P.O. Box 1446, Pasco, WA 99301-1446 509-547-2112; Rev. Donald Thayer, exec. dir.

Union Gospel Mission, adm. office: 7101 Martin Luther King, Jr. Way •S., 206-723-0767; men's services: 2nd Ave. Ext., 206-622-5177; women's services: 6th & King, 206-622-5177; for mail use: P.O. Box 202, Seattle, WA 98111 206-723-0767; Rev. Stephen E. Burger, exec. dir.

Union Gospel Mission, 219 1/2 N. Browne; for mail use: P.O. Box 1787, Spokane, WA 99210 509-624-1264; Philip Altmeyer, exec. dir.

Union Gospel Mission, 13 Front St.; for mail use: P.O. Box 565, Yakima, WA 98907 509-248-4510; Rev. Roger C. Phillips, exec. dir.

Union Gospel Mission of Gray's Harbor, 405 E. Heron; for mail use: P.O. Box 859, Aberdeen, WA 98520-0913 206-533-1064; Gary Rowell, exec. dir.

Walla Walla Rescue Mission, 202 W. Birch; for mail use: P.O. Box 56, Walla Walla, WA 99362 509-525-7153; Gary Meister, exec. dir.

West Virginia

Bluefield Union Mission, 2203 Bluefield Ave.; for mail use: P.O. Box 4056, Bluefield, WV 24701 304-327-8167; Dr. Allen A. Hammond, exec. dir.

Clarksburg Mission, Inc., 312 N. 4th St.; for mail use: P.O. Box 1123, Clarksburg, WV 26301 304-622-2451; Leon Bailey, exec. dir.

Huntington City Mission, 1030 7th Ave.; for mail use: P.O. Box 3, Huntington, WV 25706 304-523-0293; Rev. James Funderburk, exec. dir.

Union Mission of Fairmont, Inc., 107 Jefferson St., Fairmont, WV 26554 304-363-0300; Rev. Robert J. Gugenheim, exec. dir.

Union Mission Settlement, Inc., 700 S. Park Rd.; for mail use: P.O. Box

112, Charleston, WV 25321 304-925-0366; Rev. James B. Moellendick, exec. dir.

Wisconsin

Milwaukee Rescue Mission, 830 N. 19th St., Milwaukee, WI 53233 414-271-6626

Wyoming

Central Wyoming Rescue Mission, 740 Cy; for mail use: P.O. Box 3212, Casper, WY 82602 307-265-2251; Rev. Roger Neff, minister of admin.

Canada

Kelowna Gospel Mission, 251 Leon Ave.; for mail use: P.O. Box 15, Station "A," Kelowna, British Columbia V1Y 7N3, Canada 604-763-3737; Rev. Lawson Barbour, supt.

Mission Services of Hamilton, Inc., 120 Cannon Street E.; for mail use: P.O. Box 368, Hamilton, Ontario L8N 3C8, Canada 416-528-4211; Rev. Martin B. Boughan, exec. dir.

Mission Services of London, 609 William St., London, Ontario N6B 3G1, Canada 519-433-2807; Roger Smith, exec. dir.

New Life Mission, 260 Johnston Ln.; for mail use: P.O. Box 712, Kamloops, British Columbia V2C 5M4, Canada 604-376-9898; Leonard E. Klassen, exec. dir.

Union Gospel Mission, 616 E. Corova St.; for mail use: P.O. Box 2546, Vancouver, British Columbia V6B 3W8, Canada 604-253-3323; Maurice McElrea, exec. dir.

Union Gospel Mission, 320 Princess St.; for mail use: P.O. Box 1073, Winnipeg, Manitoba R3C 2X4, Canada 204-943-9904; W. G. McNairn, exec. dir.

Union Mission for Men, 35 Waller St., Ottawa, Ontario K1N 7G4, Canada 613-234-1144; Dr. Cal Chambers, supt.

Welcome Hall Mission, 1490 St. Antoine St.; for mail use: P.O. Box 894, Sta. A, Montreal, Quebec H3C 2V8, Canada 514-935-6395; Rev. C. B. Muirhead, adm.

TRANSLATING, BIBLE MISSIONS

Wycliffe Bible Translators, 19891 Beach Blvd., Huntington Beach, CA 92648 714-536-9346

Outreach Ministries

ATHLETE OUTREACH MINISTRIES

Fellowship of Christian Athletes, 8701 Leeds Rd., Kansas City, MO 64129 816-921-0909; 800-289-0909

BUSINESS OUTREACH MINISTRIES

Christian Business & Professional Women (After 5 Clubs), (Stonecroft Ministries), P.O. Box 9609, Kansas City, MO 64134 816-763-7800

Christian Businessmen's Committee of USA, Attn: Carman G. Wolf, 1800 McCallie Ave., Chattanooga, TN 37404 615-698-4444

EVANGELISM/DISCIPLESHIP MINISTRIES

Agape Force, Inc., P.O. Box 4036 Maryville, TN 37802-4036 615-428-6085

American Bible Society, 1865 Broadway, New York, NY 10023 212-581-7400

American Remnant Mission, Inc., 2100 Monument Blvd., Ste. 17, P.O. Box 2321, Pleasant Hill, CA 94523 415-676-5886

American Rescue Workers, P.O. Box 22, Williamsport PA 17701 717-323-8401

American Tract Society, 1624 N. First St., Garland TX 75040 214-276-9408

Anchor Bay Evangelistic Association, P.O. Box 288, Aurora, IL 60507 312-896-1248

Bill Glass Evangelistic Association, P.O. Box 356, Dallas, TX 75221 214-291-7895

Billy Graham Evangelistic Association, 1300 Harmon Pl., Minneapolis, MN 55403 612-338-0500

Charles E. Fuller Institute of Evangelism and Church Growth, P.O. Box 91990, 44 S. Mentor Ave., Pasadena, CA 91106-2902 818-449-0425; 800-C-FULLER

Chosen People Ministries, 1300 Cross Beam Dr., Charlotte NC 28217-2800 704-357-9000

Christ Alongside, P.O. Box 29, Bremerton WA 98310 206-692-5305

Christ for the Nations, Inc., P.O. Box 769000, Dallas TX 75376-9000 214-376-1711

Christian Communications of Chicagoland, Inc., One N. Wacker Dr., 11th Floor, Chicago, IL 60606 312-977-3838

Christian Destiny, Inc., P.O. Box C, Hillsboro, KS 67063 316-947-2345

Christian Evangelical Association, P.O. Box 538, Port Angeles, WA 98362-0101 206-457-4163

Christian Mission for the United Nations Community, 99 Lafayette Ave., 2nd Floor, White Plains, NY 10603 913-948-5700

Christian Women's Clubs, (Stonecroft Ministries), P.O. Box 9609, Kansas City, MO 64134 816-763-7800

Christians in Action, P.O. Box 728, 37721 Rd. 200, Woodlake, CA 93286-9998 209-564-3762

Christians in Government, P.O. Box 71654, Los Angeles, CA 90071 213-250-2824

Churches Alive!, P.O. Box 3800, San Bernardino, CA 92413 714-886-5361

Clyde Dupin Ministries, Inc., P.O. Box 565, Kernersville, NC 27285 919-996-2555

Correll Missionary Ministries, P.O. Box 1269, Springfield, VA 22151 704-527-1195

Crista Ministries, Inc., 19303 Fremont Ave. N., Seattle, WA 98133 206-546-7200

Delaware County Evangelistic Association, 5101 W. Hessler Rd., Muncie, IN 47304 317-288-6566

Eastern European Bible Mission, P.O. Box 110, Colorado Springs, CO 80901 719-577-4450; 800-227-2979

Evangelistic Association of New England, 88 Tremont St., Boston, MA 02108 617-523-3579

Every Home for Christ/World Literature Crusade, 20232 Sunburst St., Chatsworth, CA 91311 818-341-7870

Faith Prayer & Tract League, 2627 Elmridge Dr., N.W., Grand Rapids, MI 49504 616-453-7695

Ford Philpot Evangelistic Association, P.O. Box 3000, Lexington, KY 40533 606-276-1479

Frontiers, P.O. Box 40159, Pasadena, CA 91104 818-798-0807

Grace Evangelistic Association, Inc., (Morning Chapel Hour), P.O. Box 900, Paramount, CA 90723 213-634-7988

Haven of Rest Ministries, 2410 Hyperion Ave., Los Angeles, CA 90027 213-664-2103

Heralds Ministries, The, (a div. of the Spoken Word, Inc.), P.O. Box 61, Newbury Park, CA 91320 805-499-3626

High Flight Foundation, P.O. Box 1387, Colorado Springs, CO 80901 303-576-7700

HIS WAY, Inc., P.O. Box 27247, San Francisco, CA 94127 415-469-7555

Holston Evangelical Fellowship, 2204 Laurinda Dr., Knoxville, TN 37914 615-877-8981

Hope Hospital Chaplains, 1800 W. Charleston Blvd., Las Vegas, NV 89102 702-383-2434

Hospital Christian Fellowship, Inc., (Evangelistic health care organiz.), P.O. Box 4004, San Clemente, CA 92672 714-496-7655

Institute for American Church Growth, 709 E. Colorado Blvd., Ste. 150, Pasadena, CA 91101 818-449-4400; 800-423-4844

Institute for Prison Ministries, Billy Graham Center, Wheaton College, Wheaton, IL 60187-5593

International Ministries to Israel, (formerly American Assoc. for Jewish Evangelism), 3323 North Ridge Ave., Arlington Hts., IL 60004 312-394-4405

International Outreach, Inc., P.O. Box 6078, Atascadero, CA 93423 805-461-1636

International Prison Ministry, P.O. Box 63, Dallas, TX 75221 214-494-2302

International Students, Inc., P.O. Box C, Colorado Springs, CO 80901 719-576-2700

James Robison Evangelistic Association, P.O. Box 18489, Ft. Worth, TX 76118 817-268-4606

Jesus Dayton, Inc., P.O. Box 403 Dayton, OH 45409, 513-298-8420

Jews for Jesus, 60 Haight St., San Francisco, CA 94102 415-864-2600

John Woodhouse Evangelistic Association, P.O. Box 205, Indian Rocks, FL 33535 813-596-2853

Josh McDowell Ministries, P.O. Box 1000, Dallas TX 75221 214-234-0645

Lamb's Players, (performing arts), P.O. Box 26, National City, CA 92050 619-474-3385; 619-474-4802

Lay Evangelism, Inc., P.O. Box 1244, Bloomington, IL 61702 309-662-6606

Leighton Ford Ministries, 6230 Fairview Rd., Ste. 220, Charlotte, NC 28210 704-366-8020; TELEX: 292124 (RCA)

Logoi, Inc., 4100 W. Flagler St., Ste. B-3, Miami FL 33134 305-446-8297

Lord's House of Glory, Inc., The, Ronald Mack, P.O. Box 2077, Washington, D.C. 20013

Luis Palau Evangelistic Team, P.O. Box 1173, Portland, OR 97207 503-643-0777

Menorah Ministries, P.O. Box 669, Palm Harbor, FL 34273 813-442-9839

Metro Ministries, Inc., 2721 S. Warren Way, Arcadia, CA 91006 213-448-5538

Mount Hermon Association, Inc., (interdenominational camp & conference ministry), Dr. Edward Hayes, executive director, Box 413, Mount Hermon, CA 95041 408-335-4466

Needle's Eye Ministries, Inc., P.O. Box 14558, Richmond VA 23221 804-358-1283

Neighborhood Bible Studies, P.O. Box 222, Dobbs Ferry, NY 10522 914-693-3273

New Covenant Evangelical Ministries, Inc., One World Ministry Center, Buffalo, NY 14223 716-876-2621

New England Fellowship of Evangelicals, P.O. Box 99, Rumney, NH 03266 603-786-9504

New Life in Christ Foundation, 4501 Wadsworth Blvd., Wheat Ridge, CO 80033 303-422-8208

Nursing Home Ministries, Inc., P.O. Box 02519, Portland, OR 97202 503-238-0647

Open Air Campaigners, P.O. Box 2440, Plainfield, NJ 07060-0740 201-757-8427

Overseas Chinese Mission, 154 Hester St., New York, NY 10013 212-226-3438

Paul Clark Ministries, P.O. Box 2112, Shawnee Mission, KS 66201 816-942-7588

Personal Ministries, P.O. Box 413, New Lenox, IL 60451 815-485-4900

Presbyterian Evangelistic Fellowship, Inc., P.O. Box 1890, Decatur, GA 30031 404-244-0740; 800-CALL PEF

Prison Fellowship, P.O. Box 17500, Washington, DC 20041-0500 703-478-0100

Railroad Evangelistic Association, Inc., R.R. 4 Box 97, Spencer, IN 47460 812-829-4667

Ravi Zacharias International Ministries, Inc., 4725 Peachtree Corners Circle, Ste. 250, Norcross, GA 30092 404-449-6766

Reach Out Evangelistic Association, P.O. Box 6651, Orange, CA 92667 714-997-2160

Robert H. Schuller Institute, 12141 Lewis St., Garden Grove, CA 92640 714-971-4133

Roger Houtsma World Outreach, P.O. Box 950, 1370 S. Novato Blvd., Novato, CA 94948 415-892-0714

Saints Alive in Jesus, P.O. Box 1076, Issaquah, WA 98027

San Francisco Careers Class, Inc., P.O. Box 14611, San Francisco, CA 94114 415-333-6019

SEA-TAC Ministries, Inc., The Airport Chaplaincy, Room 213, SEA-TAC Intl. Airport, 17800 Pacific Hwy. So., Seattle, WA 98158 206-433-5505

Search, (lifestyle evangelism), P.O. Box 521, Lutherville, MD 21093 301-252-1246

Siloam International, 1310 Broadway, Bellingham, WA 98225; P.O. Box W, Bellingham, WA 98227 206-647-2283

STEER, Inc., P.O. Box 1236, Bismarck, ND 58501 701-258-4911

Steve Wingfield Ministries, Inc., P.O. Box 1464, Harrisonburg, VA 22801 703-828-4747

Stonecroft Ministries, Intl. Hdqrtrs.: P.O. Box 9609, Kansas City, MO 64134 816-763-7800; Canadian Office: P.O. Box 1200, Willowdale, Ontario M2N 5T5, Canada 416-222-0548

Tele-Visitation, P.O. Box 71654, Los Angeles, CA 90071 213-624-2196

Tom Skinner Associates, Inc., 505 Eighth Ave., New York, NY 10018 212-563-5454

United Gospel Outreach, 7225-27 S. Main St., Los Angeles, CA 90003 213-758-1213

Venture Teams International, Box 7430, Sta. E, Calgary, Alberta, Canada, T3C 3M2 403-286-3422

Village Missions, (Stonecroft Ministries), P.O. Box 9609, Kansas City, MO 64134 816-763-7800

Waikiki Beach Chaplaincy, P.O. Box 15488 Honolulu, HI 96815 808-923-3137

Wales Goebel Ministry, (Lifeline Adoption Agency), 2908 Pump House Rd., Birmingham, AL 35243 205-967-4888

Watchmen Association, Inc., 705 Forest Park Rd., Great Falls, VA 22066 703-759-3110

Wear's Valley Bible Conference Center, Inc., R.R. 7, Sevierville, TN 37862 615-453-2382

Worldwide Dental Health Service, (Missionary Dentists), P.O. Box 7002, Seattle, WA 98133 206-546-1200; 206-771-3241

HANDICAP/DISABLED OUTREACH MINISTRIES

Bible Alliance, (Talking Book Program, the Bible on audio cassettes for blind, visually impaired and print handicapped), P.O. Box 621, Bradenton, FL 34206 813-748-3031

Broken Wing Outreach, c/o Greater Minneapolis Association of Evangelicals, 3361 Republic Ave., Minneapolis, MN 55426 612-920-8147

Children's Bible Fellowship of N.Y., Hope Town Resident Christian School, Rev. Winfield R. Ruelke, D.D., pres., P.O. Box 670, Carmel, NY 10512 914-225-2005

Christian Berets Camps & Ministries, 1325 Yosemite Blvd., Modesto, CA 95354 209-524-7993

Christian Church Foundation for the Handicapped, P.O. Box 310, Louisville, TN 37777 615-984-8066

Christian Fellowship for the Blind, International, Inc., (mission braille & cassette outreach), Dr. Franklin D. Tucker, exec. dir., 1124 Fair Oaks, P.O. Box 26, South Pasadena, CA 91030-0026 818-799-3935

Christian Fund for the Disabled, (a ministry of Joni and Friends), P.O. Box 3333, Agoura Hills, CA 91301 818-707-5664

Christian Horizons, Inc., 334, Williamston MI 48895 517-655-3463

Christian League for the Handicapped, P.O. Box 98, Walworth, WI 53184 414-275-6131

Christian Overcomers, Inc., 246A Third Ave., Westwood, NJ 07675 201-358-0055

Deaf Ministries International, P.O. Box 182, Concord, CA 94522 415-686-3966

Deaf Video Communications of America, Inc., 4624 Yackley Ave., Lisle, IL 60532 312-964-0909

Disability Communication Consultants, 540 Tubman Court, San Jose, CA 95125

Elim Christian School Special Education, 13020 S. Central, Palos Heights, IL 60463 312-389-0555

Gray Harbor Baptist Church Ministries to the Handicapped, (indep. Bapt.), P.O. Box 729, Ocean Shores, WA 98569 206-289-2540

Handi Vangelism, (BCM Intl., bereaved parents ministries), 237 Fairfield Ave., Upper Darby, PA 19082 215-352-7177

Hope Town Resident Christian School, (see Children's Bible Fellowship of N.Y.)

John Milton Society for the Blind, 475 Riverside Dr., #455, New York NY 10115 212-870-3335

Joni & Friends (Joni Eareckson Tada, founder), P.O. Box 3333, Agoura Hills, CA 91301 818-707-5664

LNE' Ministries, (mentally retarded/physically disabled people/seriously or terminally ill children), St. Andrews Presbyterian Church, P.O. Box 125, Strathmore, CA 93267 209-568-2238

Lutheran Braille Evangelism Association, 1740 Eugene St., White Bear Lake, MN 55110 612-426-0469

Missionary Vision for Special Ministries, 640 W. Briar Pl., Chicago, IL 60657 312-327-0489

National Church Conference of the Blind, P.O. Box 163, Denver, CO 80201 303-455-3430

Network, The, Christian Ministries with Disabled People, Ed & Judith Myers, 5521 Garvin Ave., Richmond, CA 94805 415-232-9114

Rainbow Acres, Inc., P.O. Box 1326, Camp Verde, AZ 86322

Shepherds Baptist Ministries, (agency for mentally retarded/Regular Baptist), P.O. Box 400, 1805 - 15th Ave., Union Grove, WI 53182 414-878-2451

Voice from the Silence, P.O. Box 182, Concord, CA 94522 415-686-3966

MILITARY OUTREACH MINISTRIES

Christian Military Fellowship, (Fellowship of Christians in U.S. Armed Forces), P.O. Box 1207, Englewood, CO 80150 303-761-1959

Overseas Christian Servicemen's Centers, P.O. Box 1268, Englewood, CO 80150 303-762-1400

PERFORMING ARTS OUTREACH MINISTRIES

A.D. Players, 2710 W. Alabama, Houston, TX 77098 713-526-2721

Artists in Christian Testimony, (ACT-artistic communication into mission strategy), (Service and Mobilization) P.O. Box 1002, 9521 Business Center Dr., Bldg. 9, Ste. A, Cucamonga, CA 91730 714-987-3274

Fellowship of Artists for Cultural Evangelism, 1605 E. Elizabeth St., Pasadena, CA 91104 213-794-7970

Jews for Jesus, 60 Haight St., San Francisco, CA 94102 415-864-2600

Lamb's Players, (performing arts), P.O. Box 26, National City, CA 92050 619-474-3385; 619-474-4802

PRISON/EX-OFFENDER OUTREACH MINISTRIES

Correctional Institutions Chaplaincy, 195 N. Main, Milpitas, CA 95035 408-263-6900

Damascus Way Re-Entry Center, (halfway house for ex-offenders), c/o (GMAE, 3361 Republic Ave., Minneapolis, MN 55426 612-920-5222

Institute for Prison Ministries, Billy Graham Center, Wheaton College, Wheaton, IL 60187-5593

International Prison Ministry, P.O. Box 63, Dallas, TX 75221 214-494-2302

Prison Chaplaincy, c/o Greater Minneapolis Association of Evangelicals, 3361 Republic Ave., Minneapolis, MN 55426 612-920-8147

Prison Fellowship, P.O. Box 17500, Washington, DC 20041-0500 703-478-0100

SPECIALIZED MINISTRIES

A.D. Players, 2710 W. Alabama, Houston, TX 77098 713-526-2721

American Family Foundation, P.O. Box 336, Weston, MA 02193 617-893-0930

Americans for a Sound AIDS Policy, W. Shepherd Smith, pres., P.O. Box 17433, Washington, D.C. 20041 703-471-7350

Artists in Christian Testimony, (ACT-artistic communication into mission strategy), (Service and Mobilization), P.O. Box 1002, 9521 Business Center Dr., Bldg. 9, Ste. A, Cucamonga, Ca 91730 714-987-3274

Billy Graham Center, Wheaton College, Wheaton, IL 60187 312-260-5157

Bread for the World, (Christian citizens' movement), 802 Rhode Island Ave. N.E., Washington, D.C. 20018 202-269-0200; 800-82-BREAD

Brethren in Christ Foster Care Ministries, (Breth. in Christ Ch.), R.D. 6, Box 174, Lancaster, PA 17603 717-872-5234

Bronx Voluntary Service Unit, (Breth. in Christ Ch.), 246 E. Tremont Ave., Bronx, NY 10457 212-583-1954

Center for Pastoral Renewal, The, P.O. Box 8617, Ann Arbor, MI 48107 313-761-8505

Chicago Mission Board of Trustees, (Breth. in Christ Ch.), 301 N. Elm St., Nappanee, IN 46550 219-773-3164

Christian Action Council, 701 W. Broad St., Ste. 405, Falls Church, VA 22046 703-237-2100

Christian Answers & Information, P.O. Box 3295, Chico, CA 95927 916-893-0567

Christian Apologetics Research & Information Service, (CARIS), P.O. Box 2067, Costa Mesa, CA 92626 714-957-0249

Christian Leaders for Responsible Television, (CLEAR-TV), P.O. Drawer 2440, Tupelo, MS 38803 601-844-5036

Christian Mandate for America, P.O. Box 2500, Culpeper, VA 22701 703-825-4040

Christian Research Associates, Inc., 6565 Gun Park Dr. #150-46, Boulder, CO 80301 303-777-1983

Christian Research Institute, P.O. Box 500, San Juan Capistrano, CA 92693; 22672 Lambert St., Ste. 615, El Toro, CA 92630 714-855-9926

Christian Resource Associates, Inc., P.O. Box 2100, Orange, CA 92626 714-997-3920

Christians for Urban Justice, One Aspinwall Rd., Dorchester, MA 02124 617-825-6080

Church Bible Studies, Inc., (interdenom.), 191 Mayhew Way, Walnut Creek, CA 94596 415-937-7286; 415-687-5555

Church Growth Center, (evangelism, discipleship), Corunna, IN 46730 219-281-2452; 800-626-8515

Church Growth Services, P.O. Box 2409, South Bend, IN 46680 219-291-4776

Churches Vitalized, Inc., 480 Brightspur Ln., Ballwin, MO 63011 314-394-2832

Citizens for Decency Through Law, Inc., William D. Swindall, national dir., 2845 E. Camelback Rd., Ste. 740, Phoenix, AZ 85016 602-381-1322

Concerned Women for America, (decency awareness), 122 C St., N.W., Ste. 800, Washington, D.C. 20001

Correctional Institutions Chaplaincy, 195 N. Main, Milpitas, CA 95035 408-263-6900

Damascus Way Re-Entry Center, (halfway house for ex-offenders), c/o GMAE, 3361 Republic Ave., Minneapolis, MN 55426 612-920-5222

Encounter Ministries, Inc., P.O. Box 757800, Memphis, TN 38175-7800 901-365-9696

Evangelical Friends Church, Eastern Region, (Evangelical Friends Alliance), 1201 30th St. N.W., Canton, OH 44709 216-493-1660

Evangelicals for Social Action, 712 G St. S.E., Washington, DC 20003 202-543-5330

Fellowship of Artists for Cultural Evangelism, 1605 E. Elizabeth St., Pasadena, CA 91104 213-794-7970

Good News, Forum for Scriptural Christianity, 308 E. Main St., P.O. Box 150, Wilmore, KY 40390 606-858-4661; 800-451-READ (for ordering subscriptions & books)

Grace Fellowship International, 3595 S. Teller #408, Denver, CO 80235 303-980-0003

Harvesting in Spanish, 245 So. Benton, Denver, CO 80226 303-232-3030

Hope Hospital Chaplains, 1800 W. Charleston Blvd., Las Vegas, NV 89102 702-383-2434

Hope House, (Breth. in Christ Ch.), 8360 Sylvan Dr., Riverside, CA 92504 714-688-9265

Hospital Chaplains' Ministry of America, Inc., 710 N. Euclid St., P.O. Box 4308, Anaheim, CA 92803-4308 714-635-4262

India Rural Evangelical Fellowship, (church planting, orphanage, Christian school), 8915 A Robin Dr., Des Plaines, IL 60016 312-297-6414

Institute of Contemporary Christianity, P.O. Box A, Oakland, NJ 07436 201-337-0005

Institute of Singles Dynamics, Box 11394, Kansas City, MO 64112 816-763-9401

Institute on Religion and Democracy, The, 729 15th St., N.W., Ste. 900, Washington, D.C. 20005 202-393-3200

Intercristo, (div. of Crista Ministries, Inc.), (provides career planning, placement & decision making services), 19303 Fremont Ave. N., Seattle, WA 98113 206-546-7330; 800-426-1342

International Evangelism Crusades, 14617 Victory Blvd., Ste. 4, Van Nuys, CA 91411 818-989-5942

John M. Perkins Foundation for Reconciliation & Development, 1581 Navarro Ave., Pasadena, CA 91103 818-791-7439

Kingdom Building Ministries, 1106 W. Spencer Ave., Marion, IN 46952

Lamb's Players, (performing arts), P.O. Box 26, National City, CA 92050 619-474-3385; 619-474-4802

Lay Renewal Ministries, P.O. Box 16807, St. Louis, MO 63105 314-727-0033

League of Prayer, Inc., P.O. Box 4038, Montgomery, AL 36104 205-284-5644

Lifeline Ministries, (Breth. in Christ Ch.), 422 Guerrero St., P.O. Box 410445, San Francisco, CA 94141 415-861-4820

Ligonier Ministris, Inc., 270 S. North Lake Blvd., Ste. 1270, Altamonte Springs, FL 32701 407-834-1633

Love & Action, (a Christian ministry of compassion to people with AIDS), Jeffrey A. Collins, exec. dir., 3 Church Circle, #108, Annapolis, MD 21401 301-268-3442

Media Management, 4736 Starkey Rd., Roanoke, VA 24014 703-989-1330

Ministerial Training Faith Homes, 2820 Eshcol Ave., Zion, IL 60099 312-746-1991

Morality in Media, (decency awareness), Morton H. Hill, pres., 475 Riverside Dr., New York, NY 10115

National Christian Association, (decency awareness), Brad Curl, dir., P.O. Box 40945, Washington, D.C. 20016

National Consultation on Pornography, Inc., (decency awareness), Jerry R. Kirk, pres., 5742 Hamilton Ave., Cincinnati, OH 45224

National Training Institute, 1000 S. Interregional Hwy., Round Rock, TX 78664 800-531-6789

Nehemiah Ministries, Inc., P.O. Box 448, Damascus, MD 20872 301-253-5433

Officer Alive/Law Enforcement Ministries, Inc., P.O. Box 1235, Hillsboro, OR 97123 503-648-5373

Overcomers Outreach, Inc., (ministry to Christian alcoholics), 17027 E. Janison Dr., Whittier, CA 90603 213-697-3994

Paxton Street Home, Inc., (Breth. in Christ Ch.), 2001 Paxton St., Harrisburg, PA 17111 717-236-5508

Peacemakers International, Inc., 411 Kipling, Wheaton, IL 60187 312-668-1205

Police Chaplain Corps, c/o Greater Minneapolis Association of Evangelicals, 3361 Republic Ave., Minneapolis, MN 55426 612-920-8147

Presbyterian Lay Committee, (Pres. Ch. [USA]), 1489 Baltimore Pike, Ste. 301, Springfield, PA 19064 215-543-0227

Presbyterian Ministers Fund, 1809 Walnut St., Philadelphia, PA 19103 800-523-4810; 800-462-4950 (PA)

Prison Chaplaincy, c/o Greater Minneapolis Association of Evangelicals, 3361 Republic Ave., Minneapolis, MN 55426 612-920-8147

Reality Ministries, Inc., 4618 S.W. Pacific Coast Hwy., Waldport, OR 97394 503-563-4764

Religious Alliance Against Pornography, (RAAP), Jerry R. Kirk, chairman, 800 Compton Rd., Ste. 9224, Cincinanti, OH 45231 513-521-6227

Seattle Area Literacy Tutors, 1013 8th Ave., Seattle, WA 98104 206-621-7323

Shepherd's Fold Ministries, Intl., 100 W. Ferry St., Ste. 4, Berrien Springs, MI 49103 616-471-4340

Specialized Christian Services, 1525 Cherry Rd., Springfield, IL 62704 217-546-7338

Spiritual Counterfeits Project, Inc., P.O. Box 4308, Berkeley, CA 94704 415-540-0300; 415-540-5767 (info line)

Spiritual Overseers Service, Intl., 4362 Vale, Irvine, CA 92714 714-852-1002

The Salvation Army, Central Territorial Hdqrtrs. 860 N. Dearborn St., Chicago, IL 60610-3392 312-440-4600

The Salvation Army, Eastern Territorial Hdqrtrs., 120 West 14th St., New York, NY 10011 212-337-7312

The Salvation Army, National Hdqrtrs., 799 Bloomfield Ave., Verona, NJ 07044 201-239-0606

The Salvation Army, Southern Territorial Hdqrtrs., 1424 Northeast Expressway, Atlanta, GA 30329-2088 404-728-1300

The Salvation Army, Western Territorial Hdqrtrs., 30840 Hawthorne Blvd., Rancho Palos Verdes, CA 90274 213-541-4721

United Evangelistic Consulting Association, 1236-42 W. 103rd St., Chicago, IL 60643 312-779-4380

U.S. Center for World Mission, 1605 Elizabeth St., Pasadena, CA 91104 818-797-1111

Violetiles, (hand-decorated ceramic tiles with scriptures), 279 Vischer Ferry Rd., Clifton Park, NY 12065 518-371-5301

Yokemates, 1135 W. 51st., Marion, IN 46953 317-674-2196

YOUTH AND CAMPUS OUTREACH MINISTRIES

AWANA Youth Association, 3201 Tollview Dr., Rolling Meadows, IL 60008 312-394-5150

BCM International, Inc., 237 Fairfield Ave., Upper Darby, PA 19082 215-352-7177

Campus Crusade for Christ International, Arrowhead Springs, San Bernardino, CA 92414 714-886-5224

Christian College Coalition, 329 Eighth St., N.E., Washington, D.C. 20002 202-293-6177

Christian Service Brigade, P.O. Box 150, Wheaton, IL 60189 312-665-0630

High School Evangelism Fellowship, Inc., (Hi-B.A.), P.O. Box 780, Tenafly, NJ 07670 201-387-1750

His Mansion, (center for troubled youth), P.O. Box G, Hillsboro, NH 03244 603-464-5555

International Society of Christian Endeavor, P.O. Box 1110, Columbus, OH 43216 614-258-9545

InterVarsity Christian Fellowship, 6400 Schroeder Rd., P.O. Box 7895, Madison, WI 53707-7895 608-274-9001

Josh McDowell Ministries, P.O. Box 1000, Dallas, TX 75221 214-234-0645

Life Line Homes, Inc., (social service agency of Free Meth. Ch. N. Am.), (endowment for youth ministries provides grants for worthy projects), P.O. Box 12366, Kansas City, KS 66112 913-262-3050

Maranatha Campus Ministries International, (Maranatha Christian Churches), Box 1799, Gainesville, FL 32602 904-375-6000

Navigators, The, P.O. Box 6000, Colorado Springs, CO 80934 719-598-1212

New Horizons Youth Ministries, 100 S. 350 E., Marion, IN 46953 317-668-4009; 800-333-4009

Olive Branch Mission, The, (Free Meth. Ch. of N. Am.), (work with inner city youth), 1047-41 W. Madison St., Chicago, IL 60607 312-243-3373

Pioneer Clubs, (weekday clubs for boys and girls), P.O. Box 788, Wheaton, IL 60189 312-293-1600

Presbyterian Evangelistic Fellowship, Inc., P.O. Box 1890, Decatur, GA 30031 404-244-0740; 800-CALL PEF

Probe Ministries International, 1900 Firman Dr., Ste. 100, Richardson, TX 75801 214-480-0240

Professional Resource Outreach to Youth, (P.R.O. Youth), 1508 N.E. 98th Ave., Vancouver, WA 98664 206-892-5343

Success With Youth Publications, Inc., P.O. Box 2789, LaJolla, CA 92038 619-578-4700

Teen Challenge, Inc., 444 Clinton Ave., Brooklyn, NY 11238 718-789-1414

Teen Challenge of Cleveland, 329 Parker St., P.O. Box 3811, Cleveland, TN 37311 615-476-6627

Teens, Inc., Box 322, 724 W. Washington Ave., South Bend, IN 46224 219-232-8523

Word of Life Fellowship, Inc., (Bible Clubs for young people aged 6 to 30), Jack Wyrtzen, founder & director, Schroon Lake, NY 12870 518-532-7111

Young Life, P.O. Box 520, 720 W. Monument St., Colorado Springs, CO 80901-0520 719-473-4262

Youth Challenge International, P.O. Box 12626, Hartford, CT 06105 203-728-5199

Youth Challenge International Bible Institute, R.D. 2, Box 33, Sunbury, PA 17801 717-286-6442; 800-222-1844 (Pa.)

Youth Development, Inc., P.O. Box 9429, San Diego, CA 92109 714-292-5683

Youth Evangelism Association, (YEA), 197 Front St., Marietta, OH 45750

Youth for Christ/USA, P.O. Box 419, Wheaton, IL 60189 312-668-6600

Youth for Christ International, 6890 S. Tucson Way, Ste. 205, Englewood, CO 80112-3923 303-790-4477

Youth Guidance, Inc., R.D. 2, Duff Rd., Sewickley, PA 15143 412-741-8550

Youth Leadership, Inc., 122 W. Franklin Ave., Minneapolis, MN 55404 612-870-3632

Youth Specialties Ministries, 1224 Greenfield Dr., El Cajon, CA 92021 619-440-2333

Youth With a Mission, (YWAM), Box 296, Sunland, CA 91040 818-896-2755

Professional Support Organizations

PROFESSIONAL ASSOCIATIONS

American Scientific Affiliation, (Fellowship of Christian Scientists), P.O. Box J, Ipswich, MA 01938 617-356-5656

Associated Church Builders, Inc., 3887 Industrial Ave., Rolling Meadows, IL 60008 312-392-6200

Association of Christian Librarians, P.O. Box 4, Cedarville, OH 45314

Business and Professional Couples' Clubs, (Stonecroft Ministries), P.O. Box 9609, Kansas City, MO 64134 816-763-7800

Cecil B. Day Foundation, Inc., 4725 Peachtree Corners Circle, Ste. 300, Norcross, GA 30092 404-446-1500

Christian Booksellers Association (CBA), (Trade Assoc. for Christian Booksellers), P.O. Box 200, Colorado Springs, CO 80901 719-576-7880

Christian Business & Professional Women (After 5 Clubs), (Stonecroft Ministries), P.O. Box 9609, Kansas City, MO 64134 816-763-7800

Christian Businessmen's Committee of USA, Attn: Carman G. Wolf, 1800 McCallie Ave., Chattanooga, TN 37404 615-698-4444

Christian Educators Association International, 1615 Howard, Pasadena, CA 91104; P.O. Box 50025, Pasadena, Ca 91105 818-798-1124

Christian Film Producers Fellowship, 5907 Meredith Dr., Des Moines, IA 50322 800-247-FILM

Christian Legal Society, P.O. Box 1492, Merrifield, VA 22116 703-642-1070

Christian Medical & Dental Society, P.O. Box 177, Sumner, IA 50674 319-578-5137

Christian Medical & Dental Society, 1616 Gateway Blvd., P.O. Box 689, Richardson, TX 75083 214-783-8384

Christian Military Fellowship, (Fellowship of Christians in U.S. Armed Forces), P.O. Box 1207, Englewood, CO 80150 303-761-1959

Christian Ministries Management Association, P.O. Box 4638, Diamond Bar, CA 91765 714-861-8861

Christian Public Relations Fellowship, c/o James Jewell, Director of Public Relations, Prison Fellowship, P.O. Box 17500, Washington, D.C. 20041 703-478-0100

Creation Research Society, 2717 Cranbrook, Ann Arbor, MI 48104 313-971-5915

Evangelical Council for Financial Accountability, P.O. Box 17456, Washington, D.C. 20041 703-435-8888; 800-3BE-WISE

Fellowship of Christian Airline Personnel, 136 Providence Rd., Fayetteville, GA 30214 404-461-9320

Fellowship of Christian Peace Officers, (Greater Minneapolis Association of Evangelicals [GMAE]), 3361 Republic Ave., Minneapolis, MN 55426 612-920-8147

Lawyers Christian Fellowship, 3931 E. Main St., Columbus, OH 43213 614-231-6614

National Association of Directors of Christian Education, 8405 N. Rockwell, 5 Plaza Square, Ste. 222, Oklahoma City, OK 73132

National Legal Foundation, The, P.O. Box 64845, Virginia Beach, VA 23464 804-424-4242

Nurses' Christian Fellowship, P.O. Box 7895, Madison, WI 53707 608-274-9001

Worldwide Dental Health Service, (Missionary Dentists), P.O. Box 7002, Seattle, WA 98133 206-546-1200; 206-771-3241

North American Associaton of Christians in Social Work (NACSW) P.O. Box S-90, St. Davids, PA 19087 215-687-5777

The North American Association of Christians in Social Work is a professional association of persons committed to the integration of Christian faith and social work practice. Our purpose is: to develop our capacity to integrate Christian faith and values with competent professional social work practice to the end of better serving others; to provide fellowship and support among persons who share this identity and concern; to support a vital Christian presence and world view in social work and social policy; and to promote a strong sense of love, justice, social service and social action within the Christian community.

Canada

NACSW, Shirley Ferguson, pres., 2 Cherrywood Dr., #408, Stoney Creek, Ontario L8G 2P6, Canada 416-937-7731, ext. 326

The Carolinas
(North Carolina, South Carolina)

NACSW, Dan Busch, 4135 Murray Hill Rd., Charlotte NC 28209 704-372-4663

Michigan
(Provisional)

NACSW, Mark Witte, 1549 Carlton N.E., Grand Rapids, MI 49505 616-942-2110

Mid-Atlantic
(District of Columbia, Delaware, Maryland, Pennsylvania, Southern New Jersey)

NACSW, Sandy Bauer, Eastern College, St. Davids, PA 19087 215-341-5876

Midwest
(Illinois, Iowa)

NACSW, Shirley Burnside, pres., 371 N. Ridgeland, Elmhurst, IL 60126 312-832-2534

Minnesota

NACSW, Laurie Goodwater, The Salvation Army, 706 1st Ave., N., Minneapolis, MN 55403 612-338-0113

New England

(Provisional)
(Maine, New Hampshire, Vermont, Massachusetts, Connecticut, Rhode Island)

NACSW, Timothy Morris, pres., The Salvation Army, 1 Franklin St., Lynn, MA 01902

Ohio

NACSW, Phyllis Thompson, 2458 Wyoming St., Apt. F, Dayton, OH 45410 513-252-0213

Oklahoma

(Provisional)

NACSW, Dr. Beverly Benton, Oral Roberts University, 7777 S. Lewis, Tulsa, OK 74171 918-592-5494 (home); 918-495-6535 (work)

Southern California

(zips 90000-93599)

NACSW, Dolores J. Reed, 6444 W. 87th St., Los Angeles, CA 90045

Texas

NACSW, R. B. Cooper, Jr., 515 McCullough, San Antonio, TX 78215 512-657-7664 (home); 512-226-0363 (work)

Wisconsin

(Provisional)

NACSW, Julie Zahn, Zahn Counseling Service, 1270 Main St., Green Bay, WI 54302 414-432-1511

FELLOWSHIP ORGANIZATIONS

American Church of the Good Samaritan, Inc., 8323 Sand Lake Rd., Orlando, FL 32811 305-422-3722

Association of Fundamental Ministers & Churches, P.O. Box 7923, 8605 E. 55th St., Kansas City, MO 64129 816-358-7789

B'rith Christian Union, P.O. Box 11437, Chicago, IL 60611 312-267-1440

Christian Holinesss Association, Asbury Manor, S. Walnut St., Wilmore, KY 40390 606-858-4091

Evangelical Church Alliance, The, P.O. Box 9, Bradley, IL 60915 815-937-0720

Fellowship of Christian Athletes, 8701 Leeds Rd., Kansas City, MO 64129 816-921-0909; 800-289-0909

Kingsway Ministries, 19th & Crocker, Attn: Mildred Nation, Des Moines, IA 50314 515-283-2049

Maranatha Campus Ministries International, (Marantha Christian Churches) P.O. Box 1799, Gainesville, FL 32602 904-375-6000

National Association of Christian Singles, 1933 W. Wisconsin Ave., Milwaukee, WI 53233 414-344-7300

National Black Evangelical Association, 5736 N. Albina St., Portland, OR 97217 503-289-0143

New England Fellowship of Evangelicals, P.O. Box 99, Rumney, NH 03266 603-786-9504

Overseas Christian Servicemen's Centers, P.O. Box 1268, Englewood, CO 80150 303-762-1400

Pentecostal Fellowship of North America, 1445 Boonville Ave., Springfield, MO 65802

Reformed Ecumenical Council, 2017 Eastern Ave., S.E., Ste. 201, Grand Rapids, MI 49507-3234 616-241-4424

Tennessee District Women's Missionary Council, (A/G), P.O. Box 24419, Nashville, TN 37202-4419 615-321-4440

Research Organizations and Theological Societies

RESEARCH ORGANIZATIONS

Billy Graham Center, Wheaton College, Wheaton, IL 60187 312-260-5157

Christian Answers & Information, P.O. Box 3295, Chico, CA 95927 916-893-0567

Christian Apologetics Research & Information Service, (CARIS), P.O. Box 2067, Costa Mesa, CA 92626 714-957-0249

Christian Research Associates, Inc., 6565 Gun Park Dr. #150-46, Boulder, CO 80301 303-777-1983

Creation Research Society, 2717 Cranbrook, Ann Arbor, MI 48104 313-971-5915

Family Research Council of America, Inc., 515 Second St., N.E., Capitol Hill, Washington, DC 20002 202-546-5400

Institute for Biblical Research, Southwestern Baptist Seminary, P.O. Box 22000, Fort Worth, TX 76122

Missions Advanced Research Center, 919 W. Huntington Dr., Monrovia, CA 91016 818-303-8811

THEOLOGICAL SOCIETIES

Conference on Faith & History, (Christians interested in history), Department of History, Indiana State University, Terre Haute, IN 47809 812-237-2707

Evangelical Theological Society, 5422 Clinton Blvd., Jackson, MS 39209 601-922-4988

Institute for Biblical Research, Southwestern Baptist Seminary, P.O. Box 22000, Fort Worth, TX 76122

Society for Pentecostal Studies, 135 N. Oakland Ave., Pasadena, CA 91182 818-584-5305

Theological Commission, World Evangelical Fellowship, 23, Norris Rd., Koramangala, Bangalore 560 025 India; Phone: 0812-571517

Wesleyan Theological Society, c/o William M. Arnett, Asbury Theological Seminary, Wilmore, KY 40390 317-674-7810

Social Support Service Organizations

Child Abuse/Orphanage/Foster Care Agencies

CHILD CARE

Brethren in Christ Foster Care Ministries, (Breth. in Christ Ch.), R.D. 6, Box 174 Lancaster, PA 17603 717-872-5234

Christian Homes for Children, Inc., 275 State St., Hackensack, NJ 07601 201-342-4235

315

Church of God Home for Children, P.O. Box 64, Kannapolis, NC 28081 704-782-8825

Covenant Children, (special focus on aiding abandoned children from Colombia/Guatemala), P.O. Box 2344, Bismarck, ND 58502 701-222-3960

Deaconess Home, (The Home of Redeeming Love), (Free Meth. Ch. of N. Am.), (care for unwed mothers & a certified adoption agency), 5401 N. Portland Ave., Oklahoma City, OK 73112 405-942-5001

Eckert Youth Home, P.O. Box 223, Williston, ND 58801 701-572-7262

Evangelical Child and Family Agency, (NAE affiliate), Doris Wheeler, executive director, 1530 N. Main St., Wheaton, IL 60187 312-653-6400

India Rural Evangelical Fellowship, (church planting, orphanage, Christian school), 8915-A Robin Dr., Des Plaines, IL 60016 312-297-6414

Mission Acres, (care for abused & neglected children), 221 Griffin Mountain Trail, Conyers, GA 30208

Pleasant Hills Children's Home, P.O. Box 1177, Fairfield, TX 75840 214-389-2641

Sunburst Youth Homes, Neillsville, WI 54456

Texas Baptist Children's Home, Drawer 7, Round Rock, TX 78664

FAMILY MINISTRIES

The following, by no means complete, is a list of family-oriented ministries. The specialized focus of many ministries is identified in parentheses for the user's convenience. While arranged according to states, this listing contains ministries that not only have area but national focus.

Alabama

Wales Goebel Ministry, (Lifeline adoption agency), 2908 Pump House Rd., Birmingham, AL 35243 205-967-4888

Arizona

Calvary Rehabilitation Center, (alcohol & drug counseling), 329 N. Third Ave., Phoenix AZ 85003 602-254-7092

Christian Family Care Agency, 1105 E. Missouri, Phoenix, AZ 85014 602-234-1935

Crisis Pregnancy Center, Inc., 1124 N. 3rd Ave., Tucson, AZ 85705-7474 602-622-5774

Arkansas

Family Ministry, 1 Shackleford Dr., Ste. 100, Little Rock, AR 72211 501-223-8663

California

Christian Marriage Enrichment, 1913 E. 17th St., Ste. 118, Santa Ana, CA 92701

Community Counseling & Psychological Services, 4800 Easton Dr., Ste. 109, Bakersfield, CA 93309 805-326-8167

Focus on the Family, Pomona, CA 91799 714-620-8500

Hotline Help Center, (crisis-intervention, prevention & treatment), P.O. Box 999, Anaheim, CA 92805 714-778-1000

Mesa Christi, Inc., 22354 Festividad Dr., Saugus, CA 91350 805-254-1796

Mount Hermon Association, Inc., (interdenom. camp & conference ministry), Edward Hayes exec. dir., Box 413, Mount Hermon, CA 95041 408-335-4466

District of Columbia

Family Research Council of America, Inc., 515 Second St., N.E., Capitol Hill, Washington, DC 20002 202-546-5400

Florida

Shepherd Care Ministries, Inc., (counseling & training program-crisis pregnancy-adoption agency), 5935 Taft St., Ste. B, Hollywood, FL 33021 305-981-2060; 305-621-1991

Georgia

Family Life Ministries, Mt. Paran Church of God, 2055 Mt. Paran Rd., Atlanta, GA 30327 404-261-0720

Mission Acres, (care for abused & neglected children), 221 Griffin Mountain Trail, Conyers GA 30208

Mission Church of God, (counseling), 380 - 14th St., Atlanta, GA 30318 404-874-2241

Illinois

Christian Camping International/U.S.A., P.O. Box 646, Wheaton, IL 60189 312-462-0300

Cornerstone Counseling Assoc., 810 N. Haddow, Arlington Heights, IL 60004 312-253-5427

Evangelical Child and Family Agency, (NAE affiliate), Doris Wheeler, exec. dir., 1530 N. Main St., Wheaton, IL 60187 312-653-6400

Family Concern, Inc., P.O. Box 53, Wheaton, IL 60189 312-668-3220

Institute of Basic Youth Conflicts, P.O. Box 1, Oak Brook, IL 60521 312-323-9800

John R. Day & Associates, Ltd., Christian Psychological Associates, 4100 War Memorial Dr., Peoria, IL 61614 309-685-7342; 923 N. Western Ave., Peoria, IL 61606 309-673-5566

Indiana

Biblical Dynamics, Inc., (Christian counseling), 1454 S. 25th St., Terre Haute, IN 47803-2946 812-238-9455

Kansas

Friends Marriage Encounter, (Evang. Friends Alliance), 2018 Maple, Wichita KS 67213 316-267-0391

Life Line Homes Inc., (social service agency of Free Meth. Ch. N. Am.), (endowment for youth ministries provides grants for worthy projects), P.O. Box 12366, Kansas City, KS 66112 913-262-3050

Menninger Foundation, (training in marriage & family counseling), Box 829, Topeka, KS 66601

Louisiana

Protestant Home for Babies, 1233 Eighth St., New Orleans, LA 70115

Michigan

Bethany Christian Services, (adoption; pregnancy counseling services), 901 Eastern Ave. N.E., Grand Rapids, MI 49503-1295 616-459-6273, corporate office; crisis pregnancy hotline, #1-800-BETHANY

Women Exploited By Abortion, 202 S. Andrews, Three Rivers, MI 49093 616-273-8476

Minnesota

Christian Counseling Center, c/o Greater Minneapolis Association of Evangelicals, 3361 Republic Ave., Minneapolis, MN 55426 612-920-6653

New Life Homes & Family Service, (Christian social service agency), c/o Greater Minneapolis Association of Evangelicals, 3361 Republic Ave.,

Ste. 201, Minneapolis, MN 55426 612-920-8117

Single Parent Christian Fellowship, c/o Greater Minneapolis Association of Evangelicals, 3361 Republic Ave., Minneapolis, MN 55426 312-920-8147

Mississippi

American Family Association, (decency awareness) Donald E. Wildmon, exec. dir., 107 Parkgate, P.O. Drawer 2440, Tupelo, MS 38803 601-844-5036

Missouri

Highlands Child Placement Services, (A/G), 1445 Boonville Ave., Springfield, MO 65802 417-862-2781

New Hampshire

His Mansion, (center for troubled youth), P.O. Box G, Hillsboro, NH 03244 603-464-5555

New Jersey

Christian Homes for Children, Inc., 275 State St., Hackensack, NJ 07601 201-342-4235

New York

Evangelical Adoption and Family Service, Inc., (NAE service agency), 119 Church Street, North Syracuse, NY 13212 315-458-1415

North Carolina

Association for Couples in Marriage Enrichment, P.O. Box 10596, Winston-Salem, NC 27108 919-724-1526

Church of God Home for Children, P.O. Box 64, Kannapolis, NC 28081 704-782-8825

North Dakota

Covenant Children, (special focus on aiding abandoned children from Colombia/Guatemala), P.O. Box 2344, Bismarck, ND 58502 701-222-3960

Eckert Youth Home, P.O. Box 223, Williston, ND 58801 701-572-7262

Ohio

Emerge Ministries, Inc., (counseling, training, education), 900 Mull Ave., Akron, OH 44313 216-867-5603; 800-621-5207

Oklahoma

Deaconess Home, (The Home of Redeeming Love), (Free Meth. Ch. of N. Am.), (care for unwed mothers & a certified adoption agency), 5401 N. Portland Ave., Oklahoma City, OK 73112 405-942-5001

Oregon

Give Us This Day, Inc., (counseling/referral/adoption services), 2207B Portland Rd., P.O. Box 796, Newberg, OR 97132 503-538-2111; 503-628-2041

PLAN (Plan Loving Adoptions Now) (adoptions) P.O. Box 667, McMinnville, OR 97128 503-472-8452

Pennsylvania

Christian Counseling & Education Foundation, 1790 E. Willow Grove Ave., Laverock, PA 19118 215-884-7676

Family Life Ministries, R.R. 4, Mountain Rd., Dillsburg, PA 17019

Handi Vangelism, (BCM Intl.) (bereaved parents ministries), 237 Fairfield Ave., Upper Darby, PA 19082 215-352-7177

Messiah Family Services, (Breth. in Christ Ch.), 5000 S. Angle St., Mt. Joy, PA 17552 717-653-8067

New Life for Girls, (women w/drug & alcohol related problems), R.D. 3, Box D700, Dover, PA 17315 717-266-5414

SOCIAL SUPPORT SERVICE ORGANIZATIONS

South Carolina

Church of God Home for Children, P.O. Box 430, Mauldin, SC 29662 803-963-5051

Tennessee

Church of God Family Life Commission, Keith at 25th St. N.W., P.O. Box 2430, Cleveland, TN 37320 615-472-3361

Cornerstone Counseling Services, 3535 Keith St. N.W., Cleveland, TN 37311 615-476-5216

F.O.C.A.S., (Fellowship of Christian Anglers Society), 1001 Market St., Chattanooga, TN 37402 615-756-2514

Teen Challenge of Cleveland, 329 Parker St., P.O. Box 3811, Cleveland, TN 37311 615-476-6627

Texas

Pleasant Hills Children's Home, P.O. Box 1177, Fairfield, TX 75840 214-389-2641

Texas Baptist Children's Home, Drawer 7, Round Rock, TX 78664

Virginia

Biblical Counseling Foundation, P.O. Box 2726, Fairfax, VA 22031 703-591-6904

Washington

Open ARMS, (abortion related ministries), National Headquarters: P.O. Box 7188, Federal Way, WA 98003 206-839-8919

Regular Baptist Child Placement Agency, Box 16353, Seattle WA 98116

Wisconsin

Christian Counseling Center, (marital/family counseling), Mission Outreach Society, P.O. Box 227, Oregon, WI 53575 608-835-5411

Sunburst Youth Homes, Neillsville, WI 54456

Canada

Christian Benefit Shop, (Breth. in Christ Ch.), 53 Southworth St. N., Welland, Ontario, L3B 1Y3, Canada 416-735-4010

Timber Bay Children's Home, (Breth. in Christ Ch.), Timber Bay, Saskatchewan S0J 2T0, Canada 306-663-5811

WOMEN'S CONCERNS ORGANIZATIONS

Christian Women's Clubs, (Stonecroft Ministries), P.O. Box 9609, Kansas City, MO 64134 816-763-7800

Concerned Women for America, (decency awareness), 122 C St., N.W., Ste. 800, Washington D.C. 20001

Tennessee District Women's Missionary Council, (A/G), P.O. Box 24419, Nashville, TN 37202-4419 615-321-4440

Women Exploited By Abortion, 202 S. Andrews, Three Rivers, MI 49093 616-273-8476